MY LIFE AS A
GODDESS

MY LIFE AS A
GODDESS

A MEMOIR THROUGH
(UN)POPULAR CULTURE

GUY BRANUM

ATRIA BOOKS

NEW YORK   LONDON   TORONTO   SYDNEY   NEW DELHI

ATRIA
BOOKS

An Imprint of Simon & Schuster, Inc.
1230 Avenue of the Americas
New York, NY 10020

First Atria Books hardcover edition July 2018

ATRIA B O O K S and colophon are trademarks of Simon & Schuster, Inc.

For information about special discounts for bulk purchases,
please contact Simon & Schuster Special Sales at
1-866-506-1949 or business@simonandschuster.com.

The Simon & Schuster Speakers Bureau can bring authors to your live event.
For more information, or to book an event, contact the Simon & Schuster Speakers
Bureau at 1-866-248-3049 or visit our website at www.simonspeakers.com.

Interior design by Kyoko Watanabe

Manufactured in the United States of America

10 9 8 7 6 5 4 3 2 1

Library of Congress Cataloging-in-Publication Data

Names: Branum, Guy, 1975– author.
Title: My life as a goddess: a memoir through (un)popular culture / Guy Branum;
    foreword by Mindy Kaling.
Description: First Atria Books hardcover edition. | New York: Atria Books,
    2018.
Identifiers: LCCN 2018016385 (print) | LCCN 2018020359 (ebook) |
    ISBN 9781501170249 (ebook) | ISBN 9781501170225 (hardback) |
    ISBN 9781501170232 (paperback)
Subjects: LCSH: Branum, Guy, 1975– | Comedians—United States—Biography. |
    Actors—United States—Biography. | BISAC: BIOGRAPHY & AUTOBIOGRAPHY /
    Personal Memoirs. | HUMOR / General. | BIOGRAPHY & AUTOBIOGRAPHY /
    Entertainment & Performing Arts.
Classification: LCC PN2287.B6835 (ebook) | LCC PN2287.B6835 A3 2018 (print) |
    DDC 792.7/6028092 [B]—dc23
LC record available at https://lccn.loc.gov/2018016385

ISBN 978-1-5011-7022-5
ISBN 978-1-5011-7024-9 (ebook)

For my father, Larry Branum, who would have hated this book.

CONTENTS

FOREWORD

GUY AND I FIRST met when we were shooting a romantic comedy movie over a decade ago, playing parts of two people nobody cared about. Our roles in the movie were pretty much the same: the desperate but appealing side characters who turned to the good-looking leads and said things like "I can't believe how single I am." Guy was our director's pet. His wife had seen him on *Chelsea Lately* and was obsessed with him. Everything Guy said made our director laugh and so I became jealous of him.

We met again years later in the writing room of *The Mindy Project*, where I hired Guy to be a writer. My plan, of course, was to hire him only to torment him for his past imprudence of being funnier and better-liked than me. To my dismay, this was thwarted almost immediately and Guy was very popular on staff. Turns out that not only was he a very funny writer, he also went to law school and could give any of us ready legal advice on any subject, no matter how arcane. Thinking about my future prenup and eventual divorce legal fees, I kept him around.

Time went by. My jealousy turned to indifference. My indifference turned to apathy. My apathy turned to light interest, interest turned to fondness, and that fondness turned to love. And the reason I loved Guy surprised me. It was because of his innate kindness. Although he is a very quick wit (a quality I assumed he gained from years of being a successful stand-up and being, well, a gay man) and could eviscerate anyone or anything he wanted, he never did, because Guy is . . . kind. I don't know many people as funny as he is who care about being compassionate. But Guy does.

But you didn't buy this book because Guy's kind. You bought it because he's funny. In this book, he writes hilariously about his career, his family, his gayness. You can live vicariously through him as he got the dream job of working for Chelsea Handler, then feel scared for him when he pissed off Chelsea Handler. It's so refreshing to read someone write truthfully about his family relationships, his love life, and his career in Hollywood, complete with juicy details. I didn't even mind the part where he called me a huge bitch (just kidding, he said I was "kind of bitchy." Just kidding, he said I was perfect). It's all so good.

And the secret bonus? You know that deep down, he's a great guy.

Mindy Kaling
Los Angeles, California

MY LIFE AS A
GODDESS

LETO AND THE LYCIAN PEASANTS

IN MY EIGHTH YEAR, my attentions turned to Greek mythology.

This is hardly unusual for children of that age, which is somewhat strange when you consider how much of Greek myth centers on rape, sexual kidnappings, and adulterous rendezvous between princesses and gods in the form of farm animals. Somehow our culture has decided Greek myths are cool for third-graders, but safe and reliable birth control is too much for a sixteen-year-old to learn about. That said, I am not here to challenge America's educational morality. I'm here to write a collection of humorous personal essays.

Like most people who write collections of humorous personal essays, I was a bookish child. Other boys my age focused most of their time on yelling, trying to fart on each other, and generally not obeying rules. The vast majority of male eight-year-olds love to break rules. It is their greatest passion. Mashing their food together in the cafeteria and pretending it's barf. Yelling "boobs" during a nice assembly where we learn about Irish step dancing. Maiming beauty. They love it. Their fierce defiance of what moms and teachers want out of them is what fuels their spirits. I have never understood these creatures.

A small but resolute minority of eight-year-old boys love the rules. Rules are our only protection from the senseless engines of chaos we share classrooms with. They are that quiet, obedient opposition who would like silence and beauty and assemblies about Irish step dancing to be preserved. I was one of those boys. Third grade is a difficult place for us, so we seek the safety of a world where systems work and laws are obeyed: age-appropriate adventure books.

I grew up in a town where absolutely nothing happened. It's a farm town in California, but not the good part of California. We will get to that later. What you need to know is that it was a place devoid of importance—political, economic, or philosophical—and any story that happened there centered on alcoholism and/or domestic violence. No one went to college, no one started a business, no one traveled anywhere but Disneyland or a lake. I grew up in a place with no dreams.

As a little kid in a little town where very little happened, Greek myths made me feel connected to the important stuff. There were kings, sorceresses, and human embodiments of abstract concepts: people who were in charge of things. If I was never going to meet any sophisticated folks in my real life, maybe I could learn how they operated from a book.

And Greek myths were full of people performing tasks I was too scared and fat and indoorsy to do myself. I wasn't like those idiots I went to school with. If one day I planned to do stuff that required being brave and bold, I would have to do a lot of research and planning first.

In the sad, poor portable building that passed for a sad, poor library at my sad, poor public elementary school, I found a series of books. They were adaptations of stories from Greek mythology by a woman named Doris Gates; they had titles like *Lord of the Sky: Zeus* and *The Warrior Goddess: Athena*. They were full of shortish episodes from *The Odyssey*, or *Theogony*, or *Metamorphoses*, made palatable for children. I consumed them with an enthusiasm I normally reserved for meatballs or banana pudding.

The Golden God: Apollo was yellow, naturally, and on its cover was a man of preternatural beauty, a 1970s decadence of oranges and yellows and black. One of the first stories in it told of the birth of the sun god, Apollo, and his sister, Artemis, the moon. I will now tell you that story to the best of my recollection.

So Zeus had sex with Leto, who was one of his sisters, as was his wife, Hera, but Hera was jealous. That was what Hera did: She got mad at Zeus about the women he fucked. She couldn't stop him, because he was the king of the gods, and she couldn't punish him. Hera got the throne and the diadem and all the perks of being the wifey, but she knew he never really loved her. This was the cruelest of tortures for one of the fairest and finest goddesses, so she did her part to spread the punishment around to the women he had sex with and the children he impregnated them with.

So Hera, regally pissed, banished Leto from Mount Olympus and placed the following curse on her sister: Not a place on earth, nor in the sea, nor under the sun, could give Leto shelter lest it be subjected to Hera's powerful wrath.

For nine months, Leto walked the earth. Slowly, she grew great with child, but no place would give her food or drink or a safe place to stay. In the hot sun of Attica, she paced and she paced, begging hills and meadows for comfort, and each one chased her away in some manner.

Finally, in the height of summer, giant with twins, she came to a pond where some peasants were washing clothes. Leto knelt down by the pond and asked if she could drink from it. The peasants noticed that she was pregnant and asked where her husband was. Leto had no answer, so the peasants mocked her for being an unwed mother and kicked around the water in the pond until it got muddy and would be gross to drink.

Leto, hot, thirsty, pregnant, tired, all of it—all of the kinds of DONE—got up and started to walk again. Where? She had no answer. How was she going to have these kids when no one would even let her sit down? Her spirit was broken.

Then she remembered that she was a goddess.

It was the most beautiful, wonderful sentence I'd ever read: Then she remembered that she was a goddess.

She turned around, raised her hands to the sky, and turned the peasants into frogs. "Kick in the mud forever, you basic amphibious bitches," she cursed.

That story changed me.

It isn't that Leto turned those asshole peasants into frogs; the frog part is an afterthought. The important part is that she remembered she was a goddess. She had been too caught up in the dirty, base realities of the life she was leading to realize the audacity of the situation. She was a goddess being condescended to by peasants. The peasants didn't know who she was, but more important, she had forgotten who she was. I didn't know you could be a goddess and forget it.

I am not supposed to be a goddess. I am very fat. I am bald. I have a faggy voice. My family is poor. My parents are uneducated. I dress like a wet three-year-old. My handwriting is bad. I sweat a lot. My parallel parking is amateurish. I'm wholly devoid of the skills required to make any ball go into any goal, hoop, or pocket.

I'm not supposed to like myself, and I'm certainly not supposed to think that I should matter. The world has spent a lot of time telling me that, and in the past thirty or so years, I often listened, because we all listen. The world is mostly full of fine facts and good lessons, but some of those facts and lessons were built to keep you down.

And I got kept down for decades. Then I remembered that I was a goddess. I may not always feel like it, but I have powers.

I am an amazing dancer. I'm quite ridiculously smart. I'm strong. I'm funny. Babies like me. I have very strong research skills. I make passingly good Punjabi okra. I have a law degree. I sparkle on panel shows. I'm very good at listening when I try.

It's not amazing. It's not lightning bolts or control of the seas, I can't turn myself into a swan and have my way with whatever man I like,[1] but it's enough for me.

---

[1] In addition to not having the power to shift my shape, I also just don't want to have to deal with all the think pieces such an act would prompt.

And Doris Gates gave me my most important power—the power to see myself. I can't control what people see when they look at me. Most people see a weird, fat, unsexy guy who is wearing cargo shorts even though he should know better. I can't decide if you think I'm beautiful, but I do get to decide if I'm going to feel beautiful, and from the moment I first tried it, I've been addicted.

So that's what this book is about, the life I was supposed to lead as a sad, fat, closeted bumpkin, and my decision to be something thoroughly more fabulous. My life has not been practical, it has not been meaningful, and it has been only periodically profitable, but it has at least stayed interesting. Because a goddess's job isn't to be good, it's to have compelling stories lyre players can tell about her at the courts of kings and princes.

Oh, and a goddess needs worshippers. You don't need a lot; in a pinch, just one will do. On that Lycian field, Leto was just about the only person who believed in Leto, but it got the job done. There have been numerous occasions when I was the only person who believed in me, but I made it through.

Thus, if you are at all interested in being a goddess, may I suggest starting this book by believing in yourself. If you're nice enough to read my book, I at least owe you enough to believe in you, too.

A POOR FIT

I WAS BORN WRONG.

The first thing I did as a legally existing human being was get lodged in my mother's vagina. I was too large. There were forceps involved, there was tugging, there was a warning that a lack of oxygen might have left me brain-damaged.

This pattern was to recur.

I don't bring this up simply to call to mind my mother's reproductive organs but to make a larger point: I am bad at fitting. I don't smoothly, comfortably integrate myself. This is possibly the dominant theme of my life. Thus, let us step back from my existence for a few pages and set ourselves a scene. Let's take a moment for some geography.

Yuba City: A Horrible Place

I was born in California, but not the California you think. I wasn't born in the urban, sun-glazed beachiness of *90210* or *The OC* or *The Hills* or any other show where physically perfect twenty-five-year-olds play high school sophomores. I don't mean to say that California doesn't exist. It does: The high school students are sexually and emotionally mature monsters who are constantly doing drugs and using their parents' money and influence to start clothing lines. They are horrifying and magnificent, but I'm not like them. If you would like to learn more about them, please consider following Patrick Schwarzenegger on Instagram. If you'd like to learn more about my sad, meager birthplace, keep reading!

I was born in Northern California, but again, not the Northern California you think of. When you think of Northern California, you think of cabernet vines and marijuana and betatted lesbian sous chefs working at three-Michelin-star restaurants and liberalism and hippies. You think of your friend's Instagram photos from that trip she took to Napa where Joel finally proposed to her (even though she swore things were over after the incident in Tulum). Northern California seems *beautiful*, and you don't know why I'm complaining about it. Again, that's not the place I'm from.

I am from a place you don't think about. I am from where almonds and peaches come from. I am from the long, wide, hot valley that begins just over the San Gabriel Mountains from Los Angeles and stretches five hundred miles north to the Siskiyou Mountains. This is where every glorious thing in your produce aisle begins its life. Just about every artichoke, almond, peach, plum, prune, walnut, kiwi, leaf of spinach, stalk of celery, bulb of garlic, floret of broccoli or cauliflower you have eaten in your life comes from this valley, and you have never thought about it. Nor should you have to.

It is a horrible place. When people from cities think about rural life, they think about the charming fiction of farming that's presented to them by tourist traps and America's national mythos. You think of Vermont. Vermont isn't farms, it's a cute place for New Yorkers to take the money they earned running America and spend it on creating wacky ice cream flavors and electing socialist senators. I know all those charming general stores and Revolutionary War cemeteries seem very authentic, but it is simply a well-textured lie. Vermont is essentially just upper, whiter Central Park.

Let's be clear: Farming isn't charming. It's the bare, base existence that people are able to scrape by on from the narrow difference between what it costs to raise crops and the pennies our cruel overlords in the city are willing to pay for them. I would know. I was raised on a farm, and every day I prayed that one day I would be able to become one of those cruel overlords in the city.

I grew up in Sutter County, California, just outside of Yuba City, a small farm town in the Sacramento Valley. It is California-small, currently around sixty-five thousand people. That would make it the fifth largest city or higher in sixteen states, the biggest city in Wyoming, West Virginia, or the aforementioned Vermont, but in California, it's less than an afterthought. A place you think you may have heard of.

When I say "farm town," you also think you know who lives there. It's a charming little community full of nice Caucasian characters who know each other and have petty arguments that last for decades but fall away in the face of an outside threat, like a flood or a big-city business lady. We've all seen that town a thousand times in movies. You're essentially just remembering a three p.m. showing of *Doc Hollywood* that you saw on TBS in the early 2000s. I'm not from there. I'm from California.

California is not a place. It's the edge of human civilization. There is no sense of community because everybody arrived six weeks ago. The orchards of Yuba City, California, are just as stark and impersonal a hellscape as any strip mall in Los Angeles; they just smell better.

All four of my grandparents came to California from the Ozark Mountains of Northwest Arkansas. In Sutter County, most people's grandparents did. Sometimes in L.A., I'll do an impression of my grandfather, emulating the bulldog bark/chicken cackle of an Ozarks accent, and people always say, "But I thought you were from California?" Then I have to explain, or start to explain, then I get tired of the entire process and just ignore it. You all read *The Grapes of Wrath* junior year of high school. I don't feel like it's incumbent on me to explain how the Okie migration worked. Invariably, people wrinkle their brows and tell me I'm being Californian the wrong way. But the truth remains that in my trashy little Northern California town, the culture was biscuits and gravy, bird dogs in your pickup truck, Mom, Jesus, midlevel racism, and pecan[1] pie.

Except that we're Jewish. Well, my mom is Jewish. Well, her mom is Jewish. My maternal grandmother is a Jew, descended from German-Jewish traders who came to the Mississippi River basin in the 1840s to sell things. They were very horrible at selling things and ended up living as sharecroppers in the Ozark Mountains. These are not nice polite southern Jews who moved south to teach physics at Ole Miss. These are not even German-Jewish shop owners who send their children to Jewish camp in Georgia and keep in touch with the relatives in New York. My grandmother is a legit hillbilly-trash Jew.[2] I know, I am also being Jewish wrong. But as my grandmother would note any time one of her descendants commented on the fragility of our Judaism, "They woulda killed you just the same." You *think* you know which "they" she's talking about, but she's from Arkansas. She's got a much more expansive definition of "they."

One time when I was visiting her house, my grandmother referenced a well-trod story of Klansmen doing something terrible to her father back in Arkansas. I was like seven or something, so I understood what the Klan was from TV movies and stuff, but not why they would be attacking a person who wasn't black. "Why did they do that to *you*?" I asked my grandmother. "Well, I reckon they wanted a change of pace," she answered.

So that is my strangely southern-white-trash Northern California town, except it isn't. See, like most farm towns in the portions of the United States that used to be Mexico, Sutter County is also about a quarter Mexican. That's not surprising. What is surprising is that another quarter of the town is South Asian. No, not the graduate-degreed Indians you're probably used to from trips to your medical provider or

---

[1] Pronounced "pick-AHN," please.

[2] Not to be confused with the West Virginian burrowing mountain Jew, or the web-toed swamp Jew of the Louisiana wetlands.

any engineering labs you may frequent, but the hillbillies of Northwest India: Punjabi Sikhs.

I'll explain more as the book goes on, but just understand the setting is a magical land where old Indian men in turbans guzzle Jack Daniel's on top of tractors slowly chugging along the road as the descendants of that lady in the Dorothea Lange Dust Bowl photo shoot guns into the air and yell racial slurs. And there are almonds everywhere. And it's very hot.

In conclusion, Yuba City doesn't make sense, but neither do I. Now back to me.

Guy Branum: Portrait of an Ungrateful Upstart

So in the middle of the 1970s, the glorious flower of the Ford administration, I came out of my mother and wanted more. It wasn't obvious at first. I spent several months just rolling around and trying to be pleasant. But I taught myself to speak as quickly as possible to try to start figuring out if better ways of living than a shitty two-bit farm town were a possibility.

I did not go over well in Yuba City. It's entirely possible that my first memory is standing outside of my grandma Branum's Southern Baptist church and having an old man ask me what I wanted to be when I grew up. I told him that I wanted to be a waitress because, at that point in my life, somewhere around three years of age, waitresses seemed like the most glamorous people imaginable. Waitresses in diners wear snappy outfits, they get to talk to the public all day long, and they have, I assumed, infinite access to pancakes. If these were so, waitressing was the line for me.

The old man did not agree. "Big boy like you?! Oughta want to be a football player." He spat these words at me. I know he had probably clung to the back of a Model T through the baking sun of Route 66, seeking a better life in the 1930s or something. I'm sure he worked a very hard life as a farm laborer or construction worker; everyone in that fucking town did. I just didn't understand why it made them so mad at *me*, and about this subject particularly. For the second five years of my life, people were persistently asking me if I wanted to be a football player. Like a woman walking down the street suffering a litany of "Hey, *smile*," I was eternally having this question posed to me as though it were some sort of favor. And for the life of me, I couldn't understand why, because professional football seemed like a ridiculously improbable career to pursue. Waitressing, however, was real, accessible, and made people's lives better by bringing them more syrup and calling them "hon."

My career aspirations were not the only thing marking me as abnormal. Let us look to another case study. Around seven or eight years of age, in Yuba City, a boy's heart turns to torturing cats. It's a farm town; there are lots of animals all over the place. Dogs, cats, chickens, pigs, and an orchard full of rats, ground squirrels, and crows. The dogs periodically eat the chickens, the cats eat the squirrels and rats and birds, and with some regularity, your mom or grandma kills a chicken for a nice dinner. A kid in a farm town *sees* death, but around third grade, most boys want to take things further and experiment with death.

One afternoon, over a tense glass of iced tea, my aunt who lived at the other end of the orchard told my mom how my cousin had drowned a cat in a bucket. My mom assured her it was nothing to worry about and advised her to punish him and make sure he never did it again. A few months later, another mom came over to chat and told my mom about her son trying to set a cat on fire. My mom dispensed the same knowing advice. Still, there was a deeper, unspoken worry. The growing concern was becoming clear. Why wasn't Guy killing any cats?

I was aware, deeply, that there was something wrong with me.

And it wasn't just issues of gender expression, charming little stories we can now tell about how I was "always gay." Hardly so. I was, in nearly every way, wrong. I was way too intellectually aggressive. I was constantly asking questions about things the people of Yuba City do not need to worry themselves over. "Who is the mayor?" was one of my obsessions for a while. No one I knew seemed to know. "What is the difference between Methodist and Presbyterian?" "What is the difference between gas and oil?" "What are the Buttes?" They all seemed to vex people.

The Sutter Buttes: Supplemental Notes
on Areas Surrounding Yuba City

I realize now I haven't explained to you what the Buttes are. I was worried you had become bored of my description of my hometown that doesn't comport with your narrow little construction of how the world works. Wouldn't it just be easier if I could say "I'm from Schenectady. Just a Jew from Schenectady!" or "Oak Park Heights Grove Lake was just a typical American suburb." But I'm not. I'm from Sutter County, CA, and to know Sutter County is to know the Buttes.

Remember how I told you about that five-hundred-mile valley full of the finest farmland in God's creation? Well, the whole thing is one long, flat trough except for one tiny aberration, the Sutter Buttes, a minuscule volcanic mountain range in the middle of the Sacramento Valley. These volcanoes have been dormant for 1.4 million years, but in Algebra II class, I would stare at them and hope they'd choose that day to come out of retirement and erupt again to *end* the *fucking boredom.*[3]

But we can say these things with the benefit of Wikipedia and hindsight. When I was seven, I just wanted to know what they were. *Why* they were. "The Indians thought they were sacred!" and "They're the littlest mountain range in the world!" is what I would get, but I didn't need fucking folk wisdom. I needed to understand.

---

[3] Aren't we lucky that isn't how I discovered I had geokinetic powers. I mean, accidentally destroying your farm town in the process of learning you have the power to control volcanoes does seem like a solid superhero origin story, and I did hate 80 percent of the people in that town. However, if I'd flooded Sutter County, California, with psychically summoned lava, it would have significantly increased the price of almonds and prunes for most of the 1990s. No one needed that.

Guy Branum: Portrait of an Ungrateful Upstart (cont.)

Working-class people are not supposed to understand. They're supposed to do. Work a job, go home, drink, beat your wife/get beaten, hunt, bake, go to church, build fences. At one point of deep familial tension, my dad built a fence, and then my uncle built a fence up against his fence, and then my dad built another fence next to the first fence. They love fences. But they don't love logic or reason or books or August Wilson's Tony Award–winning play *Fences*. With the exception of my mom and a couple of my teachers, just about everyone told me "You don't need to know that" with the same vehemence of that old guy telling me I should want to be a football player. Why would I need to know what a parliament is or how World War I started when I was just going to grow up to be a cement mason who farms almonds on the side?

Also, to be clear, my deep, deep need to understand the origins of World War I was the initial major crack in my relationship with my mother. In this world of horrid, caustic people telling me what I couldn't be, my mom was the one lady who was, on a regular basis, finding it pretty cool that I knew who the Secretary of the Interior was. She also understood that it was her responsibility to make me Jewish; thus she was constantly telling me about World War II, the Holocaust, and that one day soon people would come for the Jews again. She was always doing her best to try to texture my brain with Jewish paranoia, and it worked, but one point bugged me. She was telling me about World War II, a sequel; what was the deal with World War I? I asked about it. She was cagey, she dodged, she stammered some things about an archduke getting shot, but she had nothing for all of my follow-up questions. Finally, when I was six, she bought us a *World Book Encyclopedia*, and I was finally able to answer some fucking questions.[4] It was like scratch-

---

[4] World War I was the result of the breakdown of the post–Congress of Vienna system of European alliances, which had led to relative stability for the past hundred years. Growing nationalism was eating away at large, anachronistic imperial states

ing an itch in the middle of my brain that had plagued me since at least age four.

So I had this insatiable intellectual curiosity, and everyone found it unnatural. "Where did he come from?" people would ask, vaguely disturbed. Occasionally, I'd get a teacher (one who wasn't from Sutter County) who'd ask, "Where did he come from!?" in much more enthusiastic tones. They were the lovely people who helped me learn and taught me to teach myself, but it didn't change the underlying reality: I was very wrong for the place I lived. I wasn't great for most other places, either.[5]

I was even physically wrong. I am gigantic. My mom is five-four; my dad was five-eight. I am six-three. By the time I was twelve, I was taller than my dad. I have also always been fat, a sturdy, farm-working fat that jiggled unappealingly but could lift whatever was necessary. Slower than every boy in class but stronger than every boy in class. Taller and wider than everyone in the class photo. Always the subject of discussions about not looking my age. Even visually, I was an aberration.

My giganticness was the one thing about me that Sutter could have understood or liked about me being different, but I even managed to do this wrong. I was supposed to be a bully. I was supposed to fight. I was supposed to use my size as a source of power over people. My uncle Ray used to think it was funny to have his son, my cat-killing cousin Robby, start fights with me, because even though he was a year younger and half my size, he always won. The thing is, I didn't understand why he was fighting with me. Usually, people were yelling at me for not having friends who were boys, or yelling at me to play with my

---

in eastern Europe and had formed new, stronger states in central Europe. The attempts of the great powers to use diplomacy to preserve the status quo meant that when inevitable regional war in the Balkans occurred, all powers engaged. That was the deal with World War I.

[5] The only place where I would have really made sense in 1975 was at Nora Ephron's apartment in the Apthorp. She would have really gotten me, and if I'd grown up with parents who really got me, I would be *The Worst.*

boy cousins instead of my girl cousins, but suddenly, this boy cousin was fighting with me and I was supposed to know what to do. What I'm saying is that growing up in a working-class household is a lot like Thunderdome, and I had to figure out how to live life as Master and Blaster combined.

The subject of violence leads us to the other thing I did wrong: I listened to my mom. Since I was two, she'd been scared of me hurting other, smaller kids, so she'd encouraged me to be gentle and kind. Then my cousin and the kids at school realized that giant kid who talked weird wouldn't fight back if you did something to him, so they started coming after me. My parents told me I was supposed to hit them, that it was silly a boy as big as I was didn't just pop them one and shut them up. I was confused.

We talk about nature and nurture when analyzing a person's character.[6] We see two ways that an identity is formed. One is biological, the mean of parents' traits passed down genetically. The other is environmental: How did the world around this person guide and encourage him? The problem is that by either of these methods, I shouldn't be me. I should be shorter and dumber and not at all concerned with what pairs well with star anise syrup in a cocktail.[7] Every man I'm related to has a job that involves digging and concrete. Biologically, I am a proletarian, from many generations of rude mechanicals who did their jobs and did not ask questions. I should be pouring a concrete slab right now instead of writing what you're already sure is one of the most charming memoirs you've ever read.

One Saturday afternoon, while helping my dad in his shop—we were always in that fucking shop—I was thinking about medieval things, as young men are wont to do, and I asked my dad, "If I had lived in medieval times, do you think I could have been a knight?" My dad said, "You would have been a worker. We have never been anything fancy. We have

---

[6] By "we" I of course mean the 1983 film *Trading Places*.

[7] Notes of orange.

always been workers."[8] And he was, generally, mad. He was always mad after I asked things like that. He wouldn't have cared much for that "charming memoirs" line, either.

And the place I was from was no better, narrowing the vision of every child raised there until the only world they could imagine was working a high-paying skilled-labor job, construction or agriculture, so they could afford to drink, go to 49ers games,[9] and get a tricked-out truck. If you asked any little boy in that town, he would tell you he wanted to be a football player or a carpenter. A football player or a pesticide sprayer. Work gave you strong muscles, it let you ride on tractors, it let you play outside and never have to read a schoolbook again. The message was less explicit than my father's words but just as clear. Across all lines of race or culture, the children of Yuba City are workers, and will always be workers.

I did not want to be a worker. I didn't have the power to say "Fuck that" or even to say, resolutely, "*No!*" All I could do was cling to a hope. I hoped I didn't have to do mindless, exhausting work in the hot sun for all my remaining days. I wanted to have a life full of complex ideas, bright colors, and people who did not recreationally kill cats. I didn't know anyone for whom that was true, but still, I dreamed. If this were a musical, it would be the part of the show where I launched into a song that proudly declared my desire to study Torah, or spend a day warm on the sand, or be in America, or find Valjean, but my life was not produced by Cameron Mackintosh. I was scared of the things I wanted.

It was not my hopes, dreams, or desires that kept me from that fate, though. It was my nature. It was my curiosity, which kept me learning

---

[8] If my life were a movie, shortly after this I would have been magically transported back to the Middle Ages to prove my mettle as a knight. Unfortunately, life rarely adheres to the plotlines of Martin Lawrence films.

[9] NFL team affiliation in the Sacramento Valley is an interesting ethnarchy. White people with solid finances like the 49ers. Black, Latino, and economically marginalized whites like the Raiders. The layer in between of white people barely holding on like some other, random team. My dad liked the D.C. team whose name we do not say. The South Asian families just liked soccer.

when I wasn't supposed to. It was my gentleness, which helped me avoid the assault convictions and DUIs that sidetracked my high school classmates. It was my homosexuality, which kept me from accidentally impregnating someone so I'd have to go to work to support her. It was my social confusion, which made me more aware of how people on TV were planning their lives than the people who should have been my friends. Some kids in Sutter County wanted to get out, but they didn't. I was just so wrong at that place that Sutter County rejected me like an Rh-incompatible liver and left me with no option but a life of magic and midlevel adventure.

It would be lovely if this were a book about me finding my place. In which I fled Yuba City and found homosexuality or stand-up comedy, Hollywood or West Hollywood, Ren Faire bead sales or the Church of Scientology, and thereby my problems were resolved. We'd love it if this book were about my dramatic weight loss and my meeting Stephen, the man who made everything *make sense*.

It's not. This isn't going to be a soothing book or a book about how I've finally gotten it all figured out. This book is a survival guide.

In a world where people don't have space for you, you have to make your own space. That takes resolve, more resolve than many people have. I didn't survive because I was smart, strong, or brave. I survived because people showed me the way.

A VOCABULARY LESSON

IN THE BEGINNING WAS the word. A word I did not know.

When I was seven years old, my family went to Disneyland. To my parents, this was one of three cognizable vacations:

1. Disneyland.
2. Fort Bragg, a small, strange town on the Northern California coast with wet gray beaches where my mother would never allow us to swim because of her overwhelming fear that the undertow would carry us off to the sea's depths.
3. Camping, an activity my mother abhorred for reasons unlike those of just about any other identified Jew in America.[1]

---

[1] While most Jews' distaste for camping is a mixture of lack of exposure in their childhood, coupled with the nasty connotation the word "camp" acquired for us during the middle part of the twentieth century, my mother's distaste was the result of excessive exposure. While her mother was an Arkansas Jew, her father was just a regular impoverished, illiterate Arkansas hillbilly. Thus, my mother spent many weeks of her childhood on the side of some mountain, trying to figure out how to

So we went to Disneyland with the regularity that my father's income could afford. On this occasion, which occurred when I was seven, my parents had attempted to economize by bringing a camping trailer to avoid the expense of a hotel. They also consolidated our vacation with that of my uncle's family.

This concerned me.

First of all, my cousins Tori and Robby were comfortable with treatment I could not stomach. They ordered off the children's menu. Their opinions were not welcomed in polite conversation. They got hit with a belt. They were not afforded the luxury of daily baths. I looked at them much like the British looked at the Greeks during the formation of the European Union. How would affiliation with these savages erode *my* rights?

Second, as stated in previous chapters, Robby, in particular, seemed to me the most distasteful of traveling companions. A year younger than I was, he seemed to enjoy only cursing, fighting, and breaking rules. Playing with him was never fun and often resulted in the destruction of my finest action figures. Snake Eyes's swivel-action battle grip was rendered useless after an incident with a wheelbarrow, and He-Man, gnawed on by Robby in some fit of rage, looked like he had necrotizing fasciitis. Nevertheless, he and I were expected to socialize during all of my maternal family's events because we were the only boy cousins. Yet one cannot play with chaos.

Finally, Uncle Ray was a drinker. Until this point, it was an issue that had barely affected me. All of my mother's male relatives drank like it was their profession,[2] and generally, Ray stayed out of my way as much as I stayed out of his. The last thing a guy with a good buzz on wants is a grade-schooler explaining to him what Hobbits are in excruciating detail.

---

cook an opossum her mother would not allow her to eat because it wasn't kosher. She assures me the answer is parboiling it on its own before removing the skin and glands. "Then you just use it like squirrel," she says.

[2] This quality is, of course, derived from their gentile ancestry. I am told they were noted bootleggers of the prohibition era whose financial success was inhibited by their taste for their own product.

This trip, however, was different.

You see, on our first day at Disneyland, we left the park at noon. Traditionally, the only thing that can cause a family to leave Disneyland at noon is a toddler with churro-induced diarrhea. This was not why we left. Our parents told us that the park was going to close down for two hours so the attendants could have lunch. This seemed odd to me. However, since these facts were explained to me by my mother, that gentle creature who'd taught me what clouds were made of, how rainbows happened, and who God was, I trusted their veracity.

The second day it happened, I was less trusting. First of all, the rides kept operating as we were leaving. I pointed this out. My dad told me it was just the people who worked at Disneyland riding them. I also noted that Disney appeared to have a flawed business model: Our supermarket, for example, did not close for lunch; some people had lunch while other people worked, and with a venture as large as Disneyland, it seemed like a similar plan was possible.

My cousins and sister were dull-eyed sheep going where directed. I was stuck on the clear flaws in the story. Yes, I was mad that I was being made to leave Disneyland, but I was even madder that the story didn't make sense. I wanted someone to explain it to me, and I was demanding such an explanation very loudly.

What I never bothered to notice were the two six-packs my uncle Ray openly and notoriously consumed back at the trailer park before our return to the Happiest Place on Earth™. I was seven, so I was inattentive to alcohol sales policies—specifically, to the fact that Disneyland didn't sell booze. Uncle Ray, meanwhile, was not a human being who could spend twelve straight hours in such a place, so the story of the park shutdown had been the compromise tacitly reached. Tragically, all of this could have been avoided if we'd properly understood the science of butt-chugging in 1983.

Let's learn a lesson about me: At the age of seven, I had some instinctive understanding of the laws of economics, enough to recognize that shutting down one's business in the middle of the day was flawed, but I did not fully notice the human being in front of me gunning twelve

Budweisers. That is, theories, facts, and stories have always been very interesting to me, but I'm really great at ignoring things that are actually happening in front of my face. Kind of like if the Department of Education were a person.

Like all major family tourism attractions, Disneyland insatiably consumes the wealth of America's beleaguered working class. Also like all major family tourism attractions, it is surrounded by parasitic minor tourist attractions that survive off the leavings and spatterings of family vacation dollars that do not end up landing in the mouse's maw.[3] There's a Medieval Times, a pirate rip-off of Medieval Times, and lots of other ancillary family entertainments that tempt hardworking midwestern plumbers with the hope that an evening there will delight their children while being moderately less expensive than time spent in Tomorrowland. It's everything Adam Smith dreamed of.

One such enterprise is Knott's Berry Farm. It is an amusement park located on the farm where the boysenberry was invented.[4] I know that doesn't seem like anything particularly impressive, but California is a place without history. Virginia can build its Busch Gardens adjacent to the first democratic legislature in North America, but on the West Coast, which didn't really get going until the mid-1960s, such things were impossible. California history goes pretty quiet in between the

---

[3] Despite this derisive image of the Walt Disney Corporation, its intellectual properties, and its subsidiaries as a predator, please do not think I espouse the opinion that said entities are insidiously evil. Disneyland is a magical place that is more than worth what you pay for it, and Disney is a hell of a movie studio to boot. Essentially, I don't hold that counterintuitive position because it's super-1990s and trite. I do oppose the Disney corporation's continued lobbying efforts to extend the period of copyright to protect Mr. W. Disney's control of Mickey Mouse, mostly because I'd really like to see *Brave New World* in the public domain.

[4] You may be saying, "How can a berry be 'invented'?" This is because you are not from a farm town and have no understanding of agriculture. Basically, they bred four existing berries together into a new berry that was sweeter and less tart than its progenitors. Please learn more about fruit domestication before you try reading further in this book. It's going to keep coming up. Every event from my childhood occurred in the presence of some member of genus *Prunus*.

gold rush and the first McDonald's being built. Thus, we have a berry-themed amusement park.

Every time my family went on vacation to Southern California—or, as we children referred to the lower half of the state, "Disneyland"—we would spend one day at Knott's Berry Farm. To be clear, it has rides and shows and a high-quality, affordable fried chicken dinner. Solid entertainment, but nothing like the Imagineering of the Walt Disney corporation. Knott's Berry Farm was the clove sorbet with which we cleansed our palates before returning for another course of the Happiest Place on Earth™.

Knott's Berry Farm did offer one amusement I have not mentioned: liquor. My uncle Ray found the good time he'd been seeking the duration of our vacation. He could ride roller coasters while shitfaced. This shifted the dynamic of the vacation. We would not be returning to Disneyland. We were now spending the remainder of our vacation enjoying the off-brand delights of a former fruit stand. It was a harrowing foreshadowing of Inauguration 2017.

However, Serendipity knew the game she was playing, for if I'd had a sober uncle or if Mr. Disney hadn't inflicted his temperance upon his guests, I may never have encountered the plate of fried dough that changed my life.

One of the days we were at Knott's Berry Farm, I was playing a carnival game of some sort, doing very poorly because my targeting skills are bad and were even worse during that period when I was growing half a foot every year. If only there had been a carnival game about knowing all the plotlines on *The Love Boat*. When I turned around, my mother had a plate that she offered to me and the other kids. We broke off pieces and ate what was resoundingly the most delightful thing I'd ever experienced. Even though there were no animatronic pirates or struggling actresses dressed like princesses, I was pretty happy.

Then several months passed. Months spent back at school—the drudgery of showing my work in math, being yelled at for my handwriting, playing with G.I. Joes. I was separated by nearly 7 percent of my lived life from the days in Buena Park's most seductive tourist attraction, but I still remembered this second-best part of our trip.[5]

I approached my mother in our home and started to request that she make the dish in question. My mother and I had a rigorously understood entente within the household. I would be the obedient, studious best boy on the planet, and in exchange, she would cook me any food I desired. As time went on, certain strictures were placed upon the agreement: Once I started fifth grade, simply demanding homemade doughnuts on a Wednesday afternoon was no longer really practical, but at this time such boundaries were rare. Chronic weight problems start so beautifully, don't they?

However, I did not know what to ask for. I remembered the thing I'd eaten. Truly, its magnificence had burned its flavor, smell, and image upon my brain. I said I wanted that thing from Knott's Berry Farm. My mother didn't know what I meant, exactly, as we'd eaten lots of things at Knott's Berry Farm.

I plumbed the depths of my mind. I turned the fullness of my not inconsiderable seven-and-a-half-year-old deductive skills to the purpose of describing this Elysian treat that my mother would make for me if I simply asked for it. My mother, mind you, was not annoyed. She was going to do it; she just needed to know what I wanted.

"It was fried spaghetti. Fried spaghetti with sugar on it."

It was the best description I could muster.

My mother was having none of this. You didn't eat fried spaghetti, and you certainly didn't cover it with sugar.

"We ate it with jelly."

---

[5] The first-best part of our trip was this ride for kids, Knott's Bear-y Tales, which smelled like boysenberries. While a very fun ride on its own merits, it was primarily distinguished by the fact that my six-year-old cousin Robby LOVED it. Robby was, traditionally, an animal whose basest instincts could not be held in check by the strongest of mid-1980s ADD drugs. However, he loved that fucking ride. It was, it seemed like, the only time I saw him enjoy a thing that wasn't violent. My mom took him on the ride like fifteen times, and for a brief moment, his savage breast was soothed. Also, the boysenberry smell was nice.

By this point she was certain I was doing that kid thing where you don't make any sense and you're describing something you just dreamed. Surely this fried spaghetti with sugar was just a little fat-boy fantasy, like a kiddie pool full of Jell-O, or having a soda fountain installed in my nightstand. She went back to her housework.

I was broken. How could this have happened? My instinctive bond of understanding with my mother had failed, and I had been denied a sweet treat. I questioned my own sanity. Had I simply dreamed this impossibly perfect food?

The answer was no. It was a funnel cake. I, at seven years old, was asking my mother to make a funnel cake on what was probably a weekday. She probably would have tried it. But that wasn't the point. The point was that I didn't get a funnel cake, and I was pretty sure I'd never get a funnel cake ever again because I did not know what it was named.

I had seen the power a word could have, and I never wanted to be without that power again.

✳

After I became literate, I learned an important lesson about calendars: They list holidays. Now, most holidays don't need listing. Big holidays exist in the world, they are palpable. Christmas, Halloween, and Valentine's Day show up in stores months before they actually happen. People's houses change, TV programming changes, you get to miss school, and, yes, you get themed snacks. These are regular, American, gentile holidays.[6]

But there were other themed snacks. Every winter, there'd come this day when my mom was grating potatoes and stirring and frying and serving them to me for breakfast with sour cream. There was a day in the springtime when a cracker and a story about Moses would happen, and they were great. They were food and stories and a special feeling I

---

[6] The next time you're ready to complain about the war on Christmas, ask when was the last time a CVS reminded you how many shopping days are left until Yom Kippur.

enjoyed. After I acquired literacy, I learned to notice their names written in small letters at the bottom of the days on the calendar.

Autumn was a nice slew of events. The school-missing and the ham of Thanksgiving, the latkes and the discussion of how we weren't supposed to eat ham on Hanukkah, then the presents and school vacation and breakfast ham of Christmas. And the New Year's Day black-eyed peas and ham. It was quite a ham-based run.[7] I'd had a great time, but I had, honestly, developed a problem. I was hooked. Addicted. For the better part of two months, I'd had a steady stream of thematic treats, and my body needed more.

I think my mom got me a chocolate Advent calendar that year, too. That was not okay. No child who's getting multiple religion-based holidays should go deep enough into Christianity to receive a daily dose of chocolate counting down the days to Christmas. Not when latkes are also in play. At least there weren't enough Jews to find gelt in my town.

The point is that after New Year's Day, I crashed. I was jonesing for some biblical stories and a ritually significant cookie. I was looking everywhere for a fix. So I went to my old friend The Calendar to see what she had for me. There, in small, precise letters under January 6, was a word.

"What is 'Epiphany'?" I asked my mom.

She had never heard this word. I showed it to her. She told me it wasn't for us. It wasn't a Jewish thing, and it wasn't a regular Protestant thing, so I was getting no snacks.

It was a good word, though. It sounded nice. I didn't know why. I kept saying it to myself at school for no reason.

I went to the dictionary. It was a valuable book, not as fun as an

---

[7] You're going to need to accept that my experience of Judaism was something very distinct from your understanding of Judaism. My grandmother's ancestors emigrated from Germany to New Orleans, the heart of America's ham basket. They became peddlers in Arkansas, a place which then had little infrastructure for the practice of Judaism. My grandma's dad pissed someone off and he became dead to his family. Without kith or kin, he went native in the Ozark Mountains of Arkansas and became a sharecropper. They could rarely afford meat, and what they could afford was traif. Ergo, you will find a deeply inconsistent but passionate construction of the laws of Kashrut from my mother and grandmother in these pages.

encyclopedia,[8] but I went to it first all the same. I assiduously flipped through the E's and eventually found it: "Epiphany." It was a holiday, the commemoration of the Magi visiting the Christ child, or his baptism or his circumcision or something. But it was also another thing: "A usually sudden manifestation or perception of the essential nature of something, an intuitive grasp of reality through something usually simple and striking, an illuminating discovery, realization, or disclosure."

I hadn't known a word could carry so much in it. It described a shocking, striking power I hadn't known existed but had maybe felt the edge of. This beautiful-sounding word (almost as euphonious as the word "euphonious") had an even more beautiful, powerful meaning. Learning the meaning of the word "epiphany" was an epiphany. Again, I wanted more.

❖

The Sapir-Whorf hypothesis is an idea in linguistics that language influences the world we perceive. Edward Sapir said, "No two languages are ever sufficiently similar to be considered as representing the same social reality. The worlds in which different societies live are distinct worlds, not merely the same world with different labels attached." It's what that Amy Adams movie with the space squids is about.

Do you know what a "velleity" is? My Microsoft Word doesn't. The word has a red squiggly line under it right now. I had to check with the Internet to make sure I'd spelled it right. (I hadn't. No one said I was a good speller. That said, when I corrected the spelling, Word still had no idea what this word was.)

A velleity is the lowest valence of desire. It's a wish so slight you'd never even act on it. Can you have a velleity if you don't know what that word means? I don't know, because I do.

If you don't know the words "coral," "fuchsia," "amaranth," or "cerise,"

---

[8] The 1980 *World Book Encyclopedia* volume M was my closest personal friend between the ages of seven and eleven. This relationship will be discussed in greater detail later in the book.

can you see them as distinct colors or do they just all look pink to you? It's not a rhetorical question. That's the question the Sapir-Whorf hypothesis answers, and the answer is "Kind of and kind of not."

This strange little hunger of mine changed me. The same way my hunger for snacks made me fat, my hunger for words engorged me. It made me fit in spaces differently. Whether I realized it or not, I had wanted these words for the power they would give me. Power in the world, definitely: Prime-time television had made clear to me that the world was run by people with better vocabularies than the farmers and construction workers of my hometown. I wanted to tussle in the world of kings and princes. But there were more private and subtle powers I wanted, too. I wanted to be able to explain the ways I felt that did not make sense. I wanted to put words to lonelinesses, desires, and fears that it seemed my classmates and cousins didn't have.

Like most children, I was a shithead. I spent years voraciously consuming all the language I could, sliding it around in my brain and in my mouth to sop up all the feelings inside me. And when I finally had the words, who was there to know what any of those fucking words meant? Communication isn't a thing you can do alone.

Let's be honest: There were people. My mom and teachers, kind of. But definitely not my peers. They told me that I talked weird. They called me "Gandhi" because I was always talking fancy, which frankly was strange at a school where around a quarter of the kids were South Asian. My dad said I was "putting on airs." My dad's parents, whose education had ended at eighth grade, thought I was making fun of them when I used an unorthodox word. I just thought if we had nice words like "clergy" or "textile" or "epiphany," we ought to use them.

Books were full of words that let me see the whole world and myself with clarity and precision, but the price was that I lived in a world where the only people who seemed to really understand me lived in books. Thank God I ended up learning the word "Faustian," so I could succinctly describe this bargain to exactly no one.

But if there was a word I could never really understand the meaning of in Yuba City, California, in the 1980s, it was "normal."

On a very fundamental level, the moral of this story is that I'm not particularly observant of my fellow human beings. In the same way I couldn't see that Uncle Ray's drunkenness was what forced us out of Disneyland for the afternoon, I just never paid enough attention to the people around me at school or in my family to be able to communicate with them. A different person—by which I mean a different gay ten-year-old—could have felt his way through the texture of their world and language. He could have found the nuances of their world. He could have figured out what I was supposed to talk about and how I was supposed to talk about it. He could have used that language to camouflage himself from their scrutiny and for no other purpose. Because one of the things the Sapir-Whorf hypothesis teaches us is that the world you live in defines your language and your language defines your world, and Yuba City, California, in the 1980s was not a world that had sensitive little boys in it. It had a language that was very complex and nuanced in its descriptions of horses, rifles, and pickup trucks, but no words for things that were interesting or cathartic to me. Like, say, "catharsis."

I realized that saying the right thing was not an option. These words I'd hoped would give me power had made me a target. They marked me as an outsider in the only world I'd ever known. The young homosexual is, however, a consummate survivor. If my voice, diction, and vocabulary were going to mark me as untowardly florid, I would hide myself in the only other way I could. So, for a decade, I became quiet.

BOTHERED AND BEWILDERED

I DO NOT KNOW when I first realized I was from a bullshit[1] tiny farm town, but I remember looking at a road sign for Butte House Road, the road that led out of Yuba City and into Tierra Buena, the area where we lived, and misreading it as "Butter House," then thinking, "That's not a name for a place that matters." As I was not yet a capable reader; I would have been four or so.

It is probably *Sesame Street*'s fault. *Sesame Street* in the 1970s was obsessed with trying to help inner-city children understand that there was a wider world out there where eggs and milk came from. I remember watching a segment about a crying, screaming baby in the city and the process by which milk got from the country to him. The sadness of the baby was too much for me. Frankly, I hope the people behind that segment are reading this so that I can properly register my complaint: There were too many steps in the milk production and transport pro-

---

[1] To provide some empirical support to my repeated assertions of Yuba City's shittiness, I should note that when Rand McNally compiled a ranking of American cities in 1985, Yuba City was named the worst city in America.

cess. The milk took forever to get to that baby[2]; it was *Precious* levels of pathos.

But the point is that *Sesame Street* wanted city children to know what the country was like, but they had no interest in placing any other children in context. The "country" they presented was a Willa Cather cliché: farmhouses surrounded by acres of wheat, no one in sight for miles. *Sesame Street* could realistically portray the emotional life of an eight-foot-tall canary, but it had no idea how rural people lived, loved, or socialized; it imagined them as mythical beasts whose only interest was producing milk for that crying baby. It seems that disregard for the agrarian proletariat is a timeless hobby for everyone in a capitalist system, even Children's Television Workshop producers. Never trust anyone in a Volvo.

I would ask my mom a lot whether we lived in the city or the country. Of course, I knew that Yuba City was nearby, but even though the word "city" was in its name, I also knew it wasn't really a city and we didn't live in it. Yet, contrary to what *Sesame Street* depicted, we also weren't isolated from other houses by miles. There were, indeed, houses next to us, but across the street and behind us were orchards (peach and almond, respectively)—which I'd never seen on TV. Pomoculture has no place in the American popular imagination, I guess.

My mom answered me by saying we lived in a "rural area." What a useless answer. This was exactly the kind of too-precise response that she was always giving me for my too-precise questions—something wholly outside of my frame of reference that would force me to go out of my comfort zone and learn something about where I lived.[3] Damn her.

What I learned, in the end, is that I didn't want to live where I lived.

---

[2] The segment is currently available on YouTube. It is four and a half minutes long. That's a long time for grade school me to have to be worrying about whether that poor baby was going to get milk or die of starvation. I encourage you to watch it to witness just how emotionally draining a film it is.

[3] My comfort zone was learning about places I did not live, preferably fictitious lands full of sorceresses.

Where I lived was hot, dull, and full of people who were angry at me. It was kind of like hell, but with fewer gay people. The place should have been a boy-child's paradise, with all the gunplay, roughhousing, and messiness, but I found it excruciating. I knew there was a better, cleaner, more organized world somewhere else. I knew this because, ironically, I'd seen it on TV.

Living in a rural area, my family did not have access to cable television until I was sixteen. You see, there weren't enough people near us for it to be financially sound for the cable company to lay cable out to us. Civilization, it seemed, was a volume business. What this means is that for most of my childhood, my primary tools to learn about the wider world were the five to seven channels we could get with our TV antenna.

Let me tell you about the world on TV. It was sophisticated and full of well-dressed people saying interesting things and living in houses with few or no rats in them. Let me tell you about living in an almond orchard: There are a lot of rats. Rat food is literally falling from the trees for six months of the year. And when it wasn't rats, it was their somewhat more sartorially engaged cousins, the ground squirrels, who were constantly seeking refuge in our attic like tiny, even more hirsute Dutch Jews.[4] We didn't have cats because we wanted them; we had them because they were the thin, furry line between us and an army of rodents full of the healthy fats and calcium of California almonds. So the general absence of vermin and livestock from the lives of people on television was spectacularly appealing to me. I wanted into that world.

And the 1980s were a glorious time for sitcoms. America's thirty-year uncontested dominance in the Western world, Reagan's sweeping tax credits, and Bill Cosby's ability to keep his serial sexual abuse under wraps combined to create a nation that was ready to make sweet, sweet love to the mythos of its middle class. *Family Ties*, *The Cosby Show*, *Growing Pains*, and serried ranks of mediocre imitators presented this real America where no one was engaged in manufacturing or agricul-

---

[4] This is a hilarious Anne Frank joke.

tural work. Everyone went to college. Problems were simple and solved in a half hour. Checks never bounced unless it was due to a hilariously contrived misunderstanding, and dads were never unemployed for more than an episode. It was heaven.

But before I watched 1980s sitcoms, I watched sitcoms from earlier eras. In my observation, there are three kinds of television all kids like: Kids watch cartoons, they watch shows with singing and dancing, and they watch old sitcoms. We know these things, but we don't really think about them. Let's take a moment to think about what aspects of a kid's life these entertainments are speaking to. Well, except for the singing and dancing shows. We know why they like them: Children are dumb and you don't need to know anything to enjoy watching Kelly Clarkson sing or Rumer Willis and a Russian guy do a paso doble. Also, they're really good.

Cartoons are fantastically absurd illustrations of the basic power relationships of our culture. The ones I grew up with were obsessed with the dynamics between predators and prey. A mouse always outsmarting the cat trying to eat him, a rabbit always outsmarting the hunter trying to eat him, a roadrunner always outsmarting the coyote trying to eat him. When I was a child, this disturbed me greatly. Wile E. Coyote never got to eat. *Never*. I know that, intellectually, we're supposed to imbue the roadrunner with personhood and be shocked by the idea that a coyote would want to eat him, but a child from a farm doesn't have the privilege of psychological dissonance on this point. Some animals eat other animals (and even I, as a human, am one of those animals that eat animals). Somehow *Looney Tunes* was expecting that the only way Wile E. Coyote could be a morally upright individual was to subvert his very nature and starve.[5] While I had no idea at the age of four that I was gay, I was nevertheless recognizing and being disturbed by the very same warped cultural sentiment that would demand virginity of me until law school. Way to foreshadow, Chuck Jones.

---

[5] I never realized until this moment what a deeply Jainist sentiment this is.

Culture for children is obsessed with animals. Anthropomorphized creatures dominate storybooks, cartoons, and the world of Disney. Even before that, baby books are teaching you animal names and the culturally sanctioned sound that each barnyard animal makes. But who is the audience for these books? Most children saying "The pig says oink" will never meet or spend significant time with a pig, and those of us who had periodic social contact with a chicken could have told you what it "said" from firsthand experience.

Pardon me for a moment while I digress from my digression. To children on a farm, chickens are not cartoon creatures concerned that the sky is falling. To us, they are the enemy. Chickens are assholes. When I was four, it became one of my daily duties to go collect eggs from our chicken coop. This meant that every day, I had to stare down a rooster while I prepared to steal his unborn progeny from his harem of concubines. This rooster, descendant of the velociraptor, at nearly three feet tall, with feet that nature had seen fit to equip with little knives, didn't seem like a fun cartoon; he seemed like my equal—my nemesis. Every day, as I did my Mom-given duty, he would peck and claw at my shins, and every day I would wish him, and all his smelly, dumb chicken concubines, ill.

Periodically, one of our dogs would find its way into the chicken coop and kill all the chickens. Every time this happened, my singular thought was "Vengeance!"

Less than a year ago, I was holding my three-year-old niece, Ali, and we saw a red-tailed hawk snatch a sparrow out of the sky. We discussed what had happened, and then I asked her if the incident had upset her. Ali gently placed her hand to the side of my face and said, "Uncle, hawks eat birds." It wasn't drama. It was nature.

I guess what I've been trying to say since two digressions ago is that children's media is obsessed with animals because animals help children make sense of the hierarchies and orders in the world around them. Coyotes, cats, and men in fur caps are hunters; bears and wolves are scary; and cows, chickens, and dogs are domesticated animals you can befriend and talk to. The observed world that Ali uses as a basis of understanding—that is, a world of rural farm life—doesn't exist for most kids, so those kids have to learn to place themselves in the world through stories about animals who can stylize the orders in their own lives. Kids in suburban Dallas can't necessarily watch a fox snatch eggs from their chicken coop, so they must learn what a fox is, and what it represents, from Swiper the Fox taking Dora the Explorer's backpack. These primitive, exaggerated archetypes help them understand their own place in life. As small, weak creatures, children can identify with the small, weak prey, and imagine for a moment that they might subvert the power dynamics like Road Runner, Tweety Bird, and Jerry always manage to.

✻

What does all of this have to do with old sitcoms?

If cartoons and children's books about animals are an attempt to educate children about their place in their family and the biological order from which humans emerged, old sitcoms are repurposed culture through which kids learn about the world they're going into. Or, more simply, old sitcoms are used by children as a primer on sophistication.

You might be ready to dismiss all of my experiences as outdated and meaningless, unrelated to the lives of the cool young people of today, but kids are still watching these shows. My niece watched the entirety of *M*A*S*H* one summer and recently plowed through *The Office*. Tina Fey just told a story on *Late Night with Seth Meyers* about her eleven-year-old daughter watching all of *The Andy Griffith Show*. So my point is super-valid and contemporary, just like me.

One could respond, "Well, of course kids like sitcoms. They are silly and fun." This is missing the point. The point is that the old sitcoms that kids are watching have little to do with the contemporary world. Kids therefore consume them differently: alone, alongside sitcoms written specifically for children, as opposed to watching with their family, the way they watch contemporary sitcoms.

So why are kids watching sitcoms with Nixon jokes or references to MC Hammer or the McDLT? I think the reason is twofold. First, you're learning what adults are talking about. Encapsulated in the judgment of a joke are dense lessons about specific pieces of culture: *Barry Manilow is lame. Brad Pitt is handsome. "I have a girlfriend who lives in Canada" is a thing sad guys say to seem cool.* When I watched *The Brady Bunch* for the first time, I didn't know who fucking Davy Jones and Joe Namath were, but I can now reference them as the cultural icons they will eternally be.

Where did you learn what Harvard was? With the exception of children born to Crimson alumni or faculty, I'd hazard a guess that you learned it from a joke on a sitcom, and if you're Gen X or Millennial, that joke was probably on an old sitcom. It's where we learn the things everyone knows. Even those kids whose parents were on the Harvard School of Divinity faculty did. What did they learn from their real-life experiences? *Harvard is where Mom works. Harvard is a place in Cambridge.* Meanwhile, on TV, particularly on situation comedies, is where you learned *Harvard means smart.*

The other, more important function old sitcoms provide is a large volume of simulated adult social interactions in which kids learn about expected behavior in a low-stakes environment. Remember in *WarGames* when Matthew Broderick is trying to teach the war computer that not all games have a winner and loser? He makes the computer play tic-tac-toe over and over again, and then it starts simulating nuclear wars. *Then* it realizes that no one wins a nuclear war, so the world is saved only to go back to the Cold War for another eight years of crippling Defense Department spending.

What I'm saying is that cartoons are tic-tac-toe, and old sitcoms are simulated nuclear wars.[6] Old sitcoms involve people outside of your understood cultural context clues having a polite struggle or misunderstanding, and then someone within their group has enough social savvy to solve the problem at hand. To illustrate, let us go to America's most

---

[6] Shows with singing and dancing are Ally Sheedy in *WarGames*, a nice break from all that conflict.

beloved and prestigious sitcom: *The Facts of Life*. Tootie is obsessed with Jermaine Jackson, so she abandons a scholarship fair to go to his concert, then sneaks into his dressing room only to discover that Jermaine Jackson has nothing to say to her. Also, the papier-mâché bust she made for him is destroyed out of concern that it may be a bomb. Then, wise, noble Mrs. Garrett explains that fanatical obsession with pop stars is something that happens to teenage girls—she was obsessed with Sinatra in her day—but one mustn't let it overwhelm their identity. Everything returns to normal, and then they do it again. When I watched this, I had no idea who Jermaine Jackson was, nor Sinatra, nor scholarship fairs. I was able to piece together what they meant as cultural symbols, and accept the cultural lesson: Don't be a teen girl who sneaks into a pop star's[7] dressing room.

So why *old* sitcoms? One issue is volume: Network sitcoms have traditionally been disseminated in sums of twenty to twenty-six per year. That's fewer than one every two weeks. Old sitcoms, however, are just lying around, being broadcast six times a day on the Oxygen network. You can get through a lot of human interactions that way. The other issue is that they are removed enough to be safe. *Black-ish* may be asking necessary and relevant questions about race in the present day, but old sitcoms are discussing questions that are well settled. Alex P. Keaton does speed to get good grades, but learns drugs are bad. Jessie Spano does speed to get good grades, but learns drugs are bad. Cherie plays in a refrigerator, nearly suffocates, and Punky Brewster must use CPR on her before we learn playing in refrigerators is bad and knowing CPR is good. They are like law school casebooks for everyday life that we give to curious ten-year-olds.

So why sitcoms? Why can't old prime-time dramas do the same work? I would argue that they are not as interpretable by children. Dramas require that you react to the facts being given, and that you use your own knowledge of human interpersonal dynamics to identify the

---

[7] We're being so generous.

central conflicts. Sitcoms don't. They have constant metatext going on in the form of jokes. In the pilot of *The Mary Tyler Moore Show*, Phyllis's daughter Bess says, "Aunt Rhoda's a lot of fun. Mom hates her." The irony in the joke allows it to pack concentrated knowledge about these characters. Rhoda is fun, Phyllis hates Rhoda, Phyllis hates fun, Phyllis's job in future scenes will be to hate fun, Rhoda's job in future scenes will be to piss off Phyllis.

The much scourged laugh track is astoundingly helpful, too. Like the dramatic overpronunciation of instructional language recordings, it tells you when to identify tension in language. Mary asks, "You lied to me?" Rhoda says, "You betcha!" and the laugh track sounds. This is not how normal life works. But it's funny—as disarming as it is informative.

Sitcoms make knowing human nature a fun game, but they also provide an important window into other lives, with an emphasis on what makes those lives like yours. The sets of multicam sitcoms so frequently place the center of the perspective in the center of the living room, in front of the couch, where the sitcom family's (or young gal in the city's) television would be. It is, then, a type of fun-house mirror for your parents' living room.

The first old sitcom I fell in love with was *The Dick Van Dyke Show*. It played every day at noon and twelve thirty on one of the stations in Sacramento, so during the summers, my mother would give my sister and me our lunch, and we would forget the heat of a Sacramento Valley summer and the phalanx of rodents mounting an offense on our attic by transporting ourselves to New Rochelle in 1962. My mother gave this show to us as if it were a gift. It was the only family sitcom her father had allowed his children to watch. He apparently found the domestic simplicity of *The Donna Reed Show* too distant from his family's impoverished, alcoholic reality, but he couldn't help himself with ol' Dick Van Dyke.[8] The show was just too funny.

---

[8] Perhaps he subconsciously sensed Mr. Van Dyke's own drinking problem and could relate to him as a kindred spirit.

And it was. *The Dick Van Dyke Show* is totally the thing that taught me what a comedy writer is. It was probably one of the key early steps in directing me to my current professional path. It also, along with the dozens of other sitcoms I was watching at the time, slowly began to teach me about the suburbs.

The suburbs, it seemed, were a place of infinite access. The schools were well funded and full of clubs and programs. You could take French in high school. There was no dog shit, there were no miscarried puppies in the front yard.[9] Dads in the suburbs had these cool professional jobs: They were doctors, architects, and therapists. There was no gunplay. There were no almonds that required care. Children never had to hear stories about how recent rain patterns had depressed construction employment, making their request for a G.I. Joe an assault on the family's stability. The families were pretty and happy, and their homes were devoid of the lurking fear of Dad's anger.

My favorite old sitcom of all time is one of the suburbiest—*Bewitched*. If you don't know what *Bewitched* is, I'm super-sad and think Nick at Nite has failed you. *Bewitched* was a pleasant domestic sitcom about a good-natured ad man and his loving wife, and it represented the most compelling fantasy of what I, as a child, wanted life to be like.

Samantha and Darrin Stephens live in a suburb so suburby it isn't even named. They have a charming home with a yard, but Darrin works in the city. (The connection and access to the city are important.) Furthermore, their lives are chic. Sam makes Darrin drinks when he gets home, and they are often entertaining clients at home or in the city. This means that Sam has to dress up cute all the time. Finally, their children, when they come, are small. These are not stories about management of their brood but about their own adult lives. Also, this meant that I had no children near my age to be jealous of.

---

[9] I once ran across a miscarried Chesapeake Bay retriever fetus in the front yard. It looked like a terrifying little monster, and I was pretty sure I was in the first five minutes of a Stephen King movie. I didn't tell anyone, and it took me years to figure out what it was.

Oh, and by the way, Sam is an actual witch.

What I love about *Bewitched* is that it never *needed* the witch stuff. It could have just been a little domestic comedy about a couple like in *I Love Lucy*, but it was so solid without the magical material that the witches seemed all the more relatable. Sitting atop this well-oiled machine of 1960s American suburb were two witches and a warlock: Endora, who wore flowing robes of unnatural secondary colors and makeup a drag queen would find unsubtle; Aunt Clara, who was daffy but formidable; and Uncle Arthur, who was funny but prickly. Each represented a powerful force for impracticality and skewed perspective. There were going to be arguments about appliances, misunderstandings with neighbors, and awkward dinners with clients, why not let some fabulous people come in and use their unholy powers to make the conflict even queerer?

While the suburbs of *The Dick Van Dyke Show* represented an important place to which I did not have access, the witches of *Bewitched* allowed me to enter it. Though I loved the three-bedroom palaces of typical sitcom families, I nevertheless worried that there was no space for a boy as fat, poor, and "different" as I was. But Endora—Endora was fabulous and did not give a fuck. Her spells could turn Darrin pregnant, emasculating the patriarchal head of the family, or transform her into Samantha's seductive double to confuse the sexual order, or turn one of Darrin's clients into a cat, confusing class distinctions. From these old sitcoms, I was learning how adult society worked, but Endora was the one character who could consistently upset the fundamental forces of that order. As much as *The Dick Van Dyke Show* made me want to be a comedy writer, *Bewitched* made me want to be a witch—someone who used her powers to make her environment extraordinary instead of stifling.

*

I guess it might have been easier if I'd just wanted to slip through the bonds of class and become a suburban dad. And I half did. Up through law school, my life choices centered around doing everything I could to secure the safety and stability of a white-collar job. On some level, I always dreamed of sliding into a life of uncomplicated suburban domesticity, although I could never entirely tell where I would fit.

Deeper within me, the lust for power wanted more. I wanted to be the creature from outside who, through wit and style, had the power to vex the lives of the happy suburban men who ruled the world. I wanted to make *entrances* and to entrance. I wanted to ridicule people to their faces and get away with it. I could never be Alex P. Keaton or Theo Huxtable. I thought maybe I had it in me to be Endora.

Which was, possibly, why I loved Samantha Stephens so much. She was trapped in a world that did not respect or appreciate all she had to offer, but she was trying to fit in to it for the sake of family. She had all the magic and attitude of an Endora but was holding it in check to keep her household stable, just like me. I lived for those moments when she let loose and used her powers, be they magical or verbal. I was dying for my chance to try out mine.

And hey, if I was going to have to break out of my home and economic class, leave behind everything and everyone I'd known to be a person who mattered in the world, why stop at snagging a white-collar job? If you're going to risk it all, why not try to be magical?

CAMOUFLAGE AND PLUMAGE

I AM A GAY man, and that means I do not like the sound of my own voice.

I do not know when my voice diverged markedly enough from that of other children to be noteworthy, but to say that it's "always" been like that would be intellectually dishonest. Also, all children sound like faggots. When you're three, you're allowed to talk about how soft rose petals are, really *romance* the idea, and everyone's going to be cool with it. At three, you've spent so much of your life with people describing you and everything you own as "cute" that you don't think twice about describing your beloved stuffed horse or your own romper with that highly problematic word. At three, you're still learning how gender works, so it takes a bit longer before anyone figures out you've learned it wrong. What I'm saying is it's too early to hope that all those photos of Prince George enraptured by bubbles mean anything.

I remember, at age eight or so, actively thinking, "Ladies talk nicely." I didn't think "Ladies talk nice" because I understood grammar. I had not learned *grammar* wrong. I understood grammar as it was supposed to be used, not as it was actually used. I was a proscriptive, not descriptive, eight-year-old. I didn't use constructions that the kids around me did for the sake of fitting in. I suppose in my later life, not fitting in with people my age would be an issue and a struggle, but for me at the advent of my personhood, it wasn't a concern. I wanted to fit in, just not with the people everyone else wanted me to fit in with. I wanted to sound like a mom. I wanted to drink coffee. I wanted to not yell—because in my ideal world, I wouldn't need to.

Soon I was stuck with a larynx full of problems. I'd open my mouth and kids would know there was something wrong with me. I mean, adults did, too. From the first sound, they understood that I wasn't playing by the rules. It was tone, it was syntax, it was grammar, it was content. There was no portion of my speech that fit with my unusually large male frame. They let their distaste be known.

It was at this point in my life that I was first diagnosed as gay. Not by a physician or a drag queen or whomever the state-certified professional would be to make such a ruling.[1] It was my classmates. My parents, you see, had been foolish enough to name me after my paternal grandfather. They didn't intend to call me by his name, Guy; they intended to participate in a strange southern custom where you give a kid a preposterous first name, then call him by his middle name or some weird nickname like Butch or Tubby. However, my parents were deeply unimaginative on the middle-name front, selecting one of the most blandly popular boys' names of the 1970s: Michael. For the first four years of my life, I was known as Mikey to all. However, when I arrived in kindergarten, the teacher summarily informed my mother that with five other Michaels in the class, Michaeling for me would not be an option. I was to be Guy. From archangel to generic man in under a day.

Through this unexpected chain of events, I was positioned in third grade at a California public school with a name that was one letter away from the word "gay." My classmates very quickly parsed this out for themselves and began a rich, exciting tradition of calling me "Gay Guy"

---

[1] The Commissioner of Major League Sodomy.

on the playground. If educators could only structure more deductive reasoning to end in the ridicule of a classmate, student engagement would skyrocket.

Now, let's be clear: As an eight-year-old, I wasn't having that much recreational sex. I hadn't bottomed, almost never went to gay bars, had no Streisand albums, and had seen Judy only in *The Wizard of Oz* and *Meet Me in St. Louis*. These kids weren't calling me gay because of whom I was having sex with, or because of my participation in a subculture, they were calling me gay because of my gender expression. These days we love to describe sexuality and gender as independent, unrelated axes: Gay is about whom you have sex with; trans is about how you express your gender. It sounds like an intelligent construction but was proved to be sorely misguided by the fieldwork I did on the playground of Tierra Buena Elementary School between 1984 and 1989.

I told my parents about the bullying. They told me I wouldn't have these problems if I acted more like a boy. For so many kids, that is the real fear when it comes to being bullied about being gay. It's not that other kids around you are mocking you, it's the fact that you know if you go to the authority figures, they will not sympathize with your situation. Actually, I don't know if that's the real fear for other people, I just knew it was for me. When I told my parents, "They called me a fag," my parents didn't say, "That's horrible. We will stop them." My parents said, "That's horrible. Stop being a fag."

I was supposed to hit Joe Mendoza, the central fag-caller: This was my parents' proposed solution. You were supposed to start a fight when someone called you gay, and if you didn't start a fight when someone called you gay, there was clearly something very wrong with you. You were probably a fag.

I tried. Joe just danced out of my way, then ran back in and punched me. Joe was gifted with excesses of speed and strength long before such skills were augmented by the powers of puberty, and he had older brothers who beat the shit out of him all the time, teaching him the refined, nuanced points of the shit-beating-out arts. I had no idea what I was doing; fighting was the least natural thing for me. If you could silence a bully by drawing a family tree of the Greek gods, or synopsizing the plot of *Time Bandits*, I would have been really good at that. For fighting I had nothing. I thought we weren't supposed to fight, I thought we were supposed to discuss our problems. The way I thought the world was supposed to work and the way it was working were at a significant disjuncture.

And let's make something else clear: These cruel, evil children in the schoolyard, these heinous bullies, all they were doing was calling me something that I was. They lived in a world where media told them gay people existed, and gave them adequate tools to be able to locate me as a gay when I was just eight years old. They received essentially no guidance about how to deal with gay people from their parents; they relied upon a pop culture that told them gay people were ridiculous and risible. Those bullies in the schoolyard weren't monsters or even bullies, they were children trying to make sense of the world. They called me the thing I am; the teachers, administrators, and parents around us just couldn't bring themselves to respond to it.

Mrs. Carol Sanger was my third- and fourth-grade teacher. She was the best teacher. No teacher ever liked me more than she did, and when she realized this was going on, we had a classroom discussion about it. She was going to fix it. Guy being made fun of was brought out in the open, and she said it wasn't acceptable. Guy being made fun of for being fat. That was what we talked about in class, how people were calling me fat. No one ever called me fat. I was super-fat, but a lot of them were, too. No, what they called me was gay, but Mrs. Sanger couldn't say that. I don't think anyone in 1985 was culturally equipped to deal with the possibility of a nine-year-old being gay. We just had to collectively pretend that gay people emerged fully grown from pods cultivated at liberal arts colleges, or were formed from Judith Light's tears.

In fourth grade, I learned that there was something about me that made me audibly different from the other boys my age. I could not mask it, I could not change it, I couldn't fight so well that I could earn the respect of my classmates. So I became quiet, very quiet, for a long time.

That's not what everyone does. Some people get really good at making the right noises. They listen closely, they shape and shade their words, becoming a perfect sign and semblance of a man. When you are prey, you learn to camouflage.

Much is made of the fact that gay people do not look distinctly different from straight people. The idea that we can pass is supposed to make our marginalization easier. *Oh, if you can hide, why not just hide?* Well, first of all, who wants to send their personality to live in a secret annex above the pectin company?[2] The idea that gays would be fine if we just hated ourselves into zombie facsimiles of straight people is gross.

Also, it's what we do a lot of the time. Some people get really good at it. The ability to shift between codes is common in many minority groups, but when you're an invisible minority, some people turn into chameleons. That's what Matt Bomer is. Do you know Matt Bomer? He's that gay actor who stared on the USA series *White Collar* and looks like if someone imagined what being a happy, handsome, well-adjusted straight guy would look like. I'm willing to bet that at some point in time in Matt Bomer's origin story, he was so deeply ashamed of who he was that he vowed to be the perfectest, normalest image of man possible. And he succeeded. Now he can be anyone.

It's the speech that Mystique gives in *X2*, the terribly named 2003 X-Men movie. Mystique is a mutant with the literal power to chameleon into any shape or voice she chooses, so Nightcrawler says to her, "I heard you can imitate anyone . . . then why not stay in disguise all the time?" Mystique says, "Because we shouldn't have to." I know we're supposed to hate Bryan Singer for his various sexual improprieties, but I nevertheless treasure the amount of real queer sentiment hidden in that film. Few lines have so incisively characterized the rage I feel that we're expected to spend our lives hiding.

But I don't really mean "our," because the other side of "You can't expect us to spend our lives hiding" is that some people can't hide.

---

[2] This is also a hilarious Anne Frank joke.

I am one of those people. I wish I'd spent all of my closeted years of self-hatred turning into a perfect simulation of a masculine, muscular straight guy. I wish I'd learned their ways enough to manipulate them. I didn't. I'm one of the gay guys whose voices always marked us as men outside masculinity. I came to understand it as a test. I would open my mouth, speak, then wait to see how the room reacted. A gay voice, a truly, magnificently gay voice isn't just a weakness, though. Plumage is an adaptation just as much as camouflage.

Before 2010, people loved to say, "They can be gay; I just don't want them to shove it in my face." First, no one is shoving their gayness in your face. Unless you're on the street watching a parade in a major American city in June. Then it's entirely possible someone's shoving their homosexuality in your face. If you don't like it, go half a block away and return to the nice, boring world of straight people shoving straightness in your face. What they were really saying is that they don't want to hear the audible parts of being gay. This is people policing expressive gayness. This is Mitt Romney and friends holding down a gay classmate in 1964 and cutting off his too-noticeable bangs. Plumage is all of the parts of male homosexuality that culture wants to tell you are unnecessary. Films and TV are always showing you gay guys like Adam Pally on *Happy Endings* or Andy Samberg in *I Love You, Man* or Woody Harrelson in *Friends with Benefits* or any number of other gay characters who aren't like those *other* gay guys. They exist to remind gay guys that a virtuous path exists if only they can manage to ape the behaviors and culture of straight men. That is why they're not fun or cool.

I have one question: How is any gay guy supposed to know if some other guy is gay?

Yes, we have telephones now with nice apps like Grindr, but before that, outside of that, how were these gay guys supposed to locate and identify other gay guys?

No one thought about that when building these characters, because they weren't characters. They were props, symbols of gay men that exist only to serve a straight story, performed by straight men who haven't really thought about what it's like to be gay. No one ever thought, "What will it take for this guy to be happy?" They just thought, "Why do gay guys have to sound all faggy like that?"[3]

We have to sound all faggy like this so we can find each other. Gays are a small, diffuse, physically invisible minority. This is deeply isolating. We spend most of our lives in your world, where only 70 to 80 percent of our actual life is executable. It takes other gay people for us to have sex, but also other, less basic operations of identity. Sharing experiences, building relationships, and fighting for equality. We have to locate mates; otherwise, how are we going to make more gay people?

At nearly anywhere in the world that isn't a gay bar, we must assume the people around us are straight. If we make a mistake about that, we could get killed. In forty-eight states, you are allowed to say you murdered a man because he was gay and hit on you, and that can be considered an affirmative defense that reduces your crime from murder, which can carry a sentence of twenty-plus years, to voluntary manslaughter, which can involve as short a sentence as three years. Identifying other gay people is a delicate science. Staring at dudes like they're a piece of meat is useful, but it can't do all the work.

One time I was doing comedy on a cruise ship at a comedy festival run by the podcast network I work with. The festival-goers constituted about 10 percent of the ship's guests. The rest of the ship was occupied by nice families, grandparents and grandkids, family reunion parties. One afternoon I was walking past the pool and I heard fun. I heard a male voice that didn't feel a need to sound particularly male. I walked up and introduced myself, and the moment he heard my voice, he knew why.

---

[3] Let's define the specific texture of this gay voice of which I speak. It is characterized by a careful pronunciation, a rapid variation in pitch, elements of upspeak, possible nasality, and *s*'s so sibilant they might be described as a lisp. Such modes of speech are now hardly exclusive to gay men, as anyone who's heard David Beckham speak can attest. Vocabulary, emphasizing florid adjectives, and strong opinions are also factors, as is subject matter, which can incorporate areas traditionally reserved for women. However, like Justice Stewart with his pornography, mostly you just know it when you hear it.

That's what our voices do. That's what Mitt Romney's classmate's bangs did. It's what gay men's tank tops and capri pants and jumpsuits do. It's what my friend Karen assures me gay women's nose rings and flouncy, athletic ponytails do. They provide a device for us to locate each other, but it is significant that these location devices be plausibly deniable. Now we live in a world where gay men get pride flags or the word "fag" tattooed on themselves, but for most of the history of gay men, and for most of the lives of gay men living today, such unambiguous symbols would have been deeply dangerous. We are prey, and bright plumage can get you killed.

So gay male culture demands that we be able to blend into the wallpaper when we need to, but also that we be capable of making ourselves *very* known in other situations. We deeply fear being seen and heard in the wrong way. This means two things:

1. We fear our own voices, and
2. We fear other gay men's voices even more.

I think you get now that while I literally mean the tone and timbre of the sounds that come out of our mouths, I also mean the uncamouflaged content of those voices. Our real stories and lives.

What I'm saying is that E. M. Forster could publish *A Room with a View* about a butt-hungry young Brit looking for romantic satisfaction in the Mediterranean during his lifetime because that Brit was a woman. Any gayness in his story was hidden. *Maurice,* the novel he wrote about an explicitly gay romance, wasn't published until after his death. What would people think if they knew?

For centuries, we've masked our stories to look like yours, terrified of what you'd think of us if you knew our real truth, our real butt-sex-in-the-bushes-having truth, so we remained silent, or we tried to echo your words.

Of course, the only thing worse than having to be embarrassed about your own truth is having to be embarrassed about someone else's version of your life. When I was on that playground, being faggy, there were other, better-hidden gay kids. They had to have feared me, because being associated with me would have made them less capable of hiding and protecting themselves. I know this because I felt that way myself for so long. You know in *Call Me by Your Name* when the old, unsexy faggy couple come to dinner and Elio needs to insult them? That's why: because he's terrified of what their version of gayness means about him.

In a 2004 review of *The L Word*, queer author Stacey D'Erasmo wrote one of the smartest analyses of gay representation I've ever read:

> [W]atching the series left me with a strange sense of dislocation along with my happiness. A peculiar consequence of so rarely seeing your kind on television, in movies, in plays, what have you, is that you can become, almost unwittingly, attached to a certain kind of wildness: the wildness of feeling not only unrepresented but somehow unrepresentable in ordinary terms. You get so good at ranging around unseen (and finding less obvious characters to identify with, from Tony Soprano to Seven of Nine) that it can feel a little limiting to be decanted into a group of perfectly nice women leading pleasant, more or less realistic lives. You can think, ungratefully: Is that all there is?
>
> Another consequence of living in a representational desert is that a tremendous urgency develops, a ferocious desire not only to be seen in some literal sense—we do have a lesbian character, she's that one in the back in the pantsuit; did you miss that episode?— but to be seen with all the blood and angst and magic you possess. Watching "Angels in America" on HBO last month, I was reminded of what Georgia O'Keeffe once said, that she decided to make flowers huge enough that people couldn't ignore them.

You fear a voice you cannot control representing your life and your world, but because so much is unsaid, you also hunger for it to be said with grandeur, with plumage.

Gay men don't like art about being gay. We want it, definitely, but when we're presented with it, it is unsettling. I'm a gay male stand-up comic; I want to tell jokes about being gay to audiences of gay men, at least sometimes. They are uneasy with this arrangement. How can my jokes be about them: I am fat and not hot. Why am I talking and not them? A range of issues around honest representation through art that straight people are used to negotiating, we must litigate for the first times in our brains. In the end, isn't it just easier to go laugh and love with Amy Schumer or Nikki Glaser?

In the foreword to *The Picture of Dorian Gray*, Oscar Wilde wrote, "The nineteenth century dislike of Realism is the rage of Caliban seeing his own face in a glass. The nineteenth century dislike of Romanticism is the rage of Caliban not seeing his own face in a glass." Who would have thought I would come to a point in this book where I argued that gay men are scared of mirrors? That's the thing, though: So many gay men love literal mirrors, because in a mirror (or Instagram account), you are simply an image that can be groomed to indistinguishability from straightness. Metaphorical mirrors, which reflect the fullness of our lives, will always remind us that we are different.

I was terrified of every gay narrative and person I was presented with until I turned seventeen. They were creepy, they were wrong. By the age of twelve, I knew that men were what made my dick move, but that didn't mean I was gay. Gay men wear silly shirts and make silly noises. I was something else. I could not deny my sexual attraction, but my commitment to not being merged into gay narrative was so great that I denied the basic truth of how that attraction should be labeled.

Then PBS got involved.

In 1993, Britain's Channel 4 acquired the rights to *Tales of the City*, Armistead Maupin's playful melodrama about life in San Francisco for young single people in the 1970s. Though the story centered on a naive straight girl from Ohio, the world she lived in, like Maupin himself, was exceedingly gay. The series aired in the U.S. on PBS, leading to official condemnations from the Georgia, South Carolina, and Oklahoma legislatures. They were horrified that tax dollars had gone to make a series presenting homosexuality as simply a charming way of life. They feared it might make nice God-fearing children gay. They were right.

Full of fear and fascination, I watched *Tales of the City* in my childhood bedroom. It was wrapped in the narrative of a woman, Mary Ann Singleton, played by the wholesome and relatable Laura Linney. It was fun and funny and sexy and bawdy. And the sexy part mattered. Every representation of gayness I'd seen until that time was either sanitized of sex, or suffused with coercion or predation. In *Tales of the City*, Michael Tolliver, Mary Ann's gay bestie, goes to the EndUp (a real gay bar in San Francisco), gets hit on, then enters an underwear competition despite embarrassment and uncertainty. It was hot, it was real, and it made me, on some level, wish I could go there. Eventually, I did.

This is why I hate my voice and the voices of other gay men. Heterosexual society wants to keep us weak, apart, and uneducated, so it strips us of the tools we need to find each other and learn from each other. I didn't come out of the closet at seventeen. I didn't even admit to myself that I was gay. I heard a real gay voice, though, Armistead Maupin's, that was skilled enough and brave enough to show me a real life, a whole life that could be mine. And, of course, one with enough murder, mysteries, and drugs to seem appealing to a young closeted person.

And that's why I love my voice and the voices of other gay men. They are full of beauty, culture, cooperation, music, opinions about Alfre Woodard, and sex. Paul Rudnick's *Jeffrey*, R. Zamora Linmark's *Rolling the R's*, Tony Kushner's *Angels in America*, Tarell Alvin McCraney's *Moonlight*, and all the way back to Forster's *Maurice*. These aren't just works from an underrepresented community, they're people who were trained to hide and be silent but were resolute enough to make noise despite the danger. They didn't know me, but they did it for me.

THE MAN WHO WATCHED *THE MAN WHO SHOT LIBERTY VALANCE*

MY MOTHER LOVES MANY things in her life, and one of them is me. She loves Douglas Sirk movies, responsible guard dogs, babies, very cold Coca-Colas, and the collected works of Tom Petty. And she loves me.

My father loved very few things in his life, and I was never certain I was one of them.

My mom's loves were always very apparent because she was always sharing them with me. My life, at its most basic, may just be me learning to love things from my mom, then going out and exploring those loves. I realize this is a very Freudian construction of a gay man's life, but facts is facts. On summer nights, she'd turn on the TV and explain to me that something special was going to happen. Then something special *would* happen, usually a showing of *Arsenic and Old Lace* or *Bell Book and Candle* on a UHF station.[1] Sometimes it was conver-

---

[1] For people too young to remember a world before ubiquitous cable, instead of having a designated cable network for specific types of entertainment, we just had specific dayparts. TCM was summertime at night on non-network stations, Cartoon

sations about how Fuerte avocados could never be as good as Hass, or why I owed it to myself to love the Indigo Girls. The result was the same: showing me that the world was a fun place full of game shows and tapioca pudding.

My dad did none of those things. He worked and he slept and he ate. He hunted and he watched football, but I knew him well enough to know he did not love those things. He wanted to love those things, but he didn't. He loved work and some of our dogs, but not all of them. There was no human culture for which he expressed true appreciation other than a well-finished concrete slab. However, if you asked him what his favorite movie was, he would always say *The Man Who Shot Liberty Valance*.

If you ask my mom what her favorite movie is, she will not give you an answer. She loves movies. She loves *The Graduate* for its perverse humor, and *October Sky* for its simple (I do not use that word as a compliment) American (nor that) morality; she even, oddly, loved *The Lord of the Rings: The Two Towers*.

Let's take a moment to discuss this. In 2002, my mother was fifty-one years old. She had never expressed any real interest in fantasy, though it had been my greatest passion for much of my core adolescent male years (ages nine to forty-one). Out of nowhere, late in the year, she informed me that I would be taking her to see *The Two Towers*. She was raising my niece full-time[2] and essentially never left the house for anything like an interest of her own. Her seclusion was the result of a tasty cocktail of housework discipline, frugality, and growing agoraphobia. But this thing she wanted. She told me and my father that she would be going, I would drive her, and my dad would watch my niece Olivia. This woman who lived at the behest of her husband was issuing one of her rare executive orders for a thing I never would have imagined

---

Network was Saturday morning, and ESPN was Sunday afternoon. It was purest barbarism.

[2] God knows my sister wasn't going to do it.

interested her. I asked her why. I could always ask my mom why and expect a good answer. "I saw the first one on HBO. It was intense, like a good war movie," she said to me. She was fifty-one years old and she'd fallen in love with a thing I'd fallen for fifteen years earlier. She loved it, but it would not rank in her top fifty movies, if she ever took the time to list them, which she wouldn't. My mom doesn't have a favorite movie because she loves movies. And things. And me.

My dad's favorite movie was *The Man Who Shot Liberty Valance*. Until this week, I had never seen it. That's because my dad never expressed a desire to see it. My dad wasn't deferential. He didn't just watch what we wanted to watch. He was quite forward in expressing his distaste for things. My father loved little, but he had scorn to go around. He was always vetoing pieces of culture as frivolous, silly, "fruity," or boring. He watched endless TCM with my mother in his later years, rolling through decades of classic cinema, including many westerns. Through VHS, DVD, cable TV, and streaming, I never once heard him say, "I want to watch *The Man Who Shot Liberty Valance*." But I always knew it was his favorite film.

Until this week in August 2017, one year, six months, and five days since he had a heart attack at a Division of the State Architect seminar in Oakland, I had never watched *The Man Who Shot Liberty Valance*. I'd never sought it out. I'd never imagined it might have value or be a tool to knowing this man.

Because I knew him. I knew my father, Larry Michael Branum, better than anyone knew him. My mother and his mother knew him longer than I did, and my uncle Kevin worked with him every day for fifteen years, but I knew him better. And I did not know him well.

Yesterday, I got sad that I'd never asked him why he liked *The Man Who Shot Liberty Valance*, that it might have been some path into his heart I'd never seen before, but as quickly as I thought it, I remembered the truth. My dad would have said it was "a good western" or "had lots of action" or "real clear-cut good guys and bad guys." Or maybe he would have told me a story about going to see it in San Francisco when he was ten years old, and how that made him feel. That would have been the best answer. My dad didn't know why he liked things. He could only describe them in rote, normal, unchallengeable ways. He liked the things he was supposed to like, or tried really hard to do so.

My dad feared thinking in ways that would not make immediate sense to others. I did not make sense to others.

My father never said, "I want you to see *The Man Who Shot Liberty Valance*."

The Man Who Shot Liberty Valance is an achingly resonant work about my relationship with my father. In 1962, my father watched and loved a film that was fundamentally about the tensions that would make communication between the two of us difficult or impossible. It is a film about two men with fundamentally different worldviews trying to cooperate and only briefly succeeding.

The film begins with a frame tale. Jimmy Stewart plays Senator Ransom Stoddard (are you lethargic from the weight of western hokeyness yet?) who returns to the town of Shinbone (it will get worse), Generic Western State, with his wife, Hallie (the unsubtle Vera Miles), because Someone Very Important has died. A young, handsome local reporter, evocative of all the qualities of white masculinity that we, and the West, believe in, notes the coming of the senator and alerts his editor. The newsmen follow Ranse (et ux) to the undertaker's shack, where they meet Pompey, a physically imposing but responsibly subservient black man, and the simple pine box that contains Tom Doniphon, the Someone Very Important whom the senator has come to see. The newsmen are *perplexed* as to why someone so dazzling as the senator would be in town to see someone, but they would have no idea who this Tom Doniphon is. When we see the senator insist that Tom be buried with his boots and pistol on, we understand. Tom Doniphon is not the kind of fancy such effeminate folk as newspaper editors would know. Tom Doniphon is a Real Man. Of course, that means he is played by John Wayne.

My dad wouldn't have wanted to be buried in cowboy boots or with a pistol, but I think he would have liked for us to bury him in a pair of work boots, with his cement trowel. We had him cremated. I don't know what he was wearing, if anything. The thing about my dad is he would have *liked* to have been buried with pistol or trowel, but if he'd been willing to contemplate death enough to write a will or express end-of-life desires, he would have instructed us to bury him in a suit. Because that's what men do. But he didn't, so my mom had him cremated because she doesn't really care what other people think.

Ranse Stoddard tells the newspapermen the real story of Tom Doniphon. It requires us to go back thirty or so years. Fresh from law school, Ranse rode into the territory on a stagecoach that was held up by the infamous Liberty Valance, played with gleeful masochism by Lee Marvin. Valance is a general-services villain who robs, vandalizes, and batters for personal joy, and to promote the general interests of the plutocratic cattle barons who influence our plot but whom we never see in human form. Valance steals Ranse's pocket watch (a gift from his father) and soils his law books, but it's when Valance challenges the inviolable status of a widow-woman by stealing her brooch that Ranse tries to stop him.

Ranse is beaten and left for dead, but a few days later, he is brought into town on the back of Tom Doniphon's wagon. Doniphon and Pompey bring him to a chow house where a young Hallie works, and the movie starts being the movie. Ranse believes in law; he wants the town marshal to arrest Valance. Unfortunately, the town marshal, like all representatives of education, culture, or government in Shinbone, is useless: Marshal Appleyard is fat; the newspaper editor, Peabody, is a drunk; and the town doctor, Willoughby, is old, silly, and drunk. Doniphon assures everyone that Valance will respect nothing but the business end of a gun, and he will continue to cruelly dominate the people of Shinbone. Valance does just that, threatening to stop the town from sending pro-statehood delegates to a territorial convention, something about the aforementioned unseen ranchers benefiting from territorial status. The point is, Valance is nefarious chaos, and finally, the weak and lawful Ranse picks up a gun to stop him, and it works. Ranse shoots Liberty and the town is saved.

Well, not really. We later discover it was actually Tom Doniphon in the shadows who shot Liberty Valance, but what matters is that everyone in town thinks it was Ranse. He's elected governor and then senator from the juice of said murder, and when he tries to tell the newspapermen of Shinbone who *really* killed Valance, he is rebuked by the editor: "This is the West, sir. When the legend becomes fact, print the legend."

My father was very different from me. He once said that he did not understand the purpose of reading a book if it did not contain technical information you needed to consult. My father had no patience for frivolity or pleasure. He seemed to believe that life lived best was unending hard work periodically punctuated by relenting to the frivolous weaknesses of a wife who wanted to see a movie or relax for an afternoon. My father very much wanted to be a hard, dry icon of strength like Tom Doniphon.

Like the cactus rose Pompey brings Hallie early in the film, my father was raised in hard soil. I don't mean poverty or adversity: My father grew up financially more secure than my mom, and was a white heterosexual cisgendered straight man at one of the nicest times in history to be such. Pax Whitemania, if you will. His problems were more immediate: His parents were not nice. My father was an unexpected late pregnancy born into a home of stern, judgmental Southern Baptists who never particularly liked him. My grandparents moved every few years. My grandfather had dreams of farming in his native Arkansas but made real money only by working in the shipyards of San Francisco. The moves meant that no friends were permanent, and the only dependable people in his life were the family who did not like him.

Then my father got himself a new family. My parents got married three months into the unexpected gestation of my sister. He was eighteen and she was nineteen, and such was the course of nature. It was now within my father's power to love people who might love him back. My mom and my sister are women, the gender traditionally assigned responsibility for affection. My father was, in various ways, able to treasure them, like Tom treasured Hallie. An ungentle person trying at gentleness.

Then I was born.

My father's hostility is in my first memories. It looms. One of my first memories is standing before my father, who was sitting in the yellow chair, which was at an angle that *clearly* means this memory is from the 1970s. Also, he's sitting down and I'm looking up at him, which means I couldn't have been more than three. (I was always enormous.) My mother said, "Tell him. Tell him that he scares you." And I remember thinking, "Maybe if I lie, he will like me." So I refused my mother's suggestion and insisted my father didn't scare me. For years I relived this moment, knowing so concretely that if I'd just been brave enough to tell my father that he scared me, things might have changed. I blamed myself, and it would be decades before it crossed my mind that my father, an adult man (though barely so), might have chosen to be less actively angry at his toddler son all the time.

My father was not, in fact, like Tom Doniphon. Men instinctively fear and respect Doniphon, but not my dad. He was not a person who was instinctively popular. He was instinctively *un*popular. His years of moving from school to school left him desperate to prove his value to other men, but he wasn't athletic enough, or tall enough, or funny enough, or rich enough, or interesting enough to captivate others. All he had was his capacious, unending willingness to work.

So he became the boss. He worked his way from construction laborer to cement mason to foreman to contractor to construction manager to construction inspector. Through responsibility and reliability, he took a working-class skill set and turned it into a marginally middle-class life. He also had employees, all men, who were duty-bound to seek his approval and understand that his way was the right way. Through work, he finally found something that proved he mattered.

And at home, he was a boss. He wielded authority, not love. His greatest expressions of affection were declining to use the authority he would remind all of us he had. When my sister and I would misbehave during the summer, a common punishment was to be whipped with the green branches of an almond tree. We would each go and select a switch, my father would ritualistically remove the lower leaves so it would move faster, and then he would switch us. Periodically, my sister would cry, and my father would make her get the switch; he would remove the leaves, then he would symbolically cast it aside to let her know she was receiving clemency because she was a girl. I would still be switched.

My mother never hit me. She never needed to. She had a relationship with me.

My father controlled the money coming into the house. He owned the cars, he owned the house. He was bigger than any of us. My father did not want to rule through respect or law but through unquestioning obedience and a decent dose of fear.

This is a power structure that Tom Doniphon would have understood. Indeed, it is a power structure that Tom tries to explain to Ranse Stoddard. It's the system of authority that Liberty Valance uses to keep the town in check, and it's the system of power that Tom uses to stop Valance.

In *The Man Who Shot Liberty Valence*, Tom Doniphon clearly loves Hallie. He is building an extension to his house to try to create the kind of feminine comforts Hallie would require. He finishes the extension just before he shoots Valance, and afterward, drunk, comes to some kind of realization that the man he is could never provide stability or happiness to Hallie. Doniphon drives home and hurls an oil lamp at the extension and sets it on fire. Tom stops himself from trying to be the kind of man he can't be, and tries to make way for Ranse to give Hallie the happiness he cannot.

My father tried. He got a girlfriend, he got her pregnant, he married her. He had a child, then another child. He built a home for us with his own hands. He tried to give us love, but the results had all too much in common with the prickly cactus rose Pompey brings Hallie on Tom's behalf.

My father and I would spend very long days doing work in our orchard or in his shop. We would talk, but if my talk ever got too whimsical, fantastical, or happy, my dad would shut it down. Happiness, in the long run, was embarrassing or expensive.

My mom told me lots of stories ranging from the Arkansas of her ancestors—stories handed down—to her own life, to celebrities, to history, to politics. Lots of settings, lots of tones, lots of lessons. Be generous; cake stands are useful; a good dog loves you and hates everyone else; if people fuck with you, make sure you fuck with them harder; most people are secretly anti-Semitic; too much baking powder will ruin dumplings. She shared her life through stories. She was basically the Andy Cohen of my childhood.

My dad told me few stories, but one he told a lot. When he was a boy and living in Missouri, the youth Sunday school leader was going to take some boys on a fishing trip. My dad wanted to go, but he was not invited. He told his mother that this was making him sad, so she called the Sunday school leader and asked him to take my dad. My dad was embarrassed but went. "It was fun, but it would have been more fun if they'd wanted me to begin with."

My dad told me this story so many times. It was a resonant truth he wanted to impart to me. It's better to just be wanted. After Ranse Stoddard finishes his story, he heads back to Washington with Hallie, and they talk of returning to Shinbone for their golden years. Simmering under the surface of the conversation is the unsettling sense that Hallie has never been truly happy because the rugged, self-assured man she always loved pushed her away so she could be a senator's wife.

I was never what my dad wanted. Part of me thinks that a son who solidified his hopes for his own masculinity would have made him happy. A football star who got the girls and was magnetic in the way he was not. My dad always seemed fascinated with those uncomplicated guys in my class. He would point out their behavior and wonder why I couldn't be more like them.

But the real part of me, the best part of me, the Ranse Stoddard who carries books, knows that no son would have been able to make him happy. He hated me before I was sentient. He loved me, too, absolutely, but from the beginning, there was a little more hate than normally exists between a father and son. Or maybe not.

Before I was aware, I was aware that I was doing it wrong. I wasn't sure what, but I was doing it wrong. He resented me for this inchoate failure and pulled away. I was always supposed to be chasing to prove something to him I didn't really want to prove. I was supposed to have some inner desire to repair trucks, play catch, and work on construction sites. I didn't. He was mad.

My mother tells a story of my dad washing his car when I was eighteen months old or so. I saw him washing and wanted to help, so I picked up a wet rag that was on the ground and rubbed it against the car. My dad freaked out because the rag had gravel stuck to it; he was worried I'd scratched his paint. He picked me up and started hitting me. More sophisticated iterations of this interaction replayed over the following twenty-five years.

One evening during my second-grade year, I was taken to the auditorium of a school not my own. I did not know what was going on. I assumed my parents were voting. When we didn't find any polling booths in the auditorium of April Lane Elementary School, I asked. My mother informed me that I was going to play T-league and my dad was going to be coach, and that it would be very good for our relationship. I was seven, my father was thirty, and already our entire family was treating my relationship with my dad like a marriage on the rocks.

Let me be honest: I did not care for T-ball. There were no wizards involved. There was grass, but frolicking was frowned upon. There were other boys, some of whom I liked, but most of whom confused me. And there was my dad, angry at me for doing it wrong, not playing me because he couldn't be showing favoritism to me. Finally, at the end of my second season playing, he got asked to coach the all-star team. He did not put me on the team because, again, he could not be seen as showing favoritism to me, so for three weeks, I had to go to the park and watch my dad coach other people's sons. I got to play with my female cousins, and honestly, I preferred it.

In a world that seemed generally angry at me—many people other than my dad were mad at me for boying wrong—I sought the stability of books. In a book, no one calls you Gay Guy or gets mad at you that you throw wrong. Books are full of other people's problems that you can learn from. Like a young Ranse Stoddard, everywhere I went, I brought a sack with a bunch of books, prepared to remove myself from dangerous situations. My dad hated it. He didn't understand it. Over time, his anger grew, first at the size of the book bag, then baldly at the books themselves.

We spent many long car rides together, mostly during the summers when I had to work construction with him. We engaged in more of that strange conversation that could never be fun, personal, or frivolous. Once, when I was in college, he picked me up from a bus that goes from Berkeley to Davis. After light talk, I retreated to a book. When we finally got home and got out of the car, he pulled *King Lear* out of my hands, tore it in two, and threw it on the ground. His rage was a thing without words.[3]

Words are what I have. I tried, starting in high school, to solve the problem of my father. People with different skill sets would have tried better means, but I believed that all he was missing was a bit of rational, logical explanation of the problem. I was just the young lawyer to convince him that hating me was the wrong choice.

Filled with all the E. L. Konigsburg and J. S. Mill I'd consumed over the years, I structured arguments. He began by dismissing my observations, so I learned to marshal facts to respond. I made my mind keen and organized, and I kept fastidious detail of his actions. I picked the most clearly structured examples of his distaste and disrespect to position my arguments most favorably. Sound reason had ended tyranny in the United States; it had ended segregation and systemic misogyny (I believed); clearly, if I could just reason well enough, my dad would realize that he didn't need to be angry with me all the time.

But the structures and authorities of Sutter County, California, were no more capable than those of Shinbone. There were no arguments

---

[3] *Educating Rita*, discussed in a later chapter of this book, contains a scene where the protagonist's husband takes her schoolbooks and burns them in the backyard. That scene is frighteningly evocative to me.

clear enough, no grades good enough, no football victories resounding enough for him to recognize validity in my cause.

My dad was officially five feet nine inches tall, which means he was actually five-eight. I am six-three. My freshman year in high school, I weighed just under three hundred pounds. Though I lacked interest, speed, or much natural skill, I was valuable on a football field. He informed me before my freshman year that I was going to play, and I played. He came to an astounding number of my practices just to watch. He had played football. He had been not great. I started games nearly every week that I played. I was eventually a team captain, and at the end of my senior year, the head coach gave me the award for toughest player. My dad loved that I played football. And on the way home from the ceremony where I got that award, my dad said to me, "You could have tried harder. You never really tried as much as you could at football."

Maybe I could have, but in my life, I had too many things I was good at to try super-hard at a thing I wasn't good at. Which is why, decades later, I would still be trying to form arguments, phrases, constructions, to make my father see our relationship differently. To stop him from identifying every action and gesture I made as an insult and a slight. I wanted to live in a world where my gods, reason and logic, had the power to heal this injury.

One thing to understand is that, in all of these conversations with my father, these oral arguments before a Republican construction worker, I had to remain completely calm. If at any point in time my father began to register that I was raising my voice, or if I simply vexed too many of his poorly formed rebuttals, he would raise his voice. If I countered, he would approach as though to hit me. He pulled a hammer on many occasions. He was in charge, and that force was part of what kept him in charge. Subtly, underneath all of my father's social interactions with us was the gentle awareness that he might beat us like he'd beat a disobedient dog. We were, of course, all animals he owned.

Now let us remember: At the age of thirteen, I was seven inches taller than he was and outweighed him by a hundred pounds, but for the following nine years, when he glowered at me and threatened violence, I relented in fear.

I hated him. Not because he threatened violence, but because he forced me to live in a world that was governed by fear and not reason. I was offering him solidity, stability. A nice, patient teenager who will never disobey but will always offer clear, well-reasoned arguments for the things he wanted to do. I wanted rule of law, but my dad understood the world better than I did. The minute he relented to rule of law, I would be in charge. He needed Shinbone to stay a territory. He needed to be Liberty Valance.

But my relationship with my dad is not a tragedy. It is a comedy. Because in this situation, Liberty Valance was five-eight.

When I was a senior in college, my mom went to the doctor. Her stomach was doing something weird, and the doctor politely informed her that the weird thing her stomach was doing was playing host to a thirty-five-pound ovarian tumor. She went into the hospital, and my family had to start wondering how things would work when the person who makes things work wasn't there. Things at home were bad. We were all on edge, and neither my sister nor my father was inclined to de-escalate situations. I'd also spent the previous three years gently unwrapping my anxiety and resentment, mostly in the form of essays about Shakespeare plays. All the work breaking down, categorizing, analyzing, and defending arguments about relationships that had been so useless against my dad delighted my instructors at Berkeley. I had people in my life who valued the person I was, and it left me feeling what may have been my first little shreds of pride.

My father and I argued. The house was deprived of the woman who loved us both more than anyone had ever loved us, the woman who de-escalated, whose upset was to be avoided. We were in my parents' bedroom. I do not know what we argued about. That has been lost to history. He raised his voice and I did not back down. He walked toward me, arms extended from his sides like a rooster trying to seem larger before a fight. I grabbed him by the throat and shoved him against the wall.

I was Ransom Stoddard. Finally, at my wits' end, and with our Hallie gone, I relented from my belief that reason, argument, and law could solve this problem. I descended to barbarism. I took a pistol to the main street of Shinbone, and I didn't need a Tom Doniphon in the shadows to shoot for me. The simple truth was that if I'd been any other boy in Sutter County, California, I'd have kicked his ass when I was fifteen. Maybe he would have shot me, but he wouldn't have. He would have respected me. But I didn't want that respect.

It was a chilling moment that I am still living today. His neck crumpled down on my hand, the shock and fear resonating from him. Worst, even in that moment, I wasn't consumed by rage; I wasn't seeing red in the fashion of every barely literate alcoholic man I'm related to. When he walked toward me, mostly I was just thinking, "This is ridiculous," and with my arm made the clearest argument that his reliance on physical violence for authority was unsound. He didn't get that.

After that, he was better. My mom used that word years later: "Ever since you did that, he's been better." A little less tyrannical, a little less cruel.

He never respected me, in the way that I understand respect. He never deferred to my reason, he never treated my suggestion as a viable option. He respected me in his way. Mostly, that involved not driving my car unless I gave him permission.

I don't know if anyone ever really loved my dad before I met him. His parents were cold and indifferent, blaming him for his unexpected birth and their tepid relationship. My mother became his wife through an unexpected pregnancy, and spent her life understanding that her affection and housework were the tools she used to earn her room and board. My sister showed my father great affection, but she made it a game of manipulation.

Maybe my dad trying to love me was like me trying to wash his car at eighteen months. Maybe he was trying to do a thing he'd never really seen. Maybe he was scared of it. Maybe when you don't go to college and write papers about *Coriolanus*, you never pick up the things you hate about yourself and look them in the eye. Maybe when you grow up in the arid lands of Shinbone, you never get to see a real rose, and the best you know is a cactus rose.

As time went on, my father learned to be kind. When I was in high school, while we were at a convention for one for the many organizations I participated in, he saw a teacher and another student exclude me from a planned trip to Medieval Times. In a fit of solidarity, he took me to Disneyland, just for dinner. You cannot imagine what a decadent act this was for my father, paying a full day's admission to Disneyland at seven p.m. It was wonderful.

These gestures were rare and strange, but they came. Then I came out of the closet, and things got worse, but then they got better again.

Then my sister had a child and abandoned it with my parents, and my father finally had a child who wasn't crazy and who wasn't Ranse Stoddard, and I got to watch him grow to truly, and maybe generously, love someone.

In December of 2015, I called my parents on my way home from work. My dad answered, and we engaged in the stilted, bad conversation we'd had on the phone for years. The brief dance before he handed the phone to my mom. Over decades of doing it, I'd slowly learned that in that conversation, there was always a little hunger. He wanted to have more to say, he wanted us to have something we could talk about. I'd tried; occasionally, I'd ask him about work and let us feel like our relationship had texture.

On this occasion, he asked me what I was doing, and I said I was going to record my podcast.[4] You should understand that my parents have paid as little attention as possible to my creative work throughout my professional life because they are reasonably certain that everything I say is a description of anal sex or a criticism of them (or both). They

---

[4] It's called *Pop Rocket*. It's a pop culture roundtable show. Download and listen today!

do not want to know about my creative life, but that is a different story. What you need to know is my father said, "Now, your podcast. What's that?" And I had explained to him what my podcast was *repeatedly* by that point. I'd been doing it for a full two years. I had told him, and he'd not cared enough to pay attention, and I was done. I conveyed this to him as clearly as possible: "I've told you about it many times before. If you actually wanted to know what it was, you would have paid attention." And then I asked to talk to my mom.

A few days later, I called to talk to my mom, and my dad told me he'd listened to my podcast. The episode that week was a throwback where we talked about pop culture from fifty years before, 1965, a period when my dad was actually familiar with pop culture. He liked it. He talked to me about it. He tried.

And two months later, at a Division of the State Architect conference in Oakland, he had a massive heart attack and stopped being.

And now I find myself needing to ask a question about wiring, or noticing particularly good wall texture or a poorly graded slab, and I pack that thing away. I put it in the place where I put things to talk to my dad about, because conversation with Mom burns on its own, but conversation with Dad needs this fuel. Then I remember he is gone and the fuel is for no one but me.

Maybe my dad loved me. Maybe he loved me as well as he could love anyone in 1975. Maybe he learned how to love better from loving me. Maybe he watched three foreign-language movies[5] at my behest even though he hated "reading movies" and loved two of them.[6] Maybe he went to the Oregon Shakespeare Festival and SFMOMA even though he didn't want to, and he enjoyed it. Maybe he was proud of how big I was, and even, eventually, proud of how well reasoned I was. Maybe he once spent two hours playing *Catchphrase* with the family and never once suggested anyone should be working. Maybe he saw me do stand-up

---

[5] *All About My Mother, Monsoon Wedding,* and *Crouching Tiger, Hidden Dragon.*
[6] Not the gay one.

at a theater where the Beatles had played, or read an article I'd written in the *New York Times*, and realized the skills I had were something he could be proud of.

Maybe.

But this is the West, sir, and when the legend becomes fact, print the legend.

SHOULDER TO HIP

THE MEMORY IS OF bracing clarity. It involves *20/20*, a newsmagazine hosted by Barbara Walters, a dazzlingly famous person everyone talked about, and Hugh Downs, a man who exemplified everything we looked for in news anchors in the 1980s (which is to say he had no discernible qualities). That it was *20/20* also means it was Friday. It means I was *pumped*: An entire weekend lay before me, and for two whole days, I didn't have to go to school and have my handwriting criticized by adults, nor my mannerisms criticized by my peers. It means it was ten p.m., and I had just watched two hours of very good ABC children's programming. This was not *TGIF*—that quartet of hallowed sitcoms most readily associated with *Full House* or *Family Matters*—but the years before *TGIF*, when ABC could simply run a block of semi-bad family sitcoms without feeling the need to be so whorey as to brand it. *Mr. Belvedere* was probably involved.

I was having a pretty good night. Maybe my best friend, Ramon, had come over to play, as he did so frequently on Fridays. Maybe my dad had gone and picked up food from McDonald's or another of my most beloved purveyors of victuals. We cannot know for certain, but I am setting the stage to make clear to you that I was in the rather delicious mood of a young man who was well fed, played out, and unbounded by the constraints of a bedtime. And then, like that, at ten p.m., *20/20* came on.

If you are under the age of thirty-five, you probably don't really know what a newsmagazine is, but *20/20* was the gold standard. Back when we had only three to four networks, there was no cable news, so the worst parts of cable news—the sensationalist investigative stories meant only to make you upset, as well as celebrity interviews—became a nighttime fixture. Basically, *Anderson Cooper 360* was one hour of television every week that aired opposite prime-time soaps. We loved it.

Also, we needed something to do with Barbara Walters before she found her true calling: making perimenopausal women fight for sport on *The View*.

20/20 began with its opening teases of what would be on the show, and Barbara, America's non-rhotic news-reading sweetheart, started saying something about America's obesity epidemic. They ran B-roll of fat people, as you do, and the B-roll featured fat people who were shot from shoulder to hip. I realized every time I'd seen B-roll of fat people, their faces had been cut off or pixelated. As a nine-year-old fat person, I didn't entirely understand why they were doing that. Clearly, they were implying that being fat was so humiliating that no one's identity or personhood should have to be associated with such an indignity. But didn't they realize that we fat people spent our lives with our fat heads attached to our fat bodies? What were they trying to achieve?

They were trying to avoid shaming people by merely *implying* that their fatness was so horrible their identities needed to be obscured. "Oh, don't worry, lardo, we'll blur your face so people won't realize you're the wide load we're talking about. You know, the way they do when they see you in real life." This was the 1980s equivalent of the 1920s newspaper photos of men arrested in gay bar raids with black boxes over their faces to obscure their shameful identities.

The moment filled me with real anger, because it seemed evident to me that the result was basic dehumanization. Even today, when fat people are represented on the news, we are represented as meat. Lumps of meat and fat lumbering through a mall or parking lot. There is no story, no humanity. We are livestock.

I have always been fat. From my ten-pound birth to my grade school years of constantly outgrowing clothes, through high school weight training and football when I worked out four hours a day, through diets and self-hatred and sweatiness and people not wanting to sit next to me on the plane. I have been fat. So this was, I suppose, my first moment of realizing that this basic building block of my identity influenced the way people understood me.

The clearest message sent to me by popular culture is that, as a fat person, I will not do important things. Fat people are not protagonists. We are not dynamic. We do not solve the problem. We are, in fact, often seen as the problem. We can be the friend[1] or associate[2] of the person who is solving the problem, but we are usually too cowardly[3] or lazy[4] to assist that person properly. The very premise of the Eddie Murphy iteration of *The Nutty Professor* is that the lead character, Sherman Klump, is so docile and incompetent as a fat person, he must be transformed into a not-fat person, Buddy, to be brave and "get the girl," Carla.[5] When Sherman defeats Buddy through an internal war for self-acceptance, the resolution doesn't involve Carla falling for Sherman, just a platonic friendship and a chaste dance. We need not discuss Sherman's family, the perpetually eating, perpetually farting, fat-suit-wearing Klumps. Just know that we are children, ruled by our appetites, incapable of anything else.[6]

---

[1] Rob Reiner in *Sleepless in Seattle*, Rosie O'Donnell in *Sleepless in Seattle*.

[2] John Candy in *Planes, Trains and Automobiles*, Rosie O'Donnell in *A League of Their Own*.

[3] Sam Tarly in *Game of Thrones*, Rosie O'Donnell in *Another Stakeout*.

[4] Wayne Knight in *Jurassic Park*, Rosie O'Donnell in *Exit to Eden*.

[5] Because, of course, women aren't human beings, but prizes to be won.

[6] Belushi in *Animal House*, Mo'Nique in *Precious*, Fat Bastard, take your pick.

You've got Otto von Bismarck and Winston Churchill and Catherine the Great and Oprah Winfrey just sitting there in history, proving to us that fat people are perfectly capable of forging a German nation or media empire out of blood and iron. We don't usually think about those people, though. We think about fat the way *20/20* told us to: Fat people don't have heads, and heads don't have fat people.

The best example is the NBC reality competition show *The Biggest Loser*. On the show, a dozen or so fat people showed up to stop being fat. They had no other characteristics. They had race and gender, I guess, but you never got a sense that they had a life worth living. They had loved ones who worried, but not careers that rewarded them. They were sad and long-suffering, not exciting or full of ideas. The fat people who came to be on *The Biggest Loser* were arriving to have people, real humans, yell at them until they, the competitors, lost enough weight to be human beings.

There was always a moment with every competitor when one of the trainers would come and yell at them about how they weren't trying hard enough and were complicit in their own suffering. Then the fat person would blubber about Their Sad Truth. Sometimes it was a tragic loss of a family member, or someone who had never loved them, or something about food being love. The point was, we were led to believe that every fat person had a Freudian closet containing some issue that, when revealed, would break the spell, allowing them to unfat and finally turn into a real boy or girl.

We watched them lose weight by being yelled at and humiliated on-camera, then drugged and dehydrated off-camera. When someone won, we cried because we believed fatness was a dragon that could be slain, and then the person went off and gained all or most of the weight back. They never got to have a personality then, either.

This narrative illustrates the complex, nearly Calvinist construction of obesity with which America is in love. We need to believe that fat people can lose the weight. We cannot accept that it might be an aspect of their—*our*—lives created by genetic predisposition or circumstance. We need to know fat people *could* lose the weight, because if they *don't*, it's a choice. It's a question of morality. Being obese is dangerous and bad and must be opposed with every fiber of your being. And if you do that, you will be transformed. If you just eat less and exercise, you can be saved. Salvation through starvation.

Kate, the fat sister on NBC's *This Is Us*, is a fictionalized version of a *Biggest Loser* competitor. She has no qualities. She's thirty-seven years old and is wholly devoid of skills or passions other than kind of liking singing. While one of her brothers earned a graduate degree and the other bounced between acting jobs, Kate did nothing of note or merit. We can assume her time was spent romancing wheels of Camembert and being too scared to talk to a boy because she knows she's too fat to be loved.

Have any of these people met a fat girl? A real Kate, in the real world, would be awesome. She'd have tons of gay friends and go to drag bingo a lot. She'd have learned to be fearless with fashion, because people are going to judge her anyway. She'd have a joke to make when she's too sweaty. She'd have broken a chair before, and she'd know what to do when it happens the second time. Chrissy Metz gives great soul to the character, but as she's written, Kate is a cul-de-sac of a human being who has tasted nothing of the world except cheesy fries. That ain't any of the fat bitches I know.

The reason the writers of *This Is Us* cannot imagine Kate doing anything valuable is because her existence as a fat person means she is doing things that are unvaluable. If Kate is fat, she cannot have been journeying toward unfatness with all of her power. If she, say, had become one of Canada's most beloved stand-ups,[7] or become a *New York Times* columnist,[8] or become the most powerful human being in world media,[9] we might have to contemplate the idea that her time was well

---

[7] Like the delightful Debra DiGiovanni.

[8] You know, like Lindy West.

[9] In the fashion of Ms. Oprah Winfrey.

spent. We might say, "Yeah, she got fat, but she had some shit going on." Kate is deserving of personhood and dynamism only during those times when her singular purpose is unfatting herself.

Famously, this is a part of Chrissy Metz's contract. She is required to lose weight so that she can tell Kate's story of triumph. Happiness and success are there for Kate, but only in her future, only as part of her narrative of losing fat, and only if she doesn't fail.

And we need fat people to fail. We need them to be so dumb and lacking in willpower that said salvation is never actually achieved. We need to know that their immorality is inherent so we can believe our own thin morality is inherent. Our narratives about conquering fatness aren't about saving fat people, it's about letting thin people feel like they're already saved, members of the chosen people.

We fat people are bound to live our lives tied to this struggle. Until we're done being fat, the trying has to be all of who we are. We are told that we must seek exercise to rid our bodies of their fatness, but we also know we'll be ridiculed for exposing our gross bodies at a beach or gym. We are told that inside of us is a thin person screaming to get out, and we must thereby know our bodies are prisons for some other, better people.

This narrative is deeply damaging. I know you think you're doing something great when you tell me my weight predisposes me to diabetes or knee deterioration, but what you're really telling me is that I should fear using my body as it is. One time in my mid-twenties, I went to a new doctor who told me that my weight was more dangerous to my health than a crack addiction. At that moment I had to step back and legitimately consider, *should* I get a crack addiction? I'd *definitely* lose weight, and the good doctor did say it was healthier than my baseline existence.[10]

---

[10] Plus, one of the methods for acquiring crack most commonly referenced in popular culture is performing fellatio on strangers, an activity at which I have proven competency.

Popular culture demands that we fat people recognize our existence as an overwhelming crisis. It's a thing to be expunged, not managed. When I go on a hike or some other group physical activity, I'm always freaking out. Will I get too exhausted? Will I sweat too much? I'm not worried about it being painful or inconvenient for me. I'm worried about the extent to which my different physical reaction to situations will mark me as Other.

On a recent vacation, I went on a snorkeling trip. It was a physical activity with which I wasn't familiar, and I began cycling through questions about how my body would fail me this time. My traveling companion and I went to get flippers from the resort, and I discovered that they did not have any to fit my gigantic feet. They told me I could go without them if I wanted, but that it would be hard to keep up with everyone else. I slid further into panic. As the boat took us out to the coral reef we were going to swim around, I started preparing myself with the stories of shame and fatness I was certain to encounter. We got to the reef and jumped out, and I started working with determination to overcome the inadequacies of my body so I wouldn't be ashamed.

Wanna know what? I was fine. I'm a strong swimmer. I have big feet, so I didn't need flippers. I kept up with everyone. My traveling companion, the very image of masc gay gym muscle, panicked the moment we got in the water and climbed back up in the boat, but *I* did just fine. Nevertheless, it took me until halfway through the expedition to realize I didn't need to keep bracing for the moment my fat body would fail me.

Western literature's greatest fat character is Tracy Turnblad, the Baltimore high school student at the center of the 1988 John Waters film *Hairspray* and its ensuing stage adaptation.[11] Tracy is distinct from most other fat characters in that she is very good at something. Fat characters are typically slow and sad, needy and childish. They're

---

[11] And the film adaptation of the stage adaptation, and the live television adaptation of the film adaptation of the stage adaptation. I hope John Waters bought a boat or something.

generally some version of Shelley Winters in *The Diary of Anne Frank*.[12] They are obstacles for nonfat heroes. Tracy, however, is talented and she knows it. She's the best at something. She gets to be confident, she gets to challenge the social order. She gets the guy, and we understand why. Tracy is like the fat girls I know.

And the thing Tracy is good at is dancing. Her skill is her body. Fat people are told we are supposed to be obsessed with our bodies but never take pleasure in them. Our bodies are supposed to be enemies we're calculating against. Not Tracy. Her body is a source of power and pleasure. The bigots at *The Corny Collins Show* want to hate her for her poverty and her weight, but once Tracy starts to Madison, they have to admit that girl's the best.

It's also significant that the conflict of *Hairspray* does not, in any significant way, rest on Tracy's fatness. This isn't a story of a lonely girl longing for a boy who doesn't notice her thick body, and it's not about a sad girl who longs to dance on TV with the thin beautifuls. No, she just wants to be on *The Corny Collins Show* and impress people with her dancing, and she achieves it pretty quickly. (The main conflict, in fact, centers on the segregation perpetuated by the show she's on.) The movie isn't about Tracy's fight for her inclusion. Rather, it's about how her inclusion is marginal and conditional as long as others are being excluded.

I've always been a very good dancer. I know this isn't something you're supposed to say about yourself, but you don't know me, and it's true. People frequently tell me this, and when they do, it always sounds like they think I don't know or maybe have never heard it before. That's because they're surprised. They don't realize what they're implying, but it's that they don't think a body this large is supposed to be fun.

I'm not good at loving my body. In truth, my body and I have a stormy relationship. It's always growing and shrinking and not fitting

---

[12] I have never seen *The Poseidon Adventure*, so I cannot comment on Shelley Winters as a fat lady who is a good swimmer. I don't think she's a protagonist, so I'm going to stick by this "Tracy Turnblad is the best" stance.

into places, and I get mad at it and feel ashamed. Several times I've marshaled the resources of my life to losing weight. I make it a priority, I eat only lean meats and vegetables, I work out multiple times a day. I lose weight, but I'm still fat. I'm still too fat to be human, and my efforts don't exactly add up to loving my body.

I'm not good at believing I'm attractive. I'm not good at making space for physical recreation in my life. I want very deeply to emphasize that my relationship to my body and/or my fatness are not fixed or anywhere close to being healthy. What I want you to know is that I'm a very. good. dancer.

In so many ways, I haven't been there for my body along the way, but it's always been there for me. Turn on the music, and it knows what to do. Though I played sports in high school, that was never natural to me, and any skill I had was me just being very, very large and strong.[13] The only thing that my brain and body have been able to collaborate on effortlessly is knowing where to put my feet when a Curtis Mayfield song is playing. But it's what I've got, so I'm going to be proud of it.

People will continue to look at me and tell me that I'm doing it wrong. They're going to talk down to me about nutrition and exercise. They're going to treat me like a baby who cannot manage his desires. They're going to expect that inherent in my fatness is a lack of agency and capability. They're going to tell me I'm doing myself a disservice by not waging war on the 40 percent of my body mass that isn't lean. I am always, on some level, going to think they're right.

But I will also love my body. I'm going to have fun with it. And I'm going to dance. A lot.

---

[13] Also, I'm *super*-strong. Why is this never a thing we can attribute to fat people?

UNDEFENDED BORDER

I HAVE A SISTER, Lori. You have probably noticed sidelong references to her in the book thus far, so you're probably wondering why I have not discussed her in great detail. The answer is that it is exceedingly difficult to discuss her. That is not to say Lori isn't much discussed. She is a topic people love, and she is a person who loves to be a topic. Every time I start with a new therapist, there comes a point about two or three sessions in when he or she begins asking questions about Lori. Probing. The questions stop being about me entirely, as we spend twenty to ninety minutes (divided over multiple sessions) discussing just Lori and her dynamics. The therapist, who has never actually met Lori, then lands on an opinion. In most cases, that opinion speculates "untreated borderline personality disorder."

That is these therapists' opinion. If Lori threatens to sue me over this book, and she will, I can provide the names and addresses of the people who expressed those opinions, making it clear that my statements are not slanderous. Lori will not hire a lawyer, but she will threaten to.

So, the question stands for me: Do I avoid talking about this person who is a quarter of my nuclear family, who was a significant presence in my life from birth, who in many ways shaped my identity, out of fear of how she will react? It's not a new question for me. All of my life, I have been forced to base a lot of decisions on how Lori will react. Thus, instead of recounting stories and incidents that shape my understanding of Lori from an early age, I must provide you with the information about Lori that gives her the least grounds to threaten to sue over.

Here are facts we have about Lori, facts that are on public record or are widely agreed to by witnesses:

> In her early twenties, Lori stole our mother's wedding ring and
> pawned it, she said, for money to buy fast food.
> In her mid-twenties, Lori embezzled from a bank she was
> working for. She was convicted and served house arrest.
> In her later twenties, Lori embezzled from another employer and
> served a sentence in a federal prison.
> In her early thirties, Lori left her three-year-old daughter with
> our parents and has no regular contact with the child nor
> provides any meaningful support for her.

That's not my story of having a sister, but when Lori is your sister, you don't get to have a story. You get to be part of her story.

I don't know how true this was when I was young. Lori, five years older, seemed like the coolest, most glamorous person I knew. She had long hair she got to brush. She had dance costumes. She went to school. For the first five years of my life, we slept in a bed together, and those childhood memories of her telling me stories or singing to me are some of the happiest times I can remember.

But around that time, when I was four or five, I started to see that Lori would sell me out for any advantage, that she could manipulate our parents or play them against each other to meet her whims. I knew if we got the same toy, she would immediately break mine. If I spoke, she would interrupt. At the time, in context, we all told the story that it was simply sibling rivalry. At what point does the narcissism and cruelty of childhood stop being adorable and start being a possible symptom of a mental disorder?

I cannot answer this question. I don't understand Lori, despite four decades of attempts. Seeking to understand Lori is a black hole that sucks up everything around it. I'm tired of that. It meant that through much of my life in my family, I didn't get to have a story. This led me to an obsession with trying to think about the people, places, and things we don't think about.

Instead of writing a chapter about Lori, I am going to write a chapter about why I love the nation of Canada. But first I have to tell you the story of our meet-cute.

M, A Love Story

There was a time before the Internet when all knowledge was happened upon. If you needed to know something, you had to find a book, the right book, that happened to have the thing you wanted to know. If you wanted a book, you had to go to a library or a bookstore, and they would have books, but just the books they had. There was no efficiency, there was no search capacity,[1] there was simply happenstance. I'm basically saying all human culture was a messy junk drawer full of things people needed but could not find until Ask Jeeves debuted in 1996 and started organizing things.

I know that this isn't true, but it was mostly true.

Back in that world, research skills were important. Research skills were the ability to be your own Wikipedia, to be the engine of your own search, to use the books that fate had been kind enough to bring into your life to obtain the information you needed.

Luckily, I lived in a family where the very sound of my voice would

---

[1] With all due respect to Melvil Dewey and the film *Party Girl*, fuck card catalogs.

fill one member of the family with a deep need to destroy any happiness I might have. If I expressed an opinion, she would find a way to use it to remind our father what an inadequate boy I was. If I expressed a desire, she would find a way to thwart it. The one place where she could not catch me was in a book. If I was quietly in a corner reading, Lori wouldn't notice me, my dad wouldn't notice me, and I could have my liberty. Most of my mid-childhood years were spent dick-deep in a book, and the books that showed you your way around other books, reference books, those were the best. They weren't fun, they weren't full of goblins and kings like my fantasy books, but they made me feel like I had access to the information that sophisticated people use to rule the world.[2]

But in the process, sometimes you obtained information you did not need. These were the most delicious of cases.

In my tenth year, I was given the task of doing a report on a state. This was a very conventional assignment among school-going children of the time. You got assigned a state, you found an encyclopedia, you transcribed some facts onto some wide-ruled paper, you made sure everything was spelled correctly, you put your full name and today's date in the top right-hand corner, you turned it in. *Boom.* Success in the form of a tiny gold star.

When states were being allocated in class, I selected Massachusetts. I did this because fancy people were from there. I had been to the west of the United States, and frankly, I'd had enough of it. Many kids chose states that they'd been to or in which they had relatives. I wanted none of this. I wanted greener, more sophisticated pastures. I wanted the closest you can get to England on this continent: New England.

Everything went fine for most of the run of this process. I extracted

---

[2] Some of those people were actually kings. However, I was to learn that these real-life kings were way less likely to have magical swords than the ones in fantasy books, but way more likely to have gone to college in England. The current monarchs of Bahrain, Belgium, Bhutan, Brunei, Jordan, Lesotho, Luxembourg, Malaysia, Monaco, Oman, Qatar, and the United Arab Emirates all went to college in the UK. Before the existence of the Internet, determining that fact would have taken nine years.

information from our trusty 1980 *World Book Encyclopedia* about cranberry production, the Berkshires, John Quincy Adams's birth in Braintree, the statewide love of cream-based clam chowder, and typed them on an Apple IIe computer. I followed orders and did what I was supposed to do.

But I am messy. I have always been and will always be messy. At all times it seems a little bit like I have barbecue sauce on my hands. I spill stuff, I lose stuff. My shoes disappear constantly. Chaos emanates from my flesh as though I were Roseanne's Twitter account itself.[3] So I, of course, didn't just extract information about Massachusetts and carry on upon my way.

You see, the entry for Massachusetts in the 1980 *World Book Encyclopedia* happens to be located in the M volume. The M encyclopedia and I were, in my tenth year, in the midst of a very real romance. See, the M encyclopedia is a meaty tome that also included the entry for mythology. The 1980 *World Book Encyclopedia* entry for "Mythology" was, in 1986, one of my favorite places to be on the planet. I would lovingly flip through those glossy pages, reading and rereading the volumes of expatiation on Greek and Roman deities, the half-page on Norse mythology, and the paragraph or so on the remaining five inhabited continents. It was very hard to learn about people or gods who weren't white from reference books in 1986.

The point is, I was spending a lot of time with the M encyclopedia. We worked together, we played together, I really thought it might be "the one."

As in any relationship, you experiment. You start to get bored with your routines and try some stuff that pushes boundaries. What I'm saying is I started exploring the other parts of the M encyclopedia.

---

[3] For your reference, here is a list (by no means exhaustive) of people Roseanne has argued about Israel with on Twitter: Hal Sparks, John Fugelsang, Joe Rogan, Mia Farrow, John Legend, Madonna, Rosie O'Donnell, and John Cusack. She does not fight with Anthony Bourdain about Israel; they may disagree, but she respects him too much to fight. That's the chaos that Roseanne's Twitter account is bringing to the table.

J. P. Morgan, Monaco, Mary I of England. But my eyes were always most drawn to those entries that the *World Book* graphic designers of 1980 had decided to give special treatment. Elevating them from the unimportant stuff with lots of facts-in-brief inserts and graphs. States. Presidents. Countries larger than Monaco. Let me get all up in that infographic, son.

You'll understand my surprise, confusion, and allure when I came upon a state entry for a state that did. not. exist.

It *looked* just like the entry for every other state, your Massachusetts, your Maryland, your Montana, all of which I'd read repeatedly. Its name, however, was something I'd never heard of. I asked my mom, who knew *most* things except what started World War I. But she had no idea what Manitoba was. To this day, few Americans do.

This was around the age when I'd also fallen in love with fantasy novels. I'd had a record-book (don't ask) version of *The Hobbit*, then seen the Ralph Bakshi film, then read the actual book, and had a great time with all of them. They'd made clear that books with fake maps and vaguely unreal history were a good time.

The *World Book Encyclopedia* article on Manitoba had *all* of this. I assumed dragons, wizards, and a spunky princess with lavender eyes and a family history of sorcery were going to be around any corner. I was wrong. All I found were a line drawing of children sledding and a discussion of controversial provincial language-education policies in the nineteenth century. It wasn't lavender eyes, but it was weird, so I kept going.

Eventually, I figured out that Manitoba was part of Canada, a thing I'd heard of. The things I knew about Canada were:

1. It was on top of America, and
2. They spoke French there.

I know this because I once asked the president of the PTA if schools near the Canadian border had bilingual aides in their classes who spoke French the way we had aides who spoke Spanish and Punjabi. She very patiently outlined the requirements of the California Educational Code to qualify for bilingual educational aides (ten or more students in the same age range per school). She said she did not know what the requirements were in states that bordered Canada, but they were probably similar. Throughout my childhood, this was all I was looking for: a person to calmly answer my questions with a synopsis of state legal codes. I remember it clearly and fondly. Mary Henson, PTA president, you are an American hero.

But the Manitoba encyclopedia entry shifted my understanding of Canada. It was a place—an entirely different place. I knew there were other countries, France, Mexico, India. Those were places full of history and other cultures. By that I mean they were hats that animatronic dolls wore on "It's a Small World." They were also different biomes, that's very important in countries. When you're ten, you don't really understand why people would have a different country if it didn't have a jungle or a desert. Those places are cool and show up in Indiana Jones movies. People *tell* you about those places. But no one is telling you jack shit about Canada. And if you've learned anything from this book thus far, it's that my only childhood gesture of rebellion was a deep desire to learn the things the world told me I did not need to know. We had good times together, the M encyclopedia and I, but our affair was over. I had found a new love, full of tar sands and mystery.

The True North, Proud and Free

Margaret Atwood, Canada's greatest living author,[4] once described the U.S.-Canadian border as the world's longest undefended one-way mirror. Our nations share a language and a continent and—we, as Americans, would like to assert—a culture. We will make jokes about the tiny

---

[4] While I love and respect Alice Munro, she needs to learn to write something longer than a short story if she wants my respect, or that of Hulu.

differences, the ways they pronounce "drama," "about," or, most egre-
giously, "pasta,"[5] but we do not give them the dignity of imagining that
there is anything, culturally, that is theirs. To the people of the United
States, the differences between us and Canada exist only as markers of
their gentle inferiority.

The thing that's most fascinating about Canada is the overlay of culture and identities that means their story is always about somebody else.

Let's step back for a moment and remind ourselves that we know
nothing about Canadian history. No one does. Who would? You learn
about other countries only when you get conquered by them or want to
eat their food. Canada isn't conquering anyone, and their culinary offerings primarily involve frying gravy. Canada never made the world learn
about it the way the USA did, with a long series of aggressive wars and
fast-food franchises. You would have to choose to learn about Canada,
and no one does that.

Let us begin at the beginning of white people. You're probably like,
"But Guy, the REAL story is the native peoples of Canada; their narrative is forgotten." To that I would like to say, "Please, get to work unfor-
getting them. I will donate to any Kickstarter you kick-start." But you
see, you had no interest in exploring the stories of First Nations Canada
until you wanted to tell me I was telling a story of Canada wrong. This
is the resilient power of Canadian boringness to keep us from discussing
them. You will try to train on a more progressive, more relevant story
and, in the end, keep knowing nothing about Canada. Also, a bunch
of the First Nations of Canada were also in the United States, because
there weren't national borders back then, so what have you done to
learn about the Ojibwa,[6] Salish,[7] and Iroquois[8] in your own country? I

---

[5] It's "PAW-sta," not "PAST-ah."

[6] Louise Erdrich's *Love Medicine* series is a good place to start.

[7] What about Lee Maracle's *Celia's Song*?

[8] Read their constitution!

didn't think so, so shut the hell up. I want to talk about Canada as it now exists, and that is a story that requires multiple races and cultures to tell.

France colonized Canada, kind of. They basically just sent a bunch of fur trappers to buy beaver pelts from First Nations for exploitative sums. We call them "fur trappers," but really, the Huron and Iroquois and Ojibwa were doing most of the actual trapping; the French were just middlemen who bought the pelts and rowed them back to port. "Canoe Jews" might be a more accurate job title than "fur trapper." The French built two real cities, Montreal and Quebec, the primary purpose of which was to keep all the pelts in a fenced-in place, and eventually sent over some women to turn it into a real colony that could make babies and cheese for itself. Look, this is reductive, but there's a lot to cover.

In 1763, the Seven Years' War was ending. It's the war we always call the French and Indian War, but open up your minds, it's a big wide world and the war was going on all over the place, and it all started because Frederick the Great wanted to take Silesia from Austria, so it's *also* the Third Silesian war, but for our purposes, let's call it the Seven Years' War. France kind of lost and Britain kind of won, so at the Treaty of Paris,[9] Britain gave Louis XV two choices: Give up the tiny Caribbean Islands of Martinique and Guadalupe, or all of Canada from the Atlantic to the Pacific. France weighed the options and kept their beautiful islands, rich with sugar plantations, and handed over half a continent to the British. That's where Canada as we know it came from.

Also, there were seventy thousand people there. France didn't care, since it had its sugar colonies. The UK didn't care, since they had soldiers in Quebec City and no one could invade New England from the North. The British colonies didn't care. When they declared independence in 1776, they didn't think to ask the Frogs up in the woods along the St. Lawrence to join them. Then, as now, no one was particularly worried about Canada.

---

[9] Aren't they all treaties of Paris?

Then the colonies won their little war. In 1783, at yet another Paris peace conference, the United Kingdom of Great Britain and Ireland handed over its American possessions (the ones that mattered) to an upstart little republic. They were forced to deal with the question of those Americans who'd remained loyal to the crown, though. Around forty thousand Americans who'd supported the British sought relocation to another part of the empire, including four thousand Black Americans who'd been promised freedom in exchange for supporting the crown. The UK had to keep its word, though it also didn't want to promise these people a nice life in Knightsbridge.

So they went to their acres of snow.

The black loyalists were taken mostly to Nova Scotia. Some used it as a staging ground from which to return to Africa, but most decided to make lives for themselves in this country where they would at least not be enslaved. White Canadians did their best to make that "at least" as meaningful as possible. For a century, they lived on the edge of Halifax, in a town called Africville. This was the birth of a sizable black population in Canada.

The white loyalists were taken farther up the St. Lawrence River, past the francophone cities of Quebec and Montreal to the banks of Lake Ontario. Together with the refugees in the costal provinces of Nova Scotia and New Brunswick, they began the history of anglophone Canada. The Declaration of Independence states the core premise of the United States as being that "Governments . . . deriv[e] their just powers from the consent of the governed." The core premise of Canada is "Nah, I'm good."

Or, as loyalist Mather Byles put it, "Which is better—to be ruled by one tyrant three thousand miles away or three thousand tyrants one mile away?"

Thousands of nice, quiet people who didn't realize why there needed to be a fuss moved to the banks of the St. Lawrence and Lake Ontario and started building quiet farms that the cruelties of latitude would make somewhat less productive than the ones they left in the States.

America started a government, Canadians started getting left alone. That couldn't last.

We Stand on Guard for Thee

About forty years later, America tried to steal Canada. We don't like to talk about it, we don't describe it that way in history books. When we explain the War of 1812, we say some convoluted thing about how the British navy was stopping our ships, looking for draft dodgers. And we say stuff about tariffs. If you want to lie about why a war started, just say "tariffs" and everyone's eyes will glaze over and they'll believe you. But that's not what happened. In 1812, Great Britain was dick-deep in the Napoleonic wars, trying really hard to keep the little general from decimating their nation the way he'd pretty much rolled over the rest of Europe and North Africa. With the British Royal Navy indisposed, members of the Anti-Federalist[10] Party thought they had a fun opportunity to fuck over the Brits and, in the process, the fancy Federalist[11] Party from Boston and New York that liked doing business with said Brits.

Oh, because another thing about the United States is that all of our wars for a really long time were about slavery. Again, a subject we're not super-keen to talk about. In 1812, the UK had banned the slave trade but the U.S. was still buying and selling black people. British ships were regularly stopping U.S. slave ships and freeing the captives. Just know that one of the reasons the Anti-Federalists wanted to piss off the Brits is America's deep passion for owning black people as property.

So we tried to snatch Canada's wig while Britain was distracted and

---

[10] They hated government and loved slavery, so were kind of like the Neanderthal version of Republicans.

[11] They were wealthy bankers in New York and Boston who were out of touch with the common man, so basically, Democrats without all the gays, women, and POC getting in the way.

were very surprised to find out that the surly fuckers up north had no interest in being assimilated into our republic. Sure, we went and managed to blow up a chunk of the-city-which-would-become-Toronto, but as soon as the British beat Napoleon, they sent the royal navy up the Chesapeake and burned the White House to the ground. Never forget that our national anthem, in addition to having some considerably racist verses,[12] is about our flag still flying after nineteen British warships shelled the shit out of Fort McHenry.

Once it became clear that the UK would be able to defend its American holding, we sued for peace, and the U.S. and UK essentially promised to leave everything the same and never talk about it again. But Canada remembered.

Je Me Souviens[13]

One of the things I really love about Canada is its understanding of itself in the shadow of powerful, more interesting family members. Britain is the place that made Canada, that appointed its leaders until 1867, that could override its laws until 1931, that had to be asked permission for constitutional changes until 1982. That's right, Canada didn't own its own constitution until *Cheers* was on the air.

Culturally, Canada has always been striving to be Britain's good child. Teacups and *u*'s in "honour" and "colour." The queen on quarters, in classrooms and post offices. A regent's distant gaze always quietly judging the country she doesn't love enough to live in. Canada wasn't even allowed to have its own foreign minister until the 1980s: The person had to be called the "Minister for External Affairs" because they had to pretend Britain was still running their foreign policy. The UK didn't

---

[12] It was, of course, a war about keeping slavery safe and legal.

[13] *Je Me Souviens* is the provincial motto of Quebec. It means "We remember," which basically means "We remember the time before you English speakers showed up and took over," which basically means "Just you wait, Johnny Canuck, just you wait."

care; they were probably busy negotiating some coal strike or Thatcher invading Uruguay. Canada does all the hard work of winning Britain's wars for it, taking Vimy Ridge, driving in farther, faster at Juno Beach than any of the other invading forces at Normandy, but the UK is barely aware they exist.

And America, big, loud, violent, and insane, sits right next to them. We flood them with media and products and threaten to wash away whatever sense of identity they've been able to cobble together. We talk about them only to mock them.[14] Want to know why Ottawa is Canada's capital? Because it's farther away from the U.S. than the other cities that were being considered for the honor, and Queen Victoria thought that seemed safest from the Yanks. From day one, Canada has been waiting for the U.S. to come and conquer it—they just didn't realize we'd do it through every means other than military force.

We take their best and their brightest and put them into our industries, making our TV and films. They can come be successful here, we just ask that they stop being quite so Canadian. In 2005, when the Liberal Party of Canada was looking for its next leader, they had to find the best Canadian to lead Canada. So they went to the obvious place: Cambridge, Massachusetts, where Michael Ignatieff was teaching and had lived for half a decade. When R. B. Bennett was done being prime minister of Canada back in the 1930s, he retired to England and was made a viscount, even though the Canadian government had asked the king not to give Canadians titles. Bennett didn't care; he'd graduated. He was bigger than being Canadian.

I love Canada because it has to manage its identity in the shadow of these two giant identities. And I love Canada because it has an identity that's always been split and compromised. The First Nations were the real Canadians, of course, living there for millennia before the French showed. Then the British arrived and took political control, but the French and First Nations had the real, organic claim on Canadianness.

---

[14] Like this chapter!

The anglophones used their political and military might to marginalize and oppress the French, but the French were insulated from the sense of inferiority that anglophone Canadians had compared to British or U.S. culture. Questions of authenticity and loyalty were ever-present in Canada. Who is Canada? Why is Canada? These questions were always so much vaguer and smaller than the U.S. versions. But isn't "vague and small" just another way of saying "nuanced"?

In 1972, CBC radio host Peter Gzowski, as part of the long, barely motivated struggle to find a Canadian identity, decided to have a contest to create a national simile. If you want to know how barely motivated this struggle was, Canada had gotten a flag of its own less than ten years before. Nearly half the country opposed having a flag. It was a huge struggle. Canada passed national health care only as part of the compromise to push through having their stupid leaf flag. You might say, "Oh, well, they weren't that big of a deal back then." They were the eighth largest economy on the planet in 1960, but they didn't want to make a fuss by doing something showy like having a flag.

So Gzowski wanted a national simile. Something like "As American as apple pie." Hundreds of suggestions streamed in, things that make perfect sense, like "As Canadian as hockey" or "As Canadian as maple syrup." These suggestions didn't win. The winner was Heather Scott of Sarnia, Ontario, who suggested "As Canadian as possible under the circumstances." The core of their story is a flexible identity that grows and shrinks to accommodate the identities around them.

Want to know the best story from Canadian history? It's not one they're going to tell you. If they are going to talk about what made Canada, what solidified it into a viable political entity, real Canadians will probably talk about John A. Macdonald, who became Canada's first prime minister with the British North America Act of 1867.[15] They will probably not mention that Macdonald was a drunk, or that he was

---

[15] The law that created Canada as a nation was, of course, passed in London by the British parliament.

caught taking bribes from railroad companies.[16] Canadians will tell you about John A. Macdonald because they know Americans talk about George Washington, and John A. Macdonald is their corollary—their imperfect, boring, weird version of something America does better. They will talk to you about what they assume you will understand because they assume no American or British people would take the time to think outside of their own paradigms. They are right.

John A. Macdonald is not the story. The *real* story happened about twenty-five years earlier, in 1841, when Upper Canada and Lower Canada, as Ontario and Quebec were then known, were merged for political purposes. For the first time, Canada was going to have a parliament with all the English speakers and French speakers in one place. The key question was whether they would end up fighting with each other, or if they would unite to fight against the British government, church, and businesses for reform and control of their own country. One of the Ontario liberals, Robert Baldwin, reached out to the leading Quebec liberal, Louis-Hippolyte Lafontaine,[17] and said the only way they could turn Canada from a colonial wood and beaver farm for Britain into a real, independent, vital country was to work together. That was a nice idea.

Nice ideas rarely go smoothly. When Louis-Hippolyte Lafontaine and his francophone supporters were going to vote in his district outside Montreal, the Orange Order,[18] an anti-Catholic militia, showed up and threatened to beat the shit out of any Catholics who tried to vote. It could have turned into a riot or a bloodbath, so Lafontaine asked his supporters to disperse. An anglophone Protestant member was sent to parliament from Lafontaine's francophone Catholic district, and the cause of reform seemed imperiled.

---

[16] Canada, as a nation, was formed largely to make sure they could build a railroad that went from Halifax to Vancouver.

[17] I may be telling you this story only because I think his name is cool.

[18] They are the same guys who were/are assholes in Northern Ireland.

Baldwin heard about this and was pissed. There was no way a majority of Canadians could unite behind reform and equality without French voices in the movement. He needed Lafontaine. So Baldwin asked his dad, who'd been elected as an MP from Toronto,[19] to step down. Baldwin brought Lafontaine into Ontario in the depths of winter[20] and introduced him to the Protestant anglophone farmers, telling them that if Canada was going to succeed, they needed to elect Lafontaine to represent Toronto.[21] They did. And when this first united Canadian parliament formed a government, Baldwin insisted Lafontaine be the Premier. English speakers were larger in number and could have easily dominated the government. Baldwin wanted Quebec, and Lafontaine, to understand they were equal partners. When they were named to united Canada's first cabinet, they had to run for their seats again. This time the Orange Order showed up in Baldwin's district and made sure he lost.

Lafontaine knew exactly what he had to do. He had one of his francophone reformer MPs from Quebec resign and let Baldwin run for his seat.

This is the promise of Canada. Nice people thinking about each other, because if they don't, they will get pushed around by outside powers and freeze to death and be eaten by moose. Canada has failed this promise *thousands* of times. Don't get me started on their treatment of the First Nations. We could have a *chat* about the Black Loyalists who were settled in Nova Scotia, then ignored by the federal and provincial government for the following century. There's the whole Viola Desmond business.[22] We could talk about the Supreme Court saying women weren't "persons," or the searing racism of the pioneering feminists who

---

[19] York. It was called York back then.

[20] I think. Read John Ralston Saul's excellent book *Extraordinary Canadians: Louis-Hippolyte Lafontaine and Robert Baldwin* for actual history. This is mostly me telling cocktail-party stories. Winter makes it more dramatic.

[21] I really handled this Toronto/York thing poorly. I should have established this earlier in the chapter. I feel like we're *stuck* calling it Toronto now.

[22] She's the Rosa Parks of Canada! She's on the Canadian ten-dollar bill.

tried to prove that women were persons, but not blacks or Jews. I'm not saying Canada is perfect, but I'm saying Canada has a dream. A different dream from that of the United States, but one that's just as beautiful.

From Baldwin and Lafontaine committing themselves to working across religious and linguistic lines to Pierre Trudeau passing the Canadian Multiculturalism Act, to a nation rooting for a one-legged cancer patient to try to run across it,[23] Canada has tried to create a society where people from varied backgrounds get to collaborate and succeed because they take care of each other. It's almost as if they, bullied as they are by British and American culture, tried to build a nation that is the antithesis of an empire.

My sister is an empire. A very big, very warlike, uncontrollable personality. I don't want to think about her, or people or institutions like her, that keep control through threat of violence and fear. I want to talk about people and places that care about each other, that try to listen to others' needs and respect them. I want to talk about people and places and things that nobody remembers to love. I want to talk about Canada.

---

[23] His name is Terry Fox and they fucking *love* him.

FOOTBALLWALLAH

I WAS INFORMED I was to play football.

I don't know what I was doing at the end of my time in junior high, but I would imagine fantasy novels and rule books for role-playing games I did not have friends to play with were key. Until this point in my life, sports, as a concept, had been relatively avoidable. My dad had tried to get me to watch football with him, but I had no interest, and he didn't really care that much.

As previously discussed, at the age of seven I had been placed on a T-ball team against my will. By thirteen, I knew the drill. This was some hope or dream of his. I was supposed to try very hard at it, fail him, and then be told I had not tried hard enough. I did not realize that the little town I was going to high school in, Sutter, was a farm town, and farm towns are football towns. On a Friday night, the lights from Sutter's stadium would have been seen for miles, but they weren't because there was nothing but rice fields and moths for miles. It was a town where everyone from the feed store to the Church of the Nazarene was going to have an opinion about how I played. I didn't know this, I just knew I had to go and start being a man. I would have preferred the safe, indoor Torah chanting of my mother's people, but alas, my bar mitzvah was on the gridiron.

Most of the kids from my elementary school went to the big high school in the main town in our county, but my dad wanted me to go to the same high school he had. Where he had played football, and had been reasonably bad at it, but had thereby solidified his own sense of masculinity. Sutter Union High School:[1] Go Huskies. My best friend, Ramon, was going with me, so when I first went for pre-football weight training in the summer of 1989, I was, at least, not alone. I had one companion. My dad dropped us off, and we walked back to Sutter's locker room. We walked in, and Ramon and I began the end of our friendship. He slid comfortably into a place in the masculine order: mediocre football player, discusser of women's boobs, chill dude who insisted on being called 'Mon. I entered a place where I could not be comfortable, where the presence of my fellow football players meant I had to fight my instincts constantly, and which made honest communication with Ramon[2] a thing of history.

Let us step back for a moment and say I had ejaculated for the first time in my life the previous year, in eighth grade. It was not one of those glorious nocturnal emissions I've heard so much about. Rather, one night as I was falling asleep, I noticed I was hard. I touched the soft skin just beneath the urinary meatus[3] and enjoyed it. I stroked it exactly one more time, and then shame oozed out onto my nice blue comforter. During this time, I had begun noticing the strapping legs of Bo Brozner, the lower stomach hair of Dave Miehle, and the enormous bulge in the bike shorts that Joe Mendoza wore to school. I understood very well that men, and men's nudity, were arousing to me. I was also reasonably certain that I was in no way gay.

---

[1] There was a different Sutter somewhere in Northern California, so we always had to clarify "Sutter Union."

[2] I had a hard time bringing myself to call him 'Mon.

[3] Dick slit.

So when I walked into the locker room at Sutter Union High School, I had a problem. Do you know what a locker room is? It is *men*,[4] adult *men*, naked and showering. And not just adult men, *athletes*. We walked in, and I was immediately staring at the nude thighs of one of the senior halfbacks. It was the best of times, it was the worst of times.

This was before the Internet. My junior high erotica was limited to particularly muscular contestants on *The Price is Right* and occasional Calvin Klein perfume ads in *Rolling Stone*, and I think at that time, I didn't even think to hoard them. I wasn't yet masturbating on the regular, I just had a secret shame. Now, suddenly, all the porn I could possibly want was just *there*, live and right in front of my face. It was porn you could smell.[5] Reach out and touch . . . well, that would have been a bad idea.

Which brings me to the bad part. Barely a year after I discovered I had a horrible secret which, if revealed, would cause my parents and community to revile and reject me, I was placed in the location most likely to make this revelation public. My greatest fantasy and my greatest fear were combined in the form of naked men and boys merely inches away whom I was supposed to be super chill and bro-y and not at all erect around.

Being gay is a lot like being a deep-cover sleeper-cell spy. You wake up one morning and your penis, the senior agent, informs you that you are not a nice little boy trying to make his family happy, but an agent of a foreign sexuality. It's your job to sneak into to the heart of heterosexuality, get the secret documents,[6] then bring them back to your superiors

---

[4] Also boys: There were fourteen-year-olds there. I was thirteen. I was totes attracted to them. If you are going to be scandalized or offended that I was attracted to boys in my class who were my age, you need to step back and seriously reconsider your mental construction of homosexuality.

[5] Though some would argue that one of the advantages of porn is that you can't smell it.

[6] Visual memories of what the other guys look like naked.

for document analysis.[7] That's a lot of pressure for someone who still slept with the closet light on.

I was fine at football. I was even, let's say, good. It was a tiny high school where fielding a football team meant every able-bodied boy had to play. We didn't have offensive and defensive players; everyone played both ways. We ran some sort of offense that didn't have a quarterback until my senior year. I'm not sure, but I think it was to ensure that no player was irreplaceable. I never really understood. I just ran out on a cold field and crashed into strangers for no reason for two hours every Friday night while other, lither people determined the outcome of the game.

See, I was good at football only because I was twice as large as anyone on that field. I was slow and confused, but at the end of the day, they had to put two linemen on me to try to stop me at all. I have no idea if it was fun. I think the greatest pleasure I experienced in football was relief that a game was over. And sacking people, sacking people was fun.

Movies about football are rarely fun. The thing about football movies is they can never let their protagonist be interesting. He can be beleaguered, his dad can hit him, and his town can expect too much of him. He is definitely, totally the victim of forces, but at the core, he is just a white male cipher of the sort we'll discuss later in this book. In the film *Johnny Be Good*, Anthony Michael Hall plays a football star who is playfully, gently arrogant, but by the film's resolution, he still ends up being a good boy who plays by the rules. If *Johnny Be Good* is the spark of hope among the gridiron films, their darkest chasm is *Rudy*. *Rudy* is a horrible film about a pathetic person. Rudy Rudolph Rudnitsky, or whatever his name is, just wants to play football at Notre Dame so bad that he makes it the only purpose of his life. He is not good at football, but he persists, and finally, at the end of his senior year, the team takes pity on him and puts him in the game. The story is simple: If a man honors and abases himself to the male power structure long enough,

---

[7] Jackin' it!

eventually, that power structure will do him honor. *Johnny Be Good* is a gentle reversal; Johnny is much lauded by the male power structure, so in the end, instead of fabulousness, he chooses solid, responsible domesticity at the state school that didn't offer him money or whores.

Football movies aren't good because, with the exception of *Air Bud 2: Golden Receiver*, they're always about people who are supposed to be playing football. This nice, athletic boy wants to play, but he's sad. This nice, unathletic boy wants to play, but he's unathletic. They're not movies, they're recitations of the Pledge of Allegiance to the phallus. They are a reaffirmation of a male order of power and obedience.

This is why no one in a football movie ever gets to experience real joy in football. If someone did, there wouldn't be conflict, it'd just be a dude being good at something and loving it. Even Rudy, who isn't good at football, doesn't seem to love doing it. He loves the idea of who he is when he plays football. He wants to be Big Man on Campus. Just about every football movie is a bildungsroman for a Big Man on Campus. These films are all blandly romanticizing the apotheosis I was supposed to be seeking in high school, but never understood or wanted.

Here's the thing about gay guys and team sports: You're in a social dynamic that rests on homosociality. We're all supposed to be comfortable and get along and be able to talk about who we want to fuck and make fun of each other. That is very hard when the person you want to fuck is the halfback. My teammates seemed to instinctively understand the flow of the game. They liked and trusted each other, and they could process disagreements through violence, be it physical or social. I did not get how this stuff worked. I was terrible at being a guy.[8] I lived in a football town, and I loved learning, but I hadn't managed to actually learn anything about football. I'm sure I would have learned a lot more about gridiron strategy if just one of the opposing side's tailbacks had been a suffocated housewife on the verge of alcoholism, but they were mostly just farmers' kids with Trans Am hair.

---

[8] IRONY!

Here's what I did manage to learn from thirteen years in Sutter County: You take a long rectangular piece of cloth and you wrap it around your waist. You tuck the cloth into your undergarments as you go. Take the other end of the cloth, pleat it, then toss those pleats over your shoulder so they hang nicely down your back. Pleat the excess in front of you and tuck that into the front of your skirt. That was a uniform I could get behind.

(It's a sari, that's how you wrap a sari.)

This was the lesson Yuba City taught me. Not the specifics of draping and folding—that would take years and the patient instruction of girls at my school to really figure out how to turn one of my bedsheets into a quality sari. The lesson was decades of schools, restaurants, and grocery stores surrounded by South Asian women working an elegance and beauty of a sort I'd never seen on TV. To everyone's surprise, powerful forces of plate tectonics, hydrology, agriculture, and colonialism had conspired to ensure that the only football movie I will ever truly love is *Bend It Like Beckham*.

When my ancestors traveled along the American Southwest, hooked a right at Bakersfield, then made their way up the long golden bowl of California, they did not know they were going to another country. Maybe they knew they were going to a place that had been, not so long ago, a chunk of Mexico, but they almost certainly did not know they were going to Punjab.

A Geography Lesson (Again)

"Punjab" comes from Persian and means "Five Waters." This refers to five rivers in Northwest India that compose the strange geographic phenomenon of an inland delta. Normally, a delta is the triangle-shaped[9] piece of land where a river enters the sea. The low elevation of the land

---

[9] They are named for the Greek letter delta, which is a triangle.

and large accumulation of silt cause rivers to flood and move around a lot, filling the area with fertile, well-irrigated soil. It is in these glorious environments where agriculture and thereby human culture first flourished. Those are normal deltas.

But sometimes a grand, giant river has to make its way through some mountains. This is true in Northwest India, where five chilly rivers born in the Himalayas find themselves up against a mountain range, then come together to form a single river running through the lowest point in the mountains. The river they become is the Indus, a cradle of human civilization, and the inverted triangle of rich floodplain created by those five rivers is the Punjab.

Eight thousand miles away, there is another inland delta. You had no idea that buying the book by the gay guy from *Chelsea Lately* would have this much agriculture in it, did you? I never signed up for it, either. The point is, where I'm from is exactly the kind of perfect agricultural environment that Punjab is, and at some point in the early twentieth century, some Punjabi dudes figured that out. They were five railroad workers[10] who'd initially come to Vancouver to work, but during construction of the Southern Pacific Railroad, they realized there was another version of their homeland. The point is that thirty to fifty years before my white ancestors made their way to Yuba City, the land was already a little colony of Britain's largest colony.

Like I said, the first five guys were railroad workers. After the railroad work dried up, coming as they did from the breadbasket of India, they went to work on farms and, eventually, bought land of their own. They started bringing their male relatives over to work the land. By 1917, someone told Washington that all these Indian guys were showing up, and Congress passed a law banning immigration from most of Asia and the Pacific. It meant the guys were trapped. Some had come over as unmarried young men, some had left wives and families in India, but once

---

[10] This is a popular version of the story. Is it true? I don't know.

the law was passed, their only option was to stay and find a non-Indian wife or return to British India and stay there forever.

Do I need to explain to you what Sikhs are? We all know what Hindus are. They are what Madonna pretended to be briefly in 1998 before she decided to become a Jewish witch. It's the glorious polytheistic religion of a billion people, mostly in South Asia. It has the coolest gods of any religion, hands down. In Durga's case, that's a lot of hands.

And we all know what Muslims are—they're followers of the Prophet Mohammed, who built upon the teachings of the other Abrahamic religions, Judaism and Christianity, to create a faith deeply rooted in law, literature, and words.

Well, Sikhism is different.[11] It's a religion that started in the fifteenth century in Punjab. It was founded by Guru Nanak and was expanded and guided by a series of gurus who taught the unified oneness of all creation. The religion has strong musical and literary traditions and celebrates justice and equality. Functionally, they're the dudes with the beards and turbans. They're the girls with bangle bracelets and braids. They are where I'm from. The current mayor of Yuba City, Preet Didbal, is the first Sikh mayor in the United States. We did not go to high school together, but I probably know one of her cousins.

Now let's get back to those poor stranded farmworkers in the 1920s. If they left America to get wives, they could never come back, but Indian women couldn't come to the U.S. I learned their answer to the problem one afternoon in high school, at lunch. My friend Karm started speaking fluent Spanish. I was a little surprised. Karm wasn't a great student, and our high school offered only two years of Spanish. When I asked him how he knew Spanish so well, he said, "Oh, my grandma's Mexican." I soon discovered *everyone's* grandma was Mexican—specifically, all the

---

[11] This point was lost on many Americans who, after 9/11, started targeting turban-wearing Sikhs for violence because they didn't understand the difference between Islam and Sikhism. Needless to say, attacking anyone for their religion is horrifying, and the aftermath of those murders has deeply affected the Sikh community and Yuba City's community.

Indian kids' paternal grandmothers (and some great-grandmothers). The Indian farmworkers from the 1920s all the way to the 1960s took Mexican wives who converted to Sikhism, learned new uses for cumin from their husbands, and pioneered the field of ethnic fusion cuisine.

And I say Indian, but when most of their families came to Yuba City, the modern state of India had not been formed. There was just one Punjab with Hindu, Sikh, and Muslim farmers, all of whom were willing to take the risk of going to a new land with new opportunities. But in 1947, India cracked (to use Bapsi Sidhwa's word). As part of India's transition to independence, it was broken into two countries: one majority Muslim, one majority Hindu. The crack ran right through Punjab. People found themselves, their property, their lives on the wrong side of a border that had never existed before. In a chaos of violence and loss, Hindus and Muslims left behind their homes to go to the new country where their religion would form the majority, but the Sikh community, a plurality in Punjab but a tiny minority in either of these states, opted to congregate in the eastern, Indian half of Punjab.

From childhood in Yuba City, white people's understanding of Indian religions was more complex than other places in America where frog gigging[12] and muddin'[13] were popular pastimes. It was necessary and instinctual. *Sikhs have long hair: Girls have braids, boys wear a patka.*[14] *All Sikhs have bracelets. Muslim girls wear pants or long skirts. They can't share your lunch.* David Mehta was the only Hindu in my class. To

---

[12] A fun diversion where drunk people go out to a rice field full of frogs and one person shines a light at the frogs to blind them while other people use three-pronged sticks to stab the frogs in the back and put them in burlap sacks. It is a popular activity in Sutter County, and was my parents' third date. My mother cooked the frogs, but did not eat them because they are not kosher.

[13] Drunk driving your four-wheel-drive truck or SUV around in the mud so that it's very messy until your car flips over and is destroyed, forcing you to get a predatory loan to buy another car and consigning you to a life of hovering debt that will keep you working at Home Depot for decades. Also super-popular.

[14] It's like the kid's version of a turban.

my understanding, Hinduism centered on being able to get a haircut[15] but not being Muslim. There was one Indian girl in my class who had secular parents. She wore her hair in a bob and dressed like the white kids. Until third grade, I assumed—because she didn't have bracelets or braids and didn't have to eat halal food—that she was black.

Want another story about how Indian my town was? When I was in third grade, my mom started working in the school cafeteria, so she took me to my grandparents' house for the two hours between when she started work at six thirty a.m. and when I had to be at school at eight thirty. It was Valentine's Day, and in classic Guy Branum fashion, I had failed to do the work I needed to do in a timely fashion. In this case, filling out Valentine's Day cards for everyone in my class. I recruited my seventy-year-old grandfather to the task. I would tell him names of people, and he would write them on the card. He handed me one that said "Cindy."

That was preposterous. Cindy? Like from *The Brady Bunch*? I said as much to him.

He said, "You said Cindy."

I realized the problem. "No, I said SHINDI." I paused, then clarified, "Like, short for Gurshinder." To me, nothing could have been more obvious, but my grandfather who'd lived through the Dust Bowl, the Depression, and two world wars was not going to be condescended to by a fat eight-year-old, or write out a Valentine's Day card to a male Punjabi kid.

Would you like another story? Every couple of years, a kid from out of town would move to Yuba City and enroll in my school. They would make a joke about some kid being named Balbinder. We didn't understand. Balbinder was just a name, like Cory. There were four Balbinders at the school, plus a number of Baljits, Baldevs, and Balbirs. It wasn't strange, it was home.

---

[15] Sikhs are not supposed to cut their hair out of respect for the perfection of God's creation.

Enough charming stories, get back to the legislation!

In 1946, the U.S. Congress had relaxed immigration restrictions on Indians, and the loss and uncertainty of partition had left many families rootless. Just as my family was sending pioneers from the barren fields of Arkansas to the oilfields of Bakersfield and the shipyards of San Francisco, new Indian immigrants were finding their way to the place that would be my home.

No one ever explained to me how this happened.

There is one good work of art about my hometown. Chitra Banerjee Divakaruni, an Indian American poet, wrote a cycle of poems about the Punjabi American women of Yuba City. They are achingly beautiful imaginings of the lives of women like the ones I grew up around. Almost no one white in Yuba City knows these poems exist. They are not, to my knowledge, taught in our schools. It is a culture that exists next to ours, one that nearly all white people in my town take for granted but refuse to see. Plus, Yuba City wasn't built for poetry. It's prose country.

What's strangest is that these communities are so strikingly similar. When you think of South Asian Americans,[16] you may think of your friend's parents who are doctors or engineers living in a nice urban environment. They aren't the people I grew up with. I grew up with farmers. I grew up with very old men in turbans driving tractors very slowly down a rural road. I grew up with old women squatting, their saris pulled through their legs, cutting the wild mustard greens for *sarson da saag* at the side of the road in January. Guys sitting around a fire by the prune dryer, passing around a bottle of Jack Daniel's. They were just as drunk and barefoot and okra-eating and surly as everyone I was related to. I grew up with Punjabi rednecks.

I guess the most distinct memory I have on this point comes from 1984. I was in fourth grade, and it was the day after Halloween. My class had two teachers; one I've mentioned before, Mrs. Sanger, was older,

---

[16] Presuming you're not South Asian American. If you are, you're probably pretty tired of this white guy telling a story not his own.

wiser, and astoundingly competent. The other was new, both to teaching and to Yuba City.

There was *news*, and this teacher felt she had to share it with the crowd. She later told my mom—who, as I said, worked in the cafeteria—that having lived through the Kennedy assassination in 1963, she thought some of the children of the class might be experiencing trauma from the *news*. She explained to us that something had happened, then she turned to Sukhbir Badyal, the smartest girl in the class, and asked her to share the news.

"Yesterday," Sukhbir began, "our president was killed . . ." I distinctly remember her saying "our president," and I knew she meant the president of India, even though she didn't, she meant Prime Minister Indira Gandhi. This is what our teacher, whose callowness ran so deep she was even named Mrs. Young, wanted Sukhbir to say.

". . . by my cousin, a hero of Khalistan!" Then eleven children in a class of thirty went apeshit. Truly apeshit as they celebrated this glorious victory for the campaign to create an independent Sikh homeland in Punjab. This was not what Mrs. Young wanted her to say. Mrs. Young had no fucking clue what was happening. She understood only that the prime minister of India had been killed, and these kids were Indian. To her, like my parents, like every white person in Yuba City, South Asians were a monolith. My teacher couldn't imagine a diversity of political perspectives. She had no idea about the massacre of Sikhs that Mrs. Gandhi had ordered scant months before. We knew what religion all the South Asian kids were to categorize them, to know who could eat from the salad bar and who couldn't cut their hair during a lice outbreak. As kids, we talked and played together, but outside of school, we lived in different worlds.

Anyone Can Cook *Aloo Gobi*

What I've taken a long, circuitous road to tell you is that my dad wanted me to be transformed by the cleansing Gatorade of football into a real man who was chill-tight bros with the real men of Sutter Union High

School, but that didn't happen. I didn't go to parties, I didn't have any-one I could consider a real romantic possibility, I was present for all the high school drama, but I was nonparticipatory.

What this meant was that in many ways, my chill-tight bros were the other people without a viable sexuality at Sutter High: the Punjabi girls, three specifically—Ravi, Baljit, and Gurpreet. Like me, they didn't get to have a romantic life. Their brothers were off dating white girls, and each would eventually have a nice wife brought over from India. The girls couldn't date because it might impugn their chastity. And they couldn't get an arranged marriage, because being from America also impugned your chastity. I'd grown up knowing women like this, my dad's age and older. Unmarriageable daughters who kept books for their dad's farm or helped manage the prune dryer. I knew Ravi, Baljit, and Gurpreet were on that path, and it wasn't so different from mine.

We did not discuss this, of course. We didn't plot or wheedle to try to figure out how our sexual identities could fit into this world that had made us. We just gossiped about movies and celebrities. I made Baljit tell me about England, where she'd grown up, and pronounce silly Brit-ish words. Mostly, we just did our homework, followed rules, and didn't think much about why we couldn't be part of the romantic drama of high school. That, coupled with rich traditions of accessorizing, draping, and dance, made them the finest fag hags a bookish asexual closeted child homosexual could ask for.

There was one act of rebellion. In eleventh grade, Ravi—who, let's be fair, was the Carrie—went to the administration and said she wanted to have an Asian club like the one at the big high school in town. The school principal, in direct violation of several federal and state laws, told her that they couldn't have one, because none of the faculty [17] wanted to be the adviser.

Ravi was pissed. She was in a world that was in the active process of

---

[17] There were no Indian teachers at the school. Indians didn't teach school, they farmed.

forgetting her. Other Indian girls played along, became cheerleaders or played volleyball and had a lot of fun at the 80 percent of teen life they were allowed to do. Ravi wanted more—she wanted acknowledgment of her space and her place at the school and community. Maybe it was the first time I saw one of my peers being vengefully political, and I was enraptured.

The rejection of the Asian Club idea had happened in the first three weeks of school. Ravi was fuming, but then morning announcements reminded her that there was one high school club that hadn't met yet: Science Club. Science Club at Sutter High existed for one reason: to use its budget for a trip to an amusement park in Santa Clara. The official justification was that roller coasters showed us physics in action. Science Club did nothing else. No one cared about it. Since no one from our school went to a real college, no one even used it to pad their extracurriculars—except for me.

When lunch period rolled around, I went to the Science Club meeting with hopes of getting elected to some nice meaningless office I could put on my résumé. Moments later, Ravi walked in, followed by Gurpreet, then Baljit, then another Baljit, then every Indian girl at the school, plus a boy or two for good measure. It was a coup. Ravi was president, Gurp was secretary, and Sukh Dhillon was treasurer. *This* was going to be Ravi's Asian Club.

(She quite politely had me installed as vice president, not because I was an "honorary Indian" or anything, but because she knew I really wanted it on my résumé for college.)

These girls were scrappy bitches. The world had forgotten them, but they found places for themselves. Some found nice local Indian guys who were willing to take a chance on a girl with impugned chastity. Some quietly did the books for their dad's company until they got fed up and started dating white guys. Some found guys in India or Canada who were excited to have a sophisticated American wife.

I am supposed to be nostalgic for football. I am supposed to watch *Friday Night Lights* or *Remember the Titans* and be electrified by its connection to my life. Now, I do miss the grass and the lights and the cold and the excitement. But if I am feeling nostalgic, if I'm missing the world I came from, the football movie I watch is Gurinder Chadha's *Bend It Like Beckham.*

Jess Bamra, the plucky Sikh girl at the center of *Bend It Like Beckham,* has no role to fill. There is no rubric for a female soccer star. She wants to be like Beckham, but a number of factors make that impossible. It is not sad, though, because she so purely experiences joy in what she's doing. Chadha's fast-paced, joyous musical montages of soccer frenetics let us join in Jess's sense of completion and camaraderie on the football pitch. We get that it's the only place she makes sense, but for a teenage Punjabi girl, that doesn't make sense.

This brings us to the choreographic difference between American football and Association football (soccer). Soccer is graceful, fluid, and long. We see Jess running, jumping, kicking in an orchestrated flow. American football is nasty, brutish, and short. Men are hidden behind pads and helmets, they crash into a scrum, and then as soon as the action has started, it is over. Everyone collects themselves and lines up again. There's no flow; you can't make a good musical montage about it because good songs don't stop every twenty seconds to reposition for the next down. Soccer is a symphony, football is a cacophony.[18]

The narratives that were built for me weren't built for me. Yes, I'm a white guy who played football, but the simple, boring, patriarchal story football movies offered was never going to satisfy my soul. My family and town would love a Rudy story where I gave my everything to football and burned all my effort to understand it and get better at it. What a fucking waste. Just think of all the cool stuff I read and learned and thought up while I was being a flaky faggot that never would have been if I'd been trying to A-student my way into masculine respectability. I don't need those stories.

I needed stories about people who don't have a place in the narrative

---

[18] To be clear, I still hate soccer. I like watching American football more than soccer; I just don't want to watch a movie about American football.

yet. I needed to see clever people figure out how they fit in to soccer, or twenty-first-century sexuality, or America. I don't look like the women in *Bend It Like Beckham*, or the 1992 Sutter Union High School Science Club officers' board, but judging people by what they look like is for sad participants in the moribund hierarchy of football in *Rudy* or *Johnny Be Good*. Jess Bamra knows you don't judge people by how they look—you judge them by how they play.

THE RAGE OF CALIBAN

IN THE YEAR 1992, my mother arrived home with a video. This was during those loose, freewheeling days when Debbie Branum would still find herself at a video store on her own, before streaming services, glaucoma, and gentle agoraphobia made these ideas comically incongruous. Communism had fallen, Kuwait was free, George H. W. Bush was president, and the world was full of slow growth and sensible promise. Anything was moderately possible.

She brought home a video and gave it to me and said, "You need to watch this." This was not unusual. As we have established in this work, my mother sharing culture with me was foundational to our relationship and key evidence of her real and profound love for me. At this point in my life, we could go so far as to say "understanding of me," though said understanding, like a California poppy, would bloom beautiful but not long. What distinguished this piece of art was that it dated from slightly later in time than most of my mother's recommendations, and it featured in one of her medium-low rotation stories about her identification as a savvy person.

I will stop obfuscating. I'm writing a book, not doing a coin trick.

It was *The Graduate*, a film from 1967 directed by the legendary Mike Nichols. Most of the old movies we watched were older than that: classics of the 1940s, '50s, or early '60s that she'd watched on TV with her mom. *The Graduate* was a film from when my mother was sixteen, an age at which she was, by the judgments of her culture, an adult woman. By nineteen, she would have a baby and her life as a breezy, art-consuming adult would be gone. It was from that little window when she could see a sex comedy and just enjoy it.

And she did. She loved it. At least three or four times in my childhood, she told a story of seeing the film and laughing at a joke before the rest of the audience. Before the punch line of the joke played out. She saw the joke coming, and she laughed at it alone. She told this story rarely but definitively, as proof of her intelligence and sophistication. I loved it. Sophistication can be hard to come by when you're living in a place that always smells at least somewhat of rotting prunes.

Another distinguishing aspect of my consumption of *The Graduate* was that I did not watch it with her. I don't think she avoided it because of the sexual nature of the film: She would usually fast-forward through anything she deemed inappropriate, and the resounding power of my asexuality at age sixteen could assuage any parent's fear of awkwardness. I think I watched the film alone mostly because she no longer felt like she had to guide me to things. She'd done her job right; she'd taught me to be an active, intelligent consumer of culture. Here's the *actual* best picture of 1967,[1] Guy. Go crazy.

So I watched a coming-of-age comedy from another time, while I myself was supposed to be coming of age. None of this mattered to me. I loved it, but for my own reasons.

The thing about a cultural trope from your parents' generation is that you encounter it as a pop culture reference so many times before you consume the original piece of art that there's the danger of the original feeling like an afterthought. I knew what a Mrs. Robinson was

---

[1] *In the Heat of the Night* can go fuck itself.

long before I saw Mrs. Robinson.[2] I thought I knew what I was going to be watching. Then I watched it, and it changed me. Mrs. Robinson changed me. Anne Bancroft changed me.

In the film, a younger Dustin Hoffman had graduated from college, and suburban people of a sort who made no sense to me were saying suburban things to him,[3] and music cues were supposed to be telling us that he had some sort of ennui,[4] I guess. That was happening and I didn't really care. There was a lot of white midcentury interior design, and I was maybe more interested in that, and I'm almost never interested in design. Benjamin Braddock, the character Hoffman was playing, was a normalish cipher, and I'd given up feeling like there were any similarities between me and normalish ciphers years before, as we will discuss later in this chapter. I mean, it *was* cool to see a young Dustin Hoffman, but this was no *Tootsie*.

Then She stalked in. She was a jungle cat. Later, I'd see her in leopard-print lingerie, and I'd be titillated, but not for any of the reasons a teenage boy looking at a partially clothed woman is supposed to be titillated. From the first moment She spoke to him, She was predator, and he was prey. She was in complete control and completely out of control. I was bedazzled.

For much of my childhood, the David Lynch film *Dune* was one of my favorite movies. My childhood was really just a laundry list of sci-fi or fantasy shitshows that I worshipped erroneously,[5] and *Dune* was a magnificent collection of great ideas rendered into turgid crap. The bones of the story, however, came from Frank Herbert's novel, which was

---

[2] Largely through the work of sitcom reruns, as we discussed in a previous chapter.

[3] Telling a kid in 1967 to get into plastics isn't morally empty, it's just good advice.

[4] Films of the latter half of the twentieth century are very certain that we should care about the ennui of straight white men. It's like the only thing Woody Allen wrote about, other than fucking teenagers.

[5] Behaving as though this quality is no longer true is not entirely accurate. I loved *Jupiter Ascending* and honestly thought *Valerian and the City of a Thousand Planets* was pretty great, too.

a smart and sordid injection of realpolitik into genres that so frequently ended up in Tolkienesque moral simplicity. I digress so far simply to say that years after my first viewing of *The Graduate*, I realized the calm, measured, forceful way Mrs. Robinson orders Benjamin Braddock to take her home is essentially just a Pasadena version of the Bene Gesserit "Voice" from *Dune*, a hypnotic power of command that badass ladies use to get what they want. I have never wanted to be a Jedi, a Navy SEAL, a Kwisatz Haderach, or any number of other makes of heroes, but I have always wanted to be a Bene Gesserit witch, just like Mrs. Robinson.

You can see why I fell for her. I also fell for her complexity, her damage, the echoes of what might have been in her life. As Anne Bancroft brings her friend's son back to her house and tries to frighten a child into fucking her, I, a sixteen-year-old boy, couldn't stop wondering, "What makes this woman tick?"

When you watch *The Graduate*, you watch for the scene in the Robinsons' den. The windows are glass and surrounded by so much lush tropical foliage that you might as well be in a zoo. You know what happens in a zoo: fighting and fucking, and Mrs. Robinson is ready to do both. Ben doesn't get this, though. Ben is an idiot, in exactly the way we insist is uniquely true of Millennials now. He's rude, self-absorbed, and generally so caught up in his own narrative that he doesn't notice the complex woman he's talking to. This is not a characteristic of generations; it's a quality of being twenty-one and dumb. Mrs. Robinson offers herself but denies that she's offering herself. She needles Ben with desire and frightens him with simply too much truth. Ben is about to turn into a man, exactly the sort of creature who runs society and keeps women like Mrs. Robinson as pets. Mrs. Robinson seduces and tortures him with the powers (sex and truth) that he does not understand. If for only a few weeks, she manages to turn Benjamin into a pet of her own.

The best line in *The Graduate* is when Mrs. Robinson and Benjamin are in the hotel bar before their first sexual rendezvous. She's trying to force this little person to be the man, to take control, to be suave. He has the capacity for none of this. She's annoyed with Ben and with herself.

When the waiter comes over, Mrs. Robinson says, "I will have a martini." It is not a request. It is an order. It's the Bene Gesserit voice. It is quiet, but it is certain. I know that her tryst is ridiculous, and that in the end she's ranting at Ben like a child who left his bike in the driveway, but I still love and respect the strength and certainty of Mrs. Robinson's cocktail order. There are moments in your life when you're not going to give anyone the chance to fuck something up. Mrs. Robinson's martini is one of those moments, and it lets us know so much about what the rest of her life is like.

The last act of *The Graduate* is a dud. Benjamin "falls in love" with Elaine Robinson and tries to wrest her away from a Berkeley frat[6] guy. Mrs. Robinson has a few diminished moments telling Ben to stay away or cursing at him in a church, but her story is done. The goddess has to be stripped of her powers. We could have access to a creature that magnificent and wild only as an impediment to some man's boring story.

It always happens. *The Devil Wears Prada* is this magnificent film about a girl getting offered the chance to learn to be a dragon lady from the very best, then she turns it down so Vinnie Chase can make her grilled cheese with ten dollars' worth of Jarlsberg in it. Nice stories need conventional endings. Mrs. Robinson isn't conventional.

The caged-beast predation of Mrs. Robinson, the polite domestic pedophilia of a woman toying with her lesser because she had nothing left to lose—I would be lying if I said it wasn't the first sexuality I saw that made sense to me. Mrs. Robinson had lived long enough in a world that did not value her. She was done asking for permission to lead a life she hated. She was going to take something, even if it was wrong. Because it was wrong.

As an intelligent, right-thinking adult, I know I should not admit that. I should not admit to finding any part of Mrs. Robinson's psychological manipulation of a barely adult Benjamin erotically appealing. In the movie, it is permissible because it was 1967 and because Mrs. Robinson is a woman. She can't be a real sexual threat. I am a gay man, thus

---

[6] Theta Xi, I believe.

a presumed manipulator, predator, and pedophile to many. My inclinations are also not ameliorated by the fact that, when I watched the film, I was five years younger than Ben is in the movie. I'm still a gay man, and admitting that age-based psychological coercion in sex interested me will make me suspect to you. I know these things as an intelligent, right-thinking adult.

But one of the key problems with our modern, liberal construction of homosexuality is that it conceives of homosexual men only as being intelligent, right-thinking adults. "Two consenting adults" are the words on which the gay rights movement was built. Gay adolescents, meanwhile, we ask not to exist. Gay children must wait. They must watch their classmates' adventures, and they have to watch movies about young, imperfect heterosexual love and dance to songs about it. And then they have to wait to get in to a good liberal arts college and become a consenting adult. But no, you will tell me. Things are better now. *Glee* happened. Shit's cool now. Gay teens now have the option of a nice dating life so long as it has the most perfect, burnished sheen of suburban domesticity on it; if the one to two out gay teens in their high school turn out to have mutual attraction, and no one's parents are religious or conservative enough to send one of the involved parties to a re-education camp when they learn about the adolescent tryst. *Love, Simon* made a modest profit! Things sure are fixed. Good luck and Godspeed, class of 2020!

But I wasn't born in 2002. I still lived in a world where gay sex was illegal in a lot of states, and I couldn't foresee a sexual life for myself that wasn't built on lies and manipulations. That Mrs. Robinson's desires chafed at social decorum (if not the law) was integral to the appeal. Don't ask me to watch and identify with stories of heterosexuals engaging in sweet, innocent adolescent love when sweet, innocent adolescent love was a thing I'd never had the option of.

I was a gay teen, and I was a housewife wasting the best years of my life. I was in a house with people who didn't give two shits about my self-actualization or happiness. I had a degree in art history, and I was doing absolutely nothing with it. I was not being sexually satisfied, but

I looked damned good in a leopard print. This upper-middle-class Gorgon was a far more realistic rendering of my teen sexuality than anyone on *Saved by the Bell*.

I was not attracted to Dustin Hoffman. I don't think anyone is, really. There are times in *Tootsie* when he's got the charismatic-actor short-guy arrogance going on and he seems attractive, but mostly, he just reminded me of a more Jewish version of my dad. Ben wasn't hot, but Mrs. Robinson's capacity to go for what she wanted, regardless of the consequences, was intoxicating.

There was recently a Netflix campaign called "The First Time I Saw Me" about members of traditionally underrepresented minorities recalling the first time they saw someone like themselves in media. It is focused primarily on visible racial minorities. Gay people, of course, don't need anything like this, because on the surface, we look like not-gay people, and surfaces are all you're looking for in art, right?

Let's jump back for a moment to that 2004 review of *The L Word* by Stacey D'Erasmo that I referenced in a previous chapter. In it, she notes, "Visibility is a tricky thing; is someone visible when you can point her out in a crowd, or when you understand what her life feels like to her?" D'Erasmo goes on: "[The] peculiar consequence of so rarely seeing your kind on television, in movies . . . you can become, almost unwittingly, attached to a certain kind of wildness: the wildness of feeling not only unrepresented but somehow unrepresentable in ordinary terms." In 1992 in America, or really, anywhere in the world, I had no options for seeing myself in media under any terms that would make rational sense to someone else. Mrs. Robinson's literal wildness brought her closer to me. Her rage was of operatic scale, and as a sixteen-year-old boy repressing all sexual or emotional desire, I needed that.

I remember when I lost this specific shred of white male entitlement. I was reading *Pawn of Prophecy*, the first book in the Belgariad, a fantasy series by David Eddings. They're these bad 1980s fantasy novels where a cipher of a boy discovers he's the wizard messiah and gets an Object of Incredible Power with which he defeats all evil. Glen Weldon of NPR's *Pop Culture Happy Hour* once described such works as Tolkien methadone—works that the primary purpose of which was to help adolescent boys taper off from the actual artistry of *The Lord of the Rings*. I was reading this adventure about a Regular Boy of No Qualities, and out of nowhere, I broke. I distinctly remember yelling at myself in my own head, "You are not like Garion." Garion was the protagonist; he was regular. I stridently reproached myself: Who did I think I was, pretending I was a regular boy, like I was a hero? I wasn't normal. I was fat, I was wrong, I was not a person on whom adventure could be overlaid. Whom, in my own head, was I trying to fool?

If you ever ask me who my favorite Disney princess is (and you should), I will answer, "Ariel." I will say this because I like *The Little Mermaid* better than any of the other Disney princess movies, because I like the songs in *The Little Mermaid* better than just about any other musical's, and I will say it because Ariel's hair is pretty. The real answer isn't Ariel, though. The real answer is that my favorite Disney princess is a sea witch.

If you're an intelligent, critical person looking on from a distance, this is hardly a surprise. Ursula, the obese, betentacled temptress of Disney's *The Little Mermaid*, is just another Mrs. Robinson. She's savvy, dejected, and willing to ruin the life of a young person to get what she needs. The difference is that she's a cartoon; she's unbounded by the restraints of suburban Pasadena. In fictitious monochromes, her manipulations are freed to be all the more buttery and delicious.

Ursula is a villain, but she isn't EVIL. She's not archly malevolent like, say, a Maleficent; she's not trying to bring people down just for the sake of evil. She's got an angle, a beef, a story we're seeing only the edges of. Triton, with his infinite power and well-muscled torso, screwed her over at some point,[7] and she's ready to take back what she can, and she doesn't really care whom she hurts in the process.

Ursula is results-oriented. If Mrs. Robinson is in an emotional cage and lashing out indiscriminately to try to feel again, Ursula is a calculat-

---

[7] As Lindy West notes in her masterful analysis of Ursula in *Shrill*, "History is written by the victors, so forgive me if I don't trust some P90X sea king's smear campaign against the radical fatty in the next grotto."

ing predator in the wild. She plays everyone from Triton to Eric to Ariel. Her greatest power isn't her "little bit of magic," it's her voice. In a world full of sentimental kings and lovers saying how they actually feel, Ursula always says what she needs to be saying. Even before she steals Ariel's voice to romance Eric, she's taking on figurative voices to be the person her prey needs in the moment. If the undersea world won't respect Ursula for her talents, she'll use those talents to fool them into giving her what she wants. She's Margaret Thatcher with tentacles. That's really all I've ever aspired to be.

I have never been that savvy or manipulative, just like I've never been as sexy or commanding as Mrs. Robinson, but in Ursula, I saw something electrifying. I don't know that I ever consciously thought that I wanted to be like her, or that her capacious body was more reminiscent of my own, but I definitely felt access to Ursula in a way that I wasn't used to finding in narrative.

Every child wants to be good, I think. I tried very hard to be good for the first twenty-odd years of my conscious life, and I eventually realized that the rules of good required too much of me. In the musical *Wicked*, Elphaba says she's sick of playing by the rules of someone else's game. She says she's spent her life constraining desires and powers to avoid losing love: "Well, if that's love, it comes at much too high a cost." We never see Mrs. Robinson or Ursula when they're still trying to be nice girls, but we know the story. They realized that "nice" is a game that ultimately benefits only Triton or Mr. Robinson. Mrs. Robinson is in an in-between place, broken and confused, but Ursula has come out the other side. The norms of morality are no longer meaningful for her. She understands that you can't save yourself by being quiet and well behaved; you can save yourself only by having power.

In *How to Be Gay*, David Halperin describes the way that gay men watch *Mildred Pierce*.[8] The story is supposed to be about a long-suffering

---

[8] If you don't know what *Mildred Pierce* is about, I don't know why you're reading this book, but it's a Joan Crawford movie about a lady who selflessly makes pies to give her daughter a better life, then her daughter fucks her boyfriend.

mother who gives too much to her daughter, but the laughter and shouts of support from gay men always back up the greedy, venomous daughter. Ironically, Halperin describes a group of gay men watching *Mommie Dearest*[9] in precisely the opposite fashion. The story is supposed to be of a cruel, vain mother demanding too much from her abused child, but the gay bar is collectively mocking Christina for putting her nice dresses on wire hangers. Yes, we identify with powerful, interesting female figures, but we are also invested in upending narrative. If the role of comic or romantic narrative is to get a happy heterosexual couple together to give us the prospect of a baby and hope that life will continue, we gay people know there will never be a place for us in the center of that story.

So we have to steal the narrative. We co-opt it, like Ursula taking Ariel's voice and Mrs. Robinson taking Ben's nuts. We can make it ours for a delightful, chaotic moment, but then the flow of narrative has to return, we have to let the conventional, boring, and normal attend to do their job of making babies. In the words of Benedick from *Much Ado About Nothing*, "The world must be peopled."

In 1981, clusters of gay men in San Francisco, New York, and Los Angeles started being diagnosed with odd combinations of opportunistic diseases, including Kaposi's sarcoma and pneumonia. It was called GRID (gay-related immune deficiency) but by 1982 had been categorized, of course, as AIDS (acquired immune deficiency syndrome). I was six. Before 1982, there were occasional gay characters in TV and film, mostly evil, mostly in art films targeted to cosmopolitan audiences, but our representation was growing. Then 1982 happened, and all gay men in film became a locus of disease, shame, pity, and death. I was still six. In 1996, Dr. David Ho pioneered treatment of HIV with a three-drug cocktail that included protease inhibitors. The number of AIDS-related deaths went from 41,000 a year to 16,000 a year, and Dr. Ho was named

---

[9] If you don't know what *Mommie Dearest* is about, I don't know why you're reading this book, but it's a Faye Dunaway movie about a Joan Crawford who selflessly makes women's weepy films to give her daughter a better life, then her daughter writes a really mean book about her.

Time's Person of the Year. On June 20, 1997, *My Best Friend's Wedding* came out in theaters, and it was a hit. I was twenty-one.

My Best Friend's Wedding is a romantic comedy starring Julia Roberts. You probably assume based on this fact that it is lame, basic, and without value. You are wrong. It tells the story of Jules (Roberts), a food critic who once made an agreement with her best friend, Michael (either Dylan McDermott or Dermot Mulroney), that if they were unmarried when they turned twenty-eight, they would get married. When she gets a call from Michael a few weeks before her twenty-eighth birthday, she assumes he's calling to invoke the pact. But she *can't*! Ugh, how dare he bring his silly love to the table. He's clearly been carrying a torch for *years*.

What Michael actually tells her is that he's getting married to twenty-year-old Kimmy (Cameron Diaz) in just a few weeks. He invites Jules to the wedding. Jules goes, but she's determined to break up his engagement and make Michael realize she is his true love.

That is the story. It is all of it. Why am I talking about it?

Because of George. Because Rupert Everett, an actual gay actor of ridiculous actual charm and handsomeness, is also in this film. From the first moments, when Jules is dragon-lady-reviewing food, she's chattering with George. Because when she is at her wits' end, she reaches out to him for help. Because he's smart and fun and loves Jules very much. *My Best Friend's Wedding* is the end of the Valley of the Shadow of Death for gay men in mainstream American films. George is *alive*.

It may seem to you that the victory I am suggesting is a flawed and meager one. This is still Jules's story. This is still about inevitable straight happiness and a love triangle with two women, neither of whom are attracted to the other. These estimations fail to understand what a deeply subversive rom-com *My Best Friend's Wedding* is.

First of all, our heroine, Jules, is trying to vex the happiness of others. She is, in her own way, a villain. She is trying to stop Michael from loving Kimmy. Under traditional rom-com rules, we would discover that Kimmy is vain or limited or cruel. She's not. She's wonderful. She's all the nice, happy, much younger wife a straight guy should people the world with. Jules is making a mistake. And George is there for her.

Romantic comedies that came after *My Best Friend's Wedding* have tried to echo the role of George and failed. They gave their heroine interchangeable sassy gay friends with a couple of one-liners and some makeup advice. I should know: I played one in 2011's *No Strings Attached.*[10] George was not a functionary; he was a force.

When things are looking worse for Jules, she calls George in. He arrives, he tells her she's doing the wrong thing, then he helps her out. He hijacks the narrative. Yes, he does it by pretending to be her fiancé, echoing and validating heteronormative rom-com tropes, but he shits on them the whole time. He understands this world. He's lived in heterosexuality his whole life, but he tap-dances around it. He's Ursula stealing voices and using them to get what he wants.

There is a moment in *My Best Friend's Wedding* when George is slinging so much magic and bullshit that he actually manages to turn the film into a musical. At lunch with Kimmy's family, he's telling the nearly impossible story of how he "fell for Jules," and he manages to make it so intoxicating, they come along for the ride. He pushes further, and he starts singing. Yeah, it's a movie, yeah, it's all made up, but why create a character who's irresponsibly heightening the farce to the point of breaking?

Because George doesn't care. He's not invested in heterosexuality. He's in a heterosexual story, he's moving it along, but he does not commit to the idea that heterosexual success for his friend is the only path. Eventually, Jules lets go and lets Michael and Kimmy get married. She finds herself alone at the reception, having done the right thing. She calls George on her ridiculously large 1997 cell phone, and he magically reappears. He narrates his own arrival: "He comes towards you . . . the

---

[10] Not to be confused with the previously referenced *Friends With Benefits*, the other fuck-buddy rom-com staring a *Black Swan* cast member and featuring a bald, gay friend. Fuck-buddy rom-coms were the dueling lambada movies of 2011.

moves of a jungle cat. Although you quite correctly sense that he is . . . gay . . . like most devastatingly handsome single men of his age are, you think . . . what the hell. Life goes on. Maybe there won't be marriage . . . maybe there won't be sex . . . but, by God, there'll be dancing." When a story doesn't know how you fit in to it, you have to do the narration yourself.

George Downes comes into a perfectly nice, respectable heterosexual romantic comedy, and he steals the narrative just like Ursula and Mrs. Robinson, but he is not thwarted by normalcy. Instead, he shows one of the characters in the very normal plot that there are options outside of that plot. He guides Jules to a very unconventional end, one without the certainty of heterosexual reproduction, and he reminds her that there's a lot of joy to be found there, too.

Rupert Everett is way more handsome than I could ever hope to be. He's astoundingly sexy and smart. Yes, he was an aspirational figure for a young gay man like me to see, but the reason I was able to so delight in his identity wasn't because I imagined I could ever be as suave, seductive, or beautiful as he. I could identify with George because he wasn't safe. He wasn't boring. George did nothing to assure Jules or me that happily ever after was our birthright. But he didn't die, either. He didn't disappear, diminish, or get sad. George knew there were other joys to be had.

Joan Didion says we tell ourselves stories to live. We seek narrative to provide rationalization to the chaos of life. Some people cling to the narrative they are given, by choice or by instinct, finding selves they should be with certain happinesses prescribed for their ends. Some of us don't. Like D'Erasmo said, we believe our stories are singular and uncapturable. I fear it. I fear I am alone, that my story is errata, that I am unlike others and a little bit gross. The truth is, though, that our stories are just not domesticated yet. They are dangerous wild things that may bite you, and I wouldn't have it any other way.

JOAN DIDION SLEPT HERE

LET'S BE HONEST, I went to college begrudgingly. Sure, I know, I've spent all of this book telling you how much I wanted to get out of Yuba City. Isn't that supposed to be my liberation? The moment when everything gets fine and my story becomes boring and I'm rendered successful and self-assured and perfect: Isn't this when I, like Oprah, become *fixed*?

No, because people are fundamentally dumb animals, and like dumb animals, we rarely accept what's good for us.

I was mad at Berkeley because I did not get in to Stanford. That is why everyone goes to Berkeley. It is a state-funded second prize for overachievers who did not overachieve quite enough. I knew one person at Berkeley who'd gotten in to Stanford and still chose to go to Berkeley. I'm sure she regrets it to this day. Hell, *Joan Didion* didn't get in to Stanford, and she invented California. It is my considered belief that not getting in to Stanford builds character.

There were other issues with going to college. First of all, no one I knew, except for my teachers, had done it. Second of all, it was a new life. I'd hungered for this life deeply. If popular culture had taught me anything, it was that going to college was a way to ensure you could be-come a person whose clothes never had roofing tar on them. But when actually presented with the opportunity to start my new, sophisticated life among people who would probably never run a trenching machine in their lives, I started to worry about how I was going to make friends.

I'd been obliged to make friends twice in my life: in first grade, when I switched schools, then in ninth grade, when I went to a different high school from most of the kids in my junior high. I hadn't done well on either of those occasions. In first grade, the closest thing I had to friends was two girls who regularly cheated off my worksheets. As discussed above, being a chill-tight bro at the beginning of high school had been impaired by my growing sexual awakening and having to spend large amounts of time around my potential bros while they were naked. It's hard to breezily chat with someone when you're terrified that he saw you staring at his abs before football practice yesterday. And I *was*.[1]

So now I had the opportunity to make friends on my own terms, to be myself, *finally*, thank God. I could just be me. Unfortunately, I had no idea who me was.

Like, you've read this book. You get that me being "the smart one" was a key part of my identity. But I was not the smart one at Berkeley. No one is the *anything* one at Berkeley. There are 40,000 students. You're at best one of the smart 3,600, and I wasn't.

The truth, which you probably have been able to suss out, is that I was reasonably terrified of what it meant that I was no longer living in a prison of ignorance and almonds. Three hours of nonconsensual football practice a day may have made my life grueling, but it at least helped me avoid some questions. And I think you know which questions I mean.

---

[1] There was this boy, Bobby Cooper, who had one of those truly *transformative* puberties. One that's essentially as effective as being bitten by a radioactive spider or having the rays of Earth's yellow sun penetrate your Kryptonian cells. He started high school as a Cabbage Patch doll, and by graduation he looked like he could break a car in half. Anyway, one time in football we were doing a drill where we had to stay in our tackle pile until the coach told us to get up, and I got to gently rub my hand along Bobby's abs. This moment is the happiest I have ever been in my life.

Now that the external barriers were removed, the barriers that remained were mostly in my own head. If I were going to change my life, first I had to change my brain.

Since childhood, I've had an obsession with movies in which lives were transformed by education. Well, mostly *Educating Rita*. It was my first Pygmalion story, and every boy's got a soft spot for his first. All I knew was that Siskel and Ebert had said that *Educating Rita* was good, and Siskel and Ebert were my real connection to the conventional wisdom of the coastal elites when I was nine. So, when I, a fourth-grader, saw the VHS at the video store, I tugged on my mom's sleeve and asked her if I could watch the film adaptation of a beloved West End stage dramedy. She said yes, because she's awesome, and we watched *Educating Rita*.

Educating Rita is about a working-class Liverpool hairdresser, Susan, who is dissatisfied with her life so starts calling herself Rita and enrolls in Britain's Open University, a then new program to allow anyone free and easy distance-learning classes. Well, it's mainly about her relationship with her professor, Frank, a jaded drunk who doesn't understand why anyone would want to learn or pretend to be fancy. Rita runs headlong into this new life, and Frank teaches her but is an asshole. Of course, they kind of fall in love, but that's not the point. The point is that Rita realizes the lives of the educated classes aren't perfect, and Frank sees the richness of his education through someone else's eyes. They learn from each other and grow, and then the movie ends with them acknowledging that and moving on to their new, separate lives.

That's a lot of emotion for a probably-going-to-be-gay fourth-grader to handle. The ending made me feel a mix of happy and sad I'd never felt before. The film loomed large in my mind, and as time went on and I was exposed to *My Fair Lady*, *Never on Sunday*, *Born Yesterday*, and even *Trading Places* and, God help me, *Back to School*. I was drawn to comedies that centered on education leading to liberty, which made the protagonist's life . . . not better, not *just* better, but bigger.

There's a moment at the beginning of *Educating Rita* when Rita/Susan is going to her professor's office for the first time. She passes a group of young, regular university students who are making fun of someone for not knowing what "assonance" is. A brief, pensive look washes over Susan's[2] face. These students are mocking someone as a moron for not knowing what this word is, and she doesn't know what it is. Susan has to wonder if she's a moron, and Rita cannot be a moron.

That look was my life. You know that by now. That look was my first seventeen years. That look isn't about education. That look is about class. We know what assonance[3] is, and we know it doesn't matter. We know that Rita knows thirty songs with good examples of assonance, and if you asked her what made the songs good, she'd be able to identify "all the words have that same 'oo' sound in them."[4] What Rita is trying to negotiate in Thatcher's stratified but purportedly meritocratic Britain is a litany of shibboleths[5] that will mark her as a person unworthy of note, along with the ability to speak the language that her betters use to discuss their management of her world.

I wasn't trying to learn things because learning is noble. I was trying to learn things so I couldn't be quite as easily turned into an economic cog as my parents had been. And their parents, and all of my ancestors back to working-class, lunch-bucket primordial ooze.

Because what I wanted wasn't to be smart—I mean, I wanted that, but it was part of a larger idea. I wanted to *succeed*. I wanted to be respectable. I wanted the centuries of dirt hosed off my genes and to know that I wasn't someone whose life was being controlled by distant other people who barely knew I existed.

I had never seen anyone do it, and I didn't precisely know how I was going to. "Get in to a good college" was the step that television had been telling me for decades. I had only moderately succeeded at that. Now what?

---

[2] No one was looking, and she's only Rita when someone's looking.

[3] Or you learned it once, then forgot it, and are now googling it on your phone.

[4] In the film she eventually defines assonance as "a bad rhyme."

[5] Shibboleths like using the word "shibboleth."

Well, one answer is "Get good grades." I didn't. I got okay grades. My first semester, my mom told me to take an unusually large course load. "You don't have a job. You can handle it." I got behind on reading, I missed morning classes, and by the end of the semester, I had a mix of A's and B's. I was proud of myself. My mom was unimpressed. I'd brought her nothing but A's while I was in high school. She wasn't happy. I was at a top-flight research university, expected to work at a caliber I never had before; I was taking way too many classes; and I was having to do my own laundry for the first time in my life. Perfection wasn't going to happen. She thought I was just being lazy, and I did, too. I slunk into a funk,[6] and my grades got worse.

Another way to "succeed" is to do something empirically noteworthy in an extracurricular activity. I did not, at this point in time, understand that extracurricular activities at Berkeley did not matter. With the exception of NCAA sports, no one really gives a shit what you do after classes. This isn't the Ivy League, with touring a capella groups or all-male musical theater troupes. It's a state-run public research university. If you want someone to care about your hobby, your hobby has to be curing lymphoma.

The practical effect was that I spent the better part of my first two years at Berkeley obsessed with student government. For someone who'd obsessively studied parliamentary procedure in high school, the idea of an actual student senate running according to parliamentary rules, governing the student activities fees of forty thousand students, was intoxicating. That's what seems interesting when you have yet to taste a dick.

My freshman year, I interned for the president of the student government. He was at least moderately corrupt and appointed me to three or four moderately powerful university committees for which I was in no way qualified or valuable, just in case he needed to pull a string. From the foot soldiers of his moderately evil administration, I learned

---

[6] This is rhyme, not assonance.

the rules of student politics at Berkeley. There was, for some reason, a highly sophisticated and stable system of student parties at Berkeley: First was a vaguely moderate party run by and for nice, privileged kids from the suburbs. While I was there, it was called the Coalition, and it actually consisted of several sub-parties that pandered to specific sub-constituencies: Asians, STEM students, members of the Greek system, and people who lived in the dorms. Then there was a deeply leftist, no-white-straight-males-need-apply party steeped in Marxism and revolution. Then there were several niche parties, including one representing the far-right students on campus, and one from the campus humor paper. Many of these parties had existed for decades, and no one at Berkeley knew they existed except the student government dorks and any fool sad enough to be fucking one of them.

At this time I still identified as a Republican. My parents were Republicans; George H. W. Bush seemed nice; Rush Limbaugh made long car rides with my dad more interesting; and Margaret Thatcher was dashing and impressive. I mean, I can't really behave as though I was just a naive idiot who hadn't thought about these things, since I've spent much of this book bragging about how I thought about everything always. My understanding of politics was deeply rooted in Thatcher's idea that it's better to create a world where people choose to be good rather than are compelled to be good. There was a lot of stuff I hadn't thought about, but mainly, I was wrapping myself in Republicanism to have one quality my dad would approve of. I was Republican in the way you like the Kansas City Royals or are Catholic.

This meant that at Berkeley, I would instinctively side with the Coalition. I even joined Berkeley College Republicans. Then I actually met them. They were all rich kids from L.A. or Orange County whose conservatism was rooted in the idea that they didn't want their dad's plastic surgeon income taxed too highly so they could afford a new beach house. They shouldn't have been at Berkeley.

Anyhoo, my first year I ran for student senate with this party of frat boys and engineers, and I'd done absolutely nothing to make myself popular or interesting, so I lost miserably. I got really sad. Around the time of the voting, Nixon had died, and I may very well have said, "They won't have Guy to kick around anymore" in my head. (This was working from the false assumption that anyone cared about me enough to kick me around.)

But this misguided run for office did have two significant externalities. The first is that it was the first time I'd spent time with gays my age. They were, of course, candidates for the opposing party, so most of our interaction involved yelling at each other and tearing signs down in the still of night, but seeing gay men who were actual people, not caricatures written by straight men for film or TV, was shocking to my mind. I kept wondering, had they played with G.I. Joes when they were young? Did they like swords? It's ridiculous in so many ways, not the least of which is that I had no fear or even awareness that I might read as *suuuuper*-gay to these other gay guys. I was lusting after boys constantly, but I refused to understand how that made me gay. Meeting real gay guys, however, forced me to start accepting that gay men were not sinister, effeminate creatures of the night. I guess this maturation was a good thing, but I kind of miss seeing all gay men as inhuman incubi—it was sexier that way.

The other thing that came from running for office was chalking. Twenty years ago, when you ran for student government at Berkeley, you were supposed to go out at night and write ads for yourself on concrete all around campus. An enthusiastic, diligent campaigner was working from dusk until dawn, we were told, and I was willing to be that campaigner, regardless of what it meant for my grades. However much I may have rejected my father's teachings, I was deeply invested in his work ethic.[7] Like, not in practice—I was mostly super-lazy—but I liked the idea of working hard. Chalking sidewalks was exactly the sort of thing that felt like work but was really just a nice waste of time.

We all know I lost, but I *did* get a lot of positive feedback on my chalking. Not for its artistic merit but for its wit. My slogan was the

---

[7] And on concrete, no less!

simple and alliterative "Guy is Good," so I tried to connect it to things around campus. Next to our campus bell tower I wrote, "Clocks are Good. Guy is Good." Outside of Café Strada, across the street from campus, I wrote, "Strada is Good, Eric Estrada[8] is Good, Guy is Good." I didn't win, but people told me I was funny, and I liked being told I was funny.

The following year, despite my assurances to politics that it would not have me to kick around anymore, I wanted revenge. I had seen the process play out, a couple of popular rich kids from one side win, a couple of shouty politicos of color from the other side win, and a couple of randos slide in. Those randos were the interesting part: They were nearly a third of the senate, and there were always one or two from the campus humor paper, *The Heuristic Squelch*.

Every college campus has a humor paper, and all of them call themselves "Tulane's Version of *The Harvard Lampoon*" or whatever. Since I am someone who, as a professional comedy writer, has spent more than enough time with alumni of *The Harvard Lampoon*,[9] I can assure you that they cannot roll their eyes enough at assertions such as this. While they will, among themselves, admit that the *Lampoon* is a work of adolescent mediocrity that barely manages to print four times a year, if you ever dared to assert that your humor paper from the University of Florida were remotely similar, they would act as though you were conflating angels and insects, then tell you about a very amusing A. S. Byatt joke that they included in the Fall 2009 edition of the *Lampoon*.

So let us not curry ire by making any such dramatic comparisons. Instead I will say that *The Heuristic Squelch* was Berkeley's version of the

---

[8] In the early 1990s, pop culture references were an unexplored science. This trite activation of a 1970s TV star's name seemed witty and dynamic. Believe me, it was much funnier back then.

[9] Hi Chris, Matt, and Charlie! I am sorry I am throwing you under the bus right now, but the unavoidable prospect of class warfare in America meant it was only a matter of time.

Florida State *Eggplant*.[10] In their antiestablishment, nihilistic comedy tear, they'd started a habit of running a slate of candidates for student office every year, and always getting a few elected. They would talk a lot of shit at senate meetings but usually end up being responsible, good kids who tried to help the university community. I realized that one way of getting in to the senate would be to join the *Squelch*.

I didn't do that. Ironically, for someone who spent his adolescent years loving running for office, I have a general assumption that no one will like me. I was certain that joining the *Squelch* would just result in awkward group politics; plus, I had a real fear of the kind of upper-middle-class Southern California gentry who populated Berkeley's least responsible diversions. I didn't trust myself to mix well with them.

I decided to do them one better. I was going to run for senate on my *own* humor platform. Specifically, I registered a party called Cal Under-graduate Masturbators (the CUM party) and established a platform to make the campus more attentive to the needs of students indulging in self-love. My victory was resounding.

I also spent the spring running the campaign of Jeff Cohen, the guy who played Chunk in *The Goonies*, for president of the student government. He was the biggest, most dazzling star our school had ever seen.[11] He was an RA, football mascot, rugby player, and cultural icon. He wanted to Schwarzenegger that popularity into political respectabil-

---

[10] I am using the *Eggplant* as a generic representative of campus humor papers you've never heard of. I can assume no one reading this book went to Florida State to pursue comedy. There are only two reasons to go to Florida State:

1. Football, or
2. If you're a Jewish, Latina, or biracial girl and want to spend four years in intense humidity having to confront the most basic truths about your hair texture before moving to more temperate climates, buying a flat iron, and getting a job in publishing.

The University of Florida, however, has produced lots of great comedy writers, like my friend Christy Stratton Mann. Go Gators!

[11] Crown Prince Haakon of Norway was also at Berkeley then, but Scandinavian royalty have lost much of the village-burning, virgin-despoiling glamour of their Viking ancestors. I did serve him popcorn at a movie theater once, though.

ity. He noticed me hanging around the student government building a little too much and asked me to be his campaign manager. He'd created a mainstream center-left party to partner up with the radical leftists of Cal-Serve, and we'd all had a nice victory and were in solid control of student government. Then, like a week into his administration, I got in a fight with him and quit as his chief of staff. We eventually made up, and he is now my entertainment lawyer.

Finally, at long last, I was an Associated Students of the University of California senator. I spent the following year bickering. It was nothing but self-righteousness, adolescent antagonism, and parliamentary procedure, and I liked only one of those things. I had gotten the thing I'd wanted, had spent far too much time and energy pursuing, and realized it was pretty lame.

This is what I hate about the musical *Wicked*: At the moment when Elphaba is offered everything she ever desired by the Wizard, but also discovers he's the person who's been persecuting the animals in Oz, she refuses. She says, "But I don't want it, I can't want it anymore." That's just so political: "I can't want it." It's a gay person who really loves Chick-fil-A not going to Chick-fil-A because Chick-fil-A doesn't like gay people. Isn't it infinitely more interesting to get the thing you want, then just realize you don't want it anymore? What if you fought your whole life to get a Chick-fil-A sandwich, and when you finally bit into one, it wasn't satisfying? That is not a good analogy, because their homophobic chicken is delicious,[12] but I think you get my point. Making a political choice isn't interesting, but to discover that your frustrated, unrealized desire was actually more satisfying than the absence of desire: That's chilling.

All that didn't happen to me, but I did start to realize a life of capital-*A* Achievement might not be as satisfying as I'd imagined it would be. At Berkeley, I wasn't the Smart One or the Important One or the Ambitious One. I was just me, and I wasn't sure what that meant.

---

[12] The only thing worse than their hatred for my sexuality is the fact that they're closed on Sundays, giving me one less day to guiltily enjoy their succulent, Christ-fearing chicken.

It never crossed my mind that I just got to decide. The purpose of my life had been to get out of Yuba City and go be a real person in the real world. Now I'd done it, and I had no idea what my life could or should look like.

A Pygmalion movie is no simple makeover movie. Look, I love a makeover movie. Any movie in which "she gets bangs" is a plot point is a movie I'm going to enjoy, but those movies are dishonest. Yes, when Mia Thermopolis from *The Princess Diaries* learns to flat-iron her hair, everything does turn around for her, but those makeovers are fatuous. She was always pretty and skinny underneath, and I always knew a new hoodie wouldn't fix my life. Makeover movies are fun, but they aren't real.

Look at *The Devil Wears Prada*, another Anne Hathaway movie in which a woman's liberation is just an eyelash curler away. The thing is, the makeover doesn't transform her so much as make her aware of her potential. It challenges her to engage a part of herself she's left fallow. But the movie is really about a bigger transformation: Does she want to learn? Does she want to study at the knee of Miranda Priestly and learn to be a dragon lady?

As I have previously stated, I am still mad at Andy Sachs for not taking the red pill and learning how to be a dragon lady. Dragon ladies are great, but you never get to see where one comes from, and movies invariably make it seem like being a dragon lady comes at incalculable personal cost. Men get to be generals or super-spies, and no one asks, "But are they there for their children?" One lady decides to make her magazine the very best, and we have to have a protagonist who scoffs and says, "I don't want to be like her." [13]

The Devil Wears Prada is at least a mature enough movie to cloud that decision with ambiguity. We understand that Miranda Priestly is great but not good, and Andy Sachs feels the loss that goes with rejecting

---

[13] Yes, I am equating the importance of our national security with a fictitious fashion magazine. Deal with it.

her mentorship. The films and books in which people let themselves be truly transformed by education always end poorly: Our protagonist has been transformed, but not enough. Eliza Doolittle can no longer be happy selling flowers on the street, but she isn't a proper lady. Illya from *Never on Sunday* can no longer be happy with her simple seaside prostitution after Homer Thrace teaches her that she's an affront to the history of Greece, but it's not like she can become a loan officer at a bank or anything. The process creates a creature incapable of living comfortably in either world.

What's great about *Educating Rita* is that Rita is a hairstylist. She gives women actual makeovers and rants about how twenty minutes under a blow dryer cannot change who you are. She's gunning for more than cosmetic transformation, and the climax of the film comes when she's educated and sophisticated enough to read and appreciate Frank's poetry. She loves it, it's "full of style . . . it has in it a direct line through to the nineteenth-century traditions of wit and classical allusion." Frank then explains to her that it's pretentious crap, full of allusions that assure the cognoscente readers that they're responsibly educated, but the poems lack legitimate passion. Frank points out the basic truth of Pygmalion tales—that they are not so different from Frankenstein stories. He thought he could fuel the intellectual ambitions of a common hairdresser, but instead he just created another upper-middlebrow, pretentious undergrad monster.

As an autodidact, I was my own Professor Higgins. Through single-minded purpose, I'd been able to transform myself into the semblance of a nice, educated person, and I'd solidly established that I wouldn't have to make my living installing HVAC equipment. But like Rita, I'd learned just enough to know that the semblance of sophistication or achievement wasn't enough. I was making choices to prove who I wasn't, and I was wholly unprepared to think about who I wanted to be.

Then something really lovely happened. The student journalist who covered the ASUC senate while I was a senator, Ryan Tate, got selected as editor in chief of the campus paper—the real campus paper, not the funny one. A week or so into my senior year, he emailed me and said that one of the weekly humor columnists for the paper had resigned, so he needed a quick replacement. He'd always found me funny and full of opinions when I was a senator, and he wanted to know if I'd be interested in submitting to be the columnist's replacement. I, of course, said yes, and a week later, my first column was running in the paper.

I don't know what I wrote about, I'm sure it was terrible, but people read it, and some of them found it funny, and some of them told me, and I loved it. Instead of trying to be like other, important people, I was just saying things I found amusing and hoping people liked it, and it was working. It was a charming drug; but, like any vaguely irresponsible person, I soon found the obligation to crank out a weekly thousand words to be a chore. Half the time I forgot I had to do it until the night of my deadline.

Which brings us to a certain Tuesday in November of 1997. I had been out at my friend Alice's house drinking, and I was wending my way home in the gentle haze of a boy who doesn't really know how to be drunk yet. I remembered it was Tuesday, and that meant I had to submit a column. Further, it was eleven p.m., and my deadline was two a.m. This was not good. This was not good at all.

I rushed home and scanned my mind for a topic. There was an obvious one: It was the week before the Big Game between Berkeley and Stanford. Look, Berkeley and Stanford do have an official sports rivalry, but how little we care about it should be evidenced by the lack of creativity in naming. We just call it the "Big Game," like the big football game in a teen movie that can't be bothered to provide any texture to the narrative. At Berkeley in the 1990s, the only sports anyone really cared about were unionizing sweatshop laborers and competitive indoor marijuana horticulture. But there was this *official* campus thing that was happening, so I figured if I could come up with a decent angle on it, it would satisfy my overlords at the paper and earn me my sweet, sweet twenty dollars for the column.

The angle was obvious. There'd been a *lot* of news that fall about the fact that Chelsea Clinton had started as a student at Stanford, and everyone was doing their best to make sure she was treated like just another student. The pressure went so far that when a campus humor columnist at Stanford referenced Ms. Clinton's presence, he was summarily fired. It was clear that I had to be writing about Stanford, and if I was going to be writing about Stanford, I was going to be writing about Chelsea.

What I wrote was an unmeasured, excessive diatribe against Stanford's elitism. I was still pissed that I hadn't gotten to go there, and I was still pissed at rich kids having advantages they don't have to think about. I essentially argued that Stanford's power and reputation were based on their exclusivity, and that Berkeley's greatness lay in its inclusion. I also talked about how our campus was gross and smelled like urine because it was inclusive, and theirs was pristine and beautiful. Thus, I encouraged Berkeley students going to Stanford to riot, destroy, and attack everything around them.

We live in a world with power disparities. Money, race, gender, class: People have different opportunities. I always thought that the glory of the First Amendment was that it allowed unfettered (not equal) access to discourse. If other people are leading better lives than you, at least you're allowed to talk shit about them. To me, that's what Joan Rivers at the Oscars always was, a person who'd never be admitted to the ranks of the blessed and beautiful sniping at whether they were blessed and beautiful enough. I know it can seem shallow and negative, but at the time, I really felt like the sharpness of my tongue was the only power I had for confronting people on course to a life much better than my own. I was super-fun at parties.

The column was fine. Not particularly inspired or funny but fine. However, we were not the only publication needing to fill their pages, so the *San Francisco Chronicle*, while putting together a special section about the Big Game rivalry, included an article about my column. It was that vague late-1990s time when we'd learned about twenty-four-hour news cycles and national obsessions, and the "Chelsea Is Off-Limits" stories were simply too good to be ignored. It was neat, someone wrote an article about my article.

Then the Associated Press picked it up, really centering on the idea that I'd threatened the life of young Ms. Clinton. In the column, I'd written the line "Chelsea Clinton represents the Stanford ethos of establishment worship which must be subverted and destroyed." The AP quoted it as "Chelsea Clinton [. . .] must be destroyed." So, you know, it didn't look great.

The following day, I was making a mad dash to finish a draft of my undergraduate history thesis[14] to show my adviser. I got a call from the campus registrar's office. Let me be clear: Berkeley doesn't call you. Berkeley may email you or send you a letter. You may call someone at Berkeley and leave a message, but the enormous bureaucracy of Sproul Hall does not deign to contact you in person over the telephone, so that seemed odd. The person said that I could be expecting a visit from the Secret Service later that day.

Fuck.

Two men, white, bland, regular. Exactly what you'd imagine of Secret Service agents showed up at my door. I was scared shitless. I wasn't a kid who broke rules or got arrested. I only challenged the order *conceptually*. Well, finally, my knife-footed chickens were coming home to roost.

At the time my apartment was truly, truly nasty. I am a fundamentally disorganized, untidy person, and my apartments in college and law school would descend into states of chaos that would frighten many, so you must understand my terror when two representatives of the Treasury Department showed up at my home and said they needed to search it. Who but a criminally insane person would let a cantaloupe get that moldy in their own home?

If I were a smarter person, I might have said no. I might have pressed my constitutional rights against illegal search and asserted that my silly little column was no reason to believe I'd do anything actually violent, and that this search was, in fact, an illegal attempt to chill and

---

[14] "Video Killed the Radio Star: The British Monarchy and Media Relations 1952–1997."

restrain free speech.[15] I *could* have done that, but all I could think was "I'm supposed to meet with my thesis adviser at three thirty." So I let them search.

They looked through my dirty clothes, my wilting salad greens, my innumerable piles of *Entertainment Weekly*. They found nothing of real concern and ended the session by taking my photo and requesting I give them access to all of my medical and psychiatric files. All this so I could have a Secret Service file of my very own opened up.

I assented, but as the Secret Service agents sped off and I carried my still-warm printout of my thesis to my meeting, the absurdity of the situation bothered me. I'd made a stupid, lame joke and politicians who didn't want to have their privilege questioned had sent some goons to scare me. I am now older, and I can imagine how Hillary felt about the danger and pain that was brought on Chelsea by dragging her into the public eye. I get why a person would have the Secret Service go check to make sure there was no potential of any real danger. I can understand it, but I don't buy it. Hillary didn't think I was going to do anything to her daughter. She thought I was shit-talking at someone who was "off-limits" and wanted to scare me and others from talking about her daughter.[16]

---

[15] You owe it to yourself to learn more about the months of harassment Kathy Griffin was subjected to after she took a photo with a bloodied replica of our president's head in the style of Judith beheading Holofernes.

[16] I think Hillary would have been a great president, and I gave five hundred dollars to her campaign in 2016. I also think she has a nasty habit of playing by the most old-school and underhanded of political strategies.

Further, arguments made at the time of my column that Chelsea should be left alone because she had not chosen to be in the public eye have been belied by the past twenty years of American political history. Chelsea is a relatively boring, talentless child of privilege who is still regularly suggested as a Democratic candidate for public office. In 2008, when she was acting as a campaign surrogate for her mother, she told a child reporter that she was off-limits for press coverage. She, a twenty-seven-year-old woman, told a fourth-grader that she was off-limits. That's my fucking problem. A few years later, Chelsea got a six-hundred-thousand-dollar-a-year job as a correspondent for NBC News. Being powerful and well connected has its perks, but it also has its downsides, and one of them is that people get to criticize you. I've been the criticizer, and God knows I now have to live with being the criticized.

I decided to do something. See, one part of the story I didn't tell you about that interrogation is that one small part of me was thinking before I opened the door to those Secret Service agents. Even though I hadn't yet been to law school and didn't yet know my rights, I grabbed a mini–tape recorder I always *intended* to use to record lectures but never did, and I pressed "record" as I opened the door. I had it in my hand as the Secret Service agents told me that Hillary had seen the AP article in the San Jose *Mercury News* and said, "Find out what the fuck is going on here." I had a record of all the times they told me what I did wasn't nice, and of them saying they were searching my home for "pictures of Chelsea with a big red X over them." Well, when I say "them," I mean the guy who was playing good cop. There was a *very* clear good cop/bad cop thing going on. The bad cop spoke only the two times I started to say no to something. Both times he told me if I refused, they'd just go get a warrant and arrest me. I didn't say "Go get a warrant," but six hours later, I was up in the offices of the *Daily Californian* with my editors, turning the tape recording into a story.

This time, the story blew up even bigger. There were stories in the *New York Times* and *Time*, and for twenty-four hours, I was part of the twenty-four-hour news cycle. The *Moscow Times* called me a "bad-boy invectivator," and the *Washington Post* called me "unfunny." A hastily written, poorly thought-out column had earned me global exposure and an odd first taste of fame.

I'd proved to myself that I had it in me to make a mark outside the confines of an almond orchard. It was messy, it was problematic, but it was mine. My time away from my family and my time spent in the loving care of old PhD's had opened me up to start expressing myself. Trying to be important hadn't worked out that well, but trial and error had shown pretty clearly that when I expressed myself creatively, people didn't always love it, but they had a reaction. I could see that doing things I loved paid off more than things I did because they seemed respectable. But I could see it only dimly.

So then I wasted three years in law school.

WHAT IS EASY-BAKE OVEN?

IN *BROADCAST NEWS*, THERE'S a moment when Holly Hunter's character, Jane, pulls her boss aside and tells him what he's doing wrong. He says, "It must be nice to always believe you know better. To always think you're the smartest person in the room."

"No," says Jane, "it's awful."

She's not supposed to say that. She's supposed to take his statement as a reproach, to accept that she cannot possibly always be the smartest person in the room. Instead of consenting to polite social modesty, she just talks about her truth.

What I'm saying is I don't know how I'm supposed to write this book. After all, you're not supposed to go around saying you're smart. You're allowed to say you weigh 140 pounds, you're allowed to say you have 4 percent body fat. I'm *not* precisely allowed to say that I could probably name five-plus Eastern Roman Emperors, and that has affected my life in ways that are good and bad.[1]

---

[1] By the way:

Constantine
Julian the Apostate
Theodosius the Great

One of the reasons it's terrible to talk about knowing too much is, say, the presumption that remembering that Basil II was known as "The Bulgar Slayer" has any bearing on anything of real importance.[2] Or, say, that the problem with Jane is the *belief* that she knows better, not that she actually thinks that she knows better.

The arrogance of thinking you're just better at problem-solving than anyone else! In the wake of thirty years of intervening feminism, we can recognize that a male executive telling a female subordinate she shouldn't make suggestions because she's not doing so passively enough probably isn't her problem. I'm not a woman, though, so I wasn't taught by the world to doubt myself and fear acting with authority.[3]

Then allow me, at the top of this chapter, to stipulate that I am an arrogant prick. There has hardly been an argument with a loved one in my adult life that did not involve the words "You think you know everything!" being launched at me. It is true. I do, often, think I know everything.

The problem with having a brain and, let's be honest, a *soul* that loves trivia is that very frequently, I *do* know the answer. In the most trivial of senses, it means that if you said, "What was the name of Eleanor of Aquitaine's uncle who ruled one of the Crusader states?" I'd say, "Raymond." It would come from my gut, before I even knew it was true, but I'd be certain it was true, because my gut trivia reactions are usually true.

But *usually* is not *always*.

Like seven guys named Michael or Basil
Irene

There. The only ones I know anything about beyond their names are Constantine, because he made everyone be Christian, and Irene, because she kept having her sons blinded so she could stay in charge. The rest of them were relatively boring.

[2] Unless you're Bulgarian, but I think even they're probably over it by now.

[3] In the SAME way. I wasn't taught that in the SAME way. Let us not too easily indulge in the game of "gay white men are STILL white men," because your little game of erasing the innumerable games of fuckery that were played on my sense of self over the course of the past forty years is no longer cute to me.

If 95 percent of the time I know a random thing I shouldn't know, just instinctively, it means that at least 5 percent of the time, I'm exceedingly wrong about something and just as certain about it as when I thought I knew.

Allow me to tell you an illustrative story.

One time I was at the bookstore in the Grove, Los Angeles's most glorious mall. Really, probably the most illustrious mall in the English-Speaking World. How illustrious is it? They used to shoot *Extra* there. That's right: The place where I go to the movies and buy hot dogs is so fancy that they shoot entertainment television there. Sometimes on a random morning, I'd rush to get a power cord for my iPhone and I'd have to push past the muscley kid from *Saved by the Bell* letting us know it was Splitsville for Blake Lively and Penn Badgley. This is the rarefied air within which the forthcoming tale takes place.

I was at the café at the top of the Barnes & Noble, in some way intending to do productive work and not doing productive work. That's like 80 percent of my life when I don't have a job. It's why my book editor, the handsome Rakesh Satyal,[4] had to wait far too long for this book. Anyway, I went to buy a coffee from the Starbucks in the bookstore. It's one of those weird things that keeps saying it's a Starbucks but isn't quite a Starbucks and won't take Starbucks gift cards. I mention this for two reasons:

1. To create a sense of displacement for the story to come. If the filming of *Extra* at the Grove reminds you that this is a sexy, rich place, the knowledge that this is a space *billed* as a Starbucks but which does not conform to the standard rules of a Starbucks should let you know that I was not exactly on stable ground.
2. To protest the very idea of such places. The sole redeeming factor of Starbucks is the standardization of rules. If you walk

---

[4] Buy his novel *No One Can Pronounce My Name*, now in paperback!

into a Starbucks, you know *everything*. You know your iced coffee will not be hot coffee poured over ice, you know that you can order a kid's temp, you know *precisely* what that turkey panini will taste like. It is an embassy of middle-class values ready to embrace you regardless of your circumstances. Things at variance with these rules are apostasies.[5]

So I was in the Barnes & Noble quasi-Starbucks, and I realized I was standing behind two friends of friends. They were my friend Cressida's sketch group partners, and one of them was her best gay. He was the kind of gay who tried to insulate himself against unfavorable social interactions by packing on as much pec meat as possible. There are some men, many of them gay, who say, "Nothing bad can ever happen to me if I have very large arms and chest." He was one of those, and I loved him for it. There are few qualities I find as fascinating in a gay man as being super-muscley, and one of those few qualities is the cocktail of self-hatred and dedication that causes them to put such energy into their striated social insurance. Can you imagine how hot I'd be if, instead of admitting all the secret shames I've reported in this book, I just tried to hide from my truth in a gym. The lats I'd have!

This meaty-peced homosexual never talked to me. We were frequently in social situations together, but he usually behaved as though I were an intangible apparition. Also, Cressida's boyfriend, my dear friend Thom, hated him.

In this particular situation, he was for some reason talking about how rare it was for someone to get to direct the film adaptation of a play he or she had directed on Broadway. I interrupted and loudly declared that Mike Nichols had directed *Who's Afraid of Virginia Woolf?* on Broadway and had gone on to direct the film.

This dude—let's call him Brian because all gay guys are named Ryan,

---

[5] Apostasies like the Iconoclasts Empress Irene crushed during her merciless reign over the Eastern Roman Empire. I bet Irene would have cut the noses off anyone who tried to run one of these pseudo-Starbucks.

and I'd love to call him that, but that's his actual name, and there's not a generic gay male first name as good as Ryan (I currently have over sixteen hundred Ryans in my contact list)—said he did not think Mike Nichols had directed *Who's Afraid of Virginia Woolf?* on Broadway. And he hadn't. I was wrong—very wrong. Mike Nichols, rather, directed *Barefoot in the Park* on Broadway, and that success had gotten him the directing gig on the *Who's Afraid of Virginia Woolf?* movie. I did not know at the time who had directed it on Broadway.[6] The point is that no one cares and you can just look it up on your phone and I was trying to show off for a cute boy who did not like me and I failed miserably and emphatically. Also, I was well past thirty at the time.

Because isn't that why people know too much? To show off? To feel useful? Isn't my vague list of the names of twenty of India's thirty or so states just an attempt to ward off uncertainty that is as pathetic and much less sexy than the massive pecs of "Brian"?

I do not know when this became part of my personality. I don't think it was, at its origin, concretely related to my desire to be something bigger and better than what my godforsaken farm town had made me. If the two *are* related, it's not that one is the parent of the other. Instead, they are sisters, shared symptoms of the disease of my childhood: a general awareness that I did not fit in.

Growing up, I had basically been Mom's little helper. I could help do the math and remember the errands. It was really just my mom being a good parent and trying to teach me to do math and do errands, but in my head, it meant I was valuable. In almost no other part of my life did I feel valuable. As we have detailed elsewhere in this book, most of the choices I made in my three- or four-year-old life were considered suspect by the people of Sutter County. But knowing things—that was something I could do right.

And that's the thing: When you're right about a fact, you're *right*. My sister was always able to know what my father or mother wanted. She

---

[6] It was Alan Schneider.

could deftly give it to them while getting what she wanted. She understood the moving target of my father's whims in ways I never could. I could do what I *thought* he wanted, but I could also be told that I was wrong. State capitals can't do that to you. You can go to a book and look up what a state capital is. It won't go anywhere. *Montpelier*. Doesn't it feel good just to say it?

As the youngest, least powerful member of a family, as a person managing hostility from several family members, and whose nascent non-gender-conforming behaviors were being heavily policed, I was maybe just trying to feel some degree of power and control. If I couldn't understand how my dad or gender norms worked, at least I had the certainty of knowing how the Calvin cycle makes photosynthesis work.

Or maybe I'm just curious. Maybe that curiosity of mine is magically real for no reason, like my homosexuality. Maybe a fairy kissed my sleeping eyelids with nerd-dew, or the argumentative demand to know how World War I started is coded into my genes. Yet three quarters of the people I was related to had no curiosity about any of this stuff at all. Only my mom and her mom seemed to think it was charming or cool.[7]

These are all plausible theories, but I'd like to offer you another. It is entirely possible that I became obsessed with knowing as much as I could—about as many things as I could—because of game shows.

I love game shows. Everyone should. People show up looking nice and well put together. They are then asked questions or given tasks to perform, and if they answer or perform correctly, there is a ding and they win a prize. I think all of us, when we are six, want to win a prize. We all want to hear a ding. We want to feel like we are worthy of celebration. I certainly did.

Game shows run during the daytime. This is TV watched only by people without jobs. When I was small, before the Early Reagan Recession destroyed the tranquility of my childhood, my mother was one of

---

[7] They were the only people in my family who identified as Jews. This is why I like Jews.

those said people without a job. She was a housewife with two kids and with a husband who wasn't particularly nice to her, nor particularly respectful of her skills. Turning the TV on at ten a.m. and knowing exactly how much that washer/dryer cost was a thing that made this woman I worshipped feel better about herself. And I wanted that glow for myself.

And let's *talk* about the daytime game shows of the 1980s! They were great, full of levels of carpeting unimaginable in our current television environment. You had a boring host, not particularly hard games and questions, and on some of them the possibility of getting to mingle with midlevel TV celebrities. A regular human being could go and rub elbows with *Mr. Belvedere* mom Ilene Graff if they only knew how to properly describe an Irish Setter without using the word "Irish" or "setter."[8]

I didn't just want to be smart. I wanted my smartness measured, and I definitely associated that measurement with being able to transition to the world of people who knew stuff and visited the larger world. It would take me through the television and into that world, which was sitcoms and entertainment, but also Congress and people who had gone to college and Europe and knowing things about the stock market. I was just waiting until I was old enough to start sending in those postcards to get to be on the *Jeopardy!* teen tournament. Then everything would change.

I did not make it on the *Jeopardy!* teen tournament. But I did experience a debased version of it my freshman year at Berkeley. A sign up on the campus bridge where clubs advertised told me that there was a quiz bowl meeting coming up. Quiz bowl. I knew that term from television. Quiz bowl meant questions, and buzzers, and rightness.

There are a lot of ways this story can go from here. More dramatic, moralistic directions. I could show up and be terrible and discover that all of my small-town pomposity had been nothing more. I could show up and be the best and realize that knowing the fact that Gdansk is Poland's largest seaport is meaningless if you've never actually been there. Or I

---

[8] This, of course, refers to *The $100,000 Pyramid.*

could win six hundred thousand dollars on *Jeopardy!* All of these would be more interesting to you than what happened.

What happened is that I showed up to quiz bowl and I was fine. I was good enough for a highly competitive team like the one at Berkeley, but not good enough to be on the main touring competitive team. I didn't care. I loved it.

Quiz Bowl, a Primer

Let me explain how a quiz bowl match works. Four people sit across from four other people; everyone's at a desk with a buzzer in front of them. A ninth person reads questions, a tenth keeps score. There are chairs for people to watch. No one is ever there to watch.

Every game consists of twenty toss-up questions that start out vague, then get progressively clearer. Each is worth ten points. No consultation is allowed; you and your team are all working independently to figure it out. You can ring in whenever you like, but if you get it wrong, your team gets minus-five points and cannot answer the question. This will piss off a dude on your team. Here's a nice example from a tournament I played at:

> An old joke about this American president was that if someone made a doll of him, you could wind it up and watch it do nothing for eight years. For ten points, name this man, the Supreme Commander of the Allied Forces in Europe during World War II, who became the thirty-fourth president when he was first elected in 1952.
> *Dwight Eisenhower*

See, it starts out with a weird fact almost no one knows, goes through a couple that make the question more gettable, then lands on the obvious "Who became president in 1952?"

If you answer a toss-up question correctly, your team gets a bonus question. They can come in different shapes and sizes, but they all are multipart and allow for collaboration. Here is a bonus question from that same mid-nineties tournament:

Did you see *Hamlet*?[9] I didn't, but I read it, so answer the following about that play where everyone is dead at the end:

(five points) This king usurps the throne that should have been Hamlet's.
Claudius

(five points) This queen keeps her position by marrying Claudius, even though Hamlet later insinuates this is incestuous.
Gertrude

(ten points) This eavesdropping noble takes a sword in the gut when he listens in on a conversation between Gertrude and Hamlet.
Polonius

(ten points) This son of Polonius gets Hamlet back by wounding him with a poisoned sword, but perishes in the attempt, though not before he says, "The king is to blame."
Laertes

That's the structure, but a game is more than a structure, it's also a feeling. The feeling of quiz bowl is readiness. It's a quiet, still listening, then an instinct, then a buzz, then an answer, then points. It's risking and winning based on your ability to identify technetium faster than seven other people who still possessed, or at least maintained until their mid-twenties, their virginity.

---

[9] Yes, this packet is from 1996, right after Kenneth Branagh's overclocked *Hamlet* that no one saw.

For seven years of my life, I recreationally sat in a room with borderline asexual, borderline Asperger's students and answered questions about school stuff. I wasn't a star, but I didn't feel mediocre. I felt capable. I wasn't mad that I wasn't the first person at the table to identify Nadine Gordimer from a set of clues about her early short stories, I was just excited that I was around a group of people who knew more about Nadine Gordimer than I did. And not that deep, complex, single-subject knowledge my professors and grad student instructors had—no, the good kind of knowledge. Fatuous, facty, and encyclopedic. They made jokes about Zeno of Elea and referenced the War of Jenkins' Ear when talking about contemporary news stories. I was in the place I'd been trying to get to all of my life.

For my years at Berkeley, I went to quiz bowl meetings at least once weekly. And there I became friends with true, complete dorks. They brushed the bad habits[10] off of me, they let me know I didn't know everything about everything, and they told me to memorize lists of things. They were harsh, antisocial clichés, almost entirely male, but this wasn't like the male harshness of my dad or football teammates. In the end, I was capable of succeeding at their game. I would get a taste of that sweet buzz. I would get to be right. I'd get to prove that if I wasn't good for anything else, at least I knew that George Eliot wrote *Middlemarch*. It was the first time I really understood why guys play basketball for fun. I didn't need to win or be the best, I just wanted to see what I could do. Get the workout. Hang out with people I thought were fun and funny and see if I could get my brain to sparkle when it needed to.[11]

---

[10] Bad quiz bowl habits. They *filled* me with bad human habits: mostly pomposity, game-based rage, and a willingness to roll my eyes when someone didn't know Madame Chiang Kai-shek was *Time*'s co-person of the year in 1937.

[11] The mind-set of quiz bowlers is best essentialized in a story about one of the great players of all time, Rob Hentzel. At least I think this story is about Hentzel—I just remember that it's about an iconic player. So Hentzel went to a quiz bowl tournament and played it solo. In every round, he alone faced off against four capable players and beat them all. Finally, he was in the game for the tournament championship, and he answered nineteen of the twenty toss-up questions correctly. On the last question, however, he had nothing. The moderator read the full question, and

It turns out I wasn't really addicted to knowing what the capital of Bangladesh is. I was addicted to having my brain feel *on*. To feeling like I was using the fullness of my powers in a way that had rarely been possible in Yuba City. I liked quiz bowl, but I liked quiz bowlers better.

When I went to law school, they started making me tour with the quiz bowl team. At Berkeley, I'd been good enough only for tournaments being held at our school. Minnesota had a much-better-funded and much-worse-at-playing team. The mediocre skills that had been drilled into me at Berkeley were now suddenly valuable, so instead of spending my weekends checking the footnotes of law review articles, I spent them in vans driving to other college towns of the Midwest to answer questions about hockey and astrophysics.[12]

In the van on the way to a quiz bowl tournament in Michigan, I fell in love. On most trips, I boarded the van with a book and we all politely listened to late-1990s indie pop as we crossed America's fruited plains, but as time wore on, our collective need for socialization crept high enough that van-wide talk began. There was a jaded conspiracy theorist who probably ended up buying a lot of Bitcoin early on; there was a bearded chemical engineer I assumed was in his mid-thirties but was actually eighteen. A Mennonite historian, a Muslim Kansan girl

---

he did not ring in. At the conclusion of the question, a girl from the opposing team rang in and answered correctly. Hentzel got up, confused about this thing he did not know, in a world of things he knew. He walked over to a friend on another team and asked, "What is Easy-Bake Oven?" That's quiz bowlers—they know everything except the stuff everyone knows.

[12] I do not know anything about either of these topics, but in quiz bowl, if you don't know about a subject, you have to teach yourself one common fact so if a question comes up, instead of just saying, "Oops, I can't help," you can at least be checking against that one thing. So here are the things I know about hockey and astrophysics:

Hockey: The award for sportsmanship in the NHL is called the Lady Byng Trophy.

Astrophysics: The space at which a mass is so concentrated that its gravitational escape velocity is equal to the speed of light is called the Schwarzschild radius.

I could be wrong about either of these things, but if I ever hear a hockey question and no one else answers, I will ring in and say, "The Lady Byng Trophy!"

whose dad owned three Dairy Queens, a dazzlingly intelligent, medium-handsome architecture student, a thirty-seven-year-old who enrolled in classes at the university only so he could play quiz bowl, and a zaftig freshman girl from North Dakota who dressed and behaved exactly as though she were an eighth-grade boy.

Guess which one I fell in love with.

Her name was Annemarie. She was a bespectacled, sarcastic misanthrope from Bismarck. I'd known her before, but only as the girl who occasionally quipped at quiz bowl tournaments and always answered exactly one toss-up per game. In the back of this Minnesota Maroon van, we politely joked around, and I said something about *The View*, and she broke the chilling news to me that Debbie Matenopoulos, one of the original panelists, had been fired. I was rattled. We then fell down a six-hour-long hole discussing minutiae of television that no one else in the world remembered. *ALF Tales*, *The Charmings*, *The Ellen Burstyn Show*. After decades of loneliness, I had found a true kindred spirit. Eyes in which I saw a soul so like my own I nearly couldn't distinguish between her and myself.

Of course I didn't respect her. Why would I respect some fat sloppy person who spent all their time thinking about TV trivia?

On that first night, we set media on fire in our own minds. We pitched ideas for what we would do if we controlled TV. *RuPaul's Celebrity Mah-Jongg*, a dramatic anthology series called *Blythe Danner Presents*, a workplace situation comedy where *everyone* was a sassy secretary called *Talk to the Hand*. I explained my long-standing theory that there was a right and wrong way to be on a talk show, and for the first time, I articulated the idea that would turn into *Talk Show the Game Show*, the TruTV show that currently pays my rent.[13]

I'd had friends before Annemarie, but never so intimate. My best

---

[13] *Talk Show the Game Show* is a talk show where guests score points by doing the sorts of things you're supposed to do on a talk show: name-drop, plug projects, and tell anecdotes. At the end, guests are evaluated by two magnificent judges, Karen Kilgariff and Casey Schreiner. Complete rules are available at TruTV's website.

friend from college, Rebecca Cohen, was funny, smart, savvy, and insightful, but we were always separated by the fact that I was an asexual dork and she was an attractive, not-mentally-broken person. With Annemarie, there was no such separation. Never was someone so like me in fears and inclinations; I was not a mystery or an enigma to her. Annemarie could look at me, into me, and see the things I was not saying. In the way I had savored the feeling that comes from trivia, that heightened, electric readiness I'd practiced while watching *Jeopardy!* and living in quiz bowl, became an aspect of my social life. Instead of facts, it was creativity and ideas. Could I be as funny as she was? Could I match her thoughts? Could I best them?

My love affair with Annemarie was, of course, going to end poorly.

You may be confused. Here's this book by this avowedly gay man, a man who interprets nearly all of his formative experiences *through* his homosexuality, and he's never once referenced being in love with a man. And here, when he finally does use the word "love" to describe a relationship, when he documents falling head over heels for someone, it's a woman.

Yes, you have solved a mystery. I am not really gay. I was just pretending because I wanted my relationship with my parents to be horrible and to always have to keep track of whether boat shoes are in.

Here's the thing: In all those years of closeted isolation, you guys—the rest of humanity who creates our culture—you guys didn't exactly make it *easy* for me to love someone. And I know love is hard for everyone, but you're going to have to consent that it's a more complex, problematic set of issues for a homosexual, particularly one who wasn't raised in a speculative fiction novel where everyone is super-chill and there are no problems for gays ever.

I have always been more likely to fall in deep, rapturous crushes with women than with men, probably mostly because there's no danger of sexual rejection associated with them. It's usually just me thinking someone's the funniest, smartest, best person ever, and wanting to know what she thinks about everything always. On the rare occasion when I've allowed myself to feel such a way about a man, I've always been terrified of showing it to him in any way, because I knew with great certainty that if he learned such a thing, he would say to me, "Guy, you are very nice, but I never, ever in my life want to be naked in the same room as you."

And don't think I'm a complete coward. I've created opportunities for many men to express the above sentiment to me. It just hurts a lot more when you actually think they're the smartest, best thing ever.

Back to Annemarie. She thought I was the smartest, best thing ever, and I thought the same of her. What I didn't realize was that, as a closeted person, I appeared to be a viable romantic interest for a woman. I didn't consider anyone would think of me romantically, ever, so it just never crossed my mind until my best law school friend, Rachel, met Annemarie and said, "That girl has a crush on you." I said that was stupid and didn't think about it after, either.

Then, in the summer between my first and second years of law school, I came out of the closet. (I'm sorry that so many of my stories use this as a breaking point. I know it's hack, but sometimes clichés really do come true.) I came out to my parents, and as part of my ritualized notification of friends, I called Annemarie and told her. She gave a desultory "Uh, yeah, we all knew" and segued to another topic of conversation. Probably the NBC soap opera *Passions*, which involved a witch and a doll that was brought to life. *Passions* was our passion back in those days.

I thought a lot about how the news would alter me. The world was full of new questions, new issues. I didn't know who I was without closet doors surrounding me. A key issue for me was that my desires were now in evidence. People knew I liked guys, so I no longer had to hide my appreciation of them. In sum, I got to flirt, and flirtation was a new, exciting search for the right answer. This time, if you got the right answer, you didn't just get ten points, you got to ejaculate with, on, or in (the prepositions seemed endless!) a boy you found attractive.[14]

The story that ends this chapter returns us to one of those University of Minnesota vans. Again, we have overnight bags and a collection of brilliant, opinionated, barely socialized delights. People who've forgot-

---

[14] I would not ejaculate in, on, or near another man for nearly a year after this.

ten more about conceptual artist Jenny Holzer than you will ever know. I got in, the same but transformed. I was talking a lot about how gay I was. I was talking about boys I liked. I was talking about how simply *everyone* was wearing powder blue this season. It was true, but I was insufferable.

So Annemarie did not suffer me. Everyone else did. None of them really noticed. They were too busy discussing what kind of pie they were going to get when we stopped off in Osseo, Wisconsin, the midpoint between Minneapolis and Chicago and the place where we got pie.[15]

There was one other significant change in the van. In the intervening year, a new guy had joined our ranks, a medical student named Dave. "Dr. Dave," we called him. He was bad at quiz bowl but still came. Also, he was handsome. Not just handsome for quiz bowl, which was as low a bar as you imagine, but regular-human hot.

I wanted his attention. I wanted it so bad. He was straight, and I knew nothing could happen, but that's exactly why I wanted to flirt with him, to get to play the game without fear of real injury. Like a shorts-and-shells practice in football. I wasn't transparent about my interest, certainly, I was just very *aware* of him. Waiting for any little moment when Dr. Dave might say something that would be a segue for me to show off just how delightful, funny, and smart I was.

Less than an hour into our drive, I was possibly on my second or third delightfully charming comment to Dr. Dave when a cry came up from the back of the van.

"NOT FUNNY."

We went back to our conversation until the next time I, in some way, tried to amuse and delight my aspiring-physician crush.

"Not funny!"

Annemarie then explained to the van just how and why I was pathetically trying to seek Dave's approval. She didn't lay all of the cards on the

---

[15] The Norske Nook in Osseo, WI. It had very good pie. There was a place next to it called We Aim to Cheese that we never went to, but has a really good name.

table. She didn't say, "Guy is trying to seem funny to make Dr. Dave like him," but only because there was an entire weekend ahead of us, and if you're going to peel someone's skin off, you really have to take your time.

I tried to lash back at her, but she would use the force of my attack to throw me with a deft "Not funny" and the occasional insult to the premise or substance of my line. In my every word or action, she knew exactly the response to make it hurt the most, and make me fear whatever would happen next.

Because Annemarie knew all the answers to me. She'd read me cover to cover and knew the strengths, weaknesses, and sensitive spots. She was pissed, maybe because she wished she could be flirting with Dr. Dave. Maybe because she wished I was flirting with her. Maybe she was just mad because I'd left her alone in the chilly waters of repressed asexuality. Now I was her Rebecca Cohen, prancing off into the sun-dappled fields of adult sexuality and leaving her behind. It didn't matter—all that mattered was that she, still steeped in plausible asexuality, could purport to need nothing. I, however, had stepped out into the world of liking boys, and that meant I could be humiliated in front of boys, so she was there to do it. Those sun-dappled fields don't leave you much cover. Annemarie and I could tell you the highest point in Oceania, the third rule of thermodynamics, and the names of first and second Becky from *Roseanne*, but how to flirt with boys, a thing everyone knows, we had no idea where to begin. So we sucked it up and focused on the parts we were good at, trivia and verbal blood sport.

However horrible and excruciating it was, I loved it. I loved trying to best her and losing. I loved watching someone know something so well, and I loved that the something she knew so well was me.

And yes, to answer your question, Annemarie is now in a committed and loving relationship with a woman who is, I hope, as masterfully cruel to her as she once was to me.

THIS MONSTROSITY

THERE'S A STORY WE all know is coming. Since you began this catalog of my homosexual whining, we've all assumed a certain bit of reportage was on its way. My college friend Alice always used to say (not in college, after I came out), "You guys have only the one story."

So why am I belaboring? Why am I not simply telling this story from the beginning? Because the belaboring is the beginning. The self-consciousness about "just telling" is what makes it a story. And I am incanting against hackness. I'm making perfectly clear to you that I know you'll think me telling my coming-out story is trite, and maybe I fear it's trite, and our sharing that construction is a gentle kind of mental colonialism. A quiet shame around the relative importance of me saying a thing that the world was very sure was important before I had the sense of self to say it.

I was in law school. I went to law school because my mom told me to. It was also to avoid having to go out into the real world. I was pretty certain I wouldn't be able to survive there. My parents had been telling me for years how frivolous and irresponsible I was, and a big part of me believed them.

My senior year of college, I said, "Maybe I could just go get a job for a couple of years and figure out what I'm doing."

"But what will you do? Be a history teacher?"

My parents, as people who had not gone to college, did not understand how majors worked. They thought people who majored in things that were high school subjects would become high school teachers, and they thought majoring in anything else was ridiculous. My mom didn't exactly understand what my poli-sci degree would be preparing me for until she found out a coworker's daughter had gotten a poli-sci degree from Chico State and gotten a job for the county. "Political science, you can be a parole officer with one of those."

When they asked me what I'd do, I didn't really have an answer. "My friends are becoming consultants," I said. They didn't know what that was. I didn't, either. My mother told me I would go to law school, because if I didn't go now, I'd never go. She was right. If I hadn't gone then, I'd never have gone, because I had no business going to law school.

Another reason I went to law school was that my grades were mediocre. Not bad, not great, but thoroughly fine. I had a severe habit of lovingly crafting papers I turned in four days late and got docked a grade and a third on.[1] I knew that law schools cared about the LSAT, and I knew I could do well on the LSAT, so I went to law school. You might not think this is explaining why and how and where and when I had a very long talk that dare not speak its name with my parents, but it's really necessary.[2]

See, I applied to lots of law schools you'd expect me to apply to: Berkeley and Stanford, the latter of which I was never going to get in to;[3] Michigan and UCLA, where I had a chance; and Davis and UC Has-

---

[1] If my editor had been allowed to dock portions of my book advance for lateness, I would currently owe Atria Books tens of thousands of dollars.

[2] Besides, what better way to spice up a banal coming-out story than with a detailed account of attending law school in the Midwest?

[3] After the Chelsea Clinton incident, their academic senate formally condemned me.

tings, where my admission was virtually guaranteed. Also, I applied to the University of Minnesota Law School for a very stupid reason.

Once, while taking BART into San Francisco, I started talking to a guy who was dorky but affable. Maybe so dorky and affable that he started the conversation with me. I have no idea who he was or why we started talking, but he told me he was in grad school for some sort of engineering, and that he'd previously gone to law school at the University of Minnesota. He was *exactly* the kind of guy who'd go to law school and then decide he'd rather be an engineer instead. Smart but willful and kind of dickish. I'm sure he "sees both sides" of Gamergate, you know? I knew a lot of those guys at Berkeley. Well, he said Minnesota was ranked seventeenth in the country. I checked, and he was right.

So, at the suggestion of a random stranger on public transportation, I applied to the University of Minnesota and got accepted, and when it came time for me to figure out which school I was going to, UCLA and Hastings told me I needed to get private loans and Michigan refused to take me off their waitlist, while the good people at Minnesota let me know they'd given me a full academic scholarship. It was very kind of them, but it did destroy my life for several years.

I didn't really think much about moving to somewhere else in the country. I figured we all watched the same TV shows, so culture had to be pretty uniform. The upper Midwest was hardly the sexiest location to go, but moving at least seemed dynamic. *Dramatic.* And at the end of it, I would have a profession, a life. And once I had that nice stable income and status . . . my life would happen, I guess? It was vague, but it felt fancy.

My parents drove me to Minnesota, I found an apartment, I started law school, and I was off on a new adventure. Then the novelty wore off. There were a lot of factors for what happened after that. Let us consider them:

1. Minnesota is cold. While I had seen snow before in my life, it was only in the context of a trip up to the Sierra Nevadas on a seventy-degree day to "play in the snow," which mainly

involved slipping in melting snow and getting very damp. I
was not used to temperatures below sixty degrees, so used
the word "winter" to describe what most Minnesotans would
call "May."

2. Law school is very serious. I thought I was going to "graduate
school" but for law. I thought it would be like Berkeley. A
lot of discussion of building blocks of the law, analysis of
the social contexts that created common law cases. That's
not what law school is. Law school is people learning to be
lawyers. At Berkeley, people wore pajamas to class and said
"Let's define our terms" a lot. At law school, people wore
business casual and tried to memorize the right answer.

3. The produce is terrible. My first couple of weeks of law school
were full of mixers and organizational breakfasts, and all of
them had fruit plates. I would invariably see a fruit plate and
think, "Ooh, strawberries!" because the strawberries looked
nice, then I'd bite into one, and it would be white, flavorless
ice on the inside.

4. Minnesotans are cold. Now, they are very nice. They always
have a smile and a "How ya doin'?," but they do not want to
hear how you're actually doing. They want you to say "Fine"
and turn down your music. Every Minnesota smile hides a
judgment; it hides an annoyance they'd never think of actually
complaining about. I was used to Californians, who wouldn't
help you but will hug and cry with you. I was used to Jews,
who would tell you exactly what they didn't like about the salad
dressing. I was used to people whose spirits were warm and
present. But the Minnesotans were like those strawberries I bit
into: Their surface was the very image of inviting flavor, but
underneath that nice was white, flavorless ice.

Basically, I had been at a shifting point in my life where, after a
couple of years at Berkeley, I was finally acknowledging the real forces
that lived inside me. I wanted to talk about ideas; I wanted to express

myself. I needed to have big emotions and engage in frivolity. I needed that from my world on a daily basis. I liked so many of the people I met at law school, and I think they enjoyed me for all of my nonsense, but we were at different places in our lives.

I may have just been immature. Most of the people starting law school with me had been out of school and in the work world for a few years. One was in his mid-thirties and had a PhD in English, one was a former sheriff in his mid-fifties, but most of them were twenty-seven-year-olds who'd decided they wanted middle-class prerogatives and were willing to work hard for three years to make that happen. Meanwhile, there was a twenty-two-year-old there because his mom told him to.

Here's a thing no one ever tells you about law school: It's just like high school. I get it, people rarely tell you anything about law school except "It was expensive" and "I went there," but you know how the people on *How to Get Away with Murder* are always researching real-life crimes and bludgeoning people to death with trophies? You will be shocked to learn that's not what happens in law school. Here's what happens in law school:

You have lockers. Like *lockers*, so you can keep all of your gigantic case books in one place and don't have to carry them around.

You have assigned seats. Like it's goddamned ninth-grade homeroom. At the beginning of class, you either get to pick a spot or you're lined up alphabetically, and where you sit is where you sit for the rest of the year.

You take classes with the same people. This isn't college, where you decide your schedule. One semester at Berkeley, I took only Tuesday and Thursday classes so I could really open up my weekends.[4] In law school, for your first year, they put you in a "section," and you all have classes with each other from eight in the morning until four or five at night.

---

[4] I did not go out or have fun on weekends. I primarily watched independent films on IFC and anything Comedy Central had to offer me.

It's *intimate*. Some law schools are bigger, but mine was
    somewhere around 400 people, which meant 130 of them
    were in my year, which meant you saw the same people all
    day long. At Berkeley, there were 400 people in my History of
    Europe survey class. I saw 400 people before I got out of bed
    every morning. At Berkeley, there was always someone new
    and dazzling to meet, and in law school, you had met pretty
    much everyone by the third day. You know the nice stable
    boyfriend the girl has at the beginning of a romantic comedy,
    but then she realizes life has more to offer her, so she leaves
    him? That's essentially everyone in law school, just a bunch of
    Bill Pullmans, Tate Donovans, and Greg Kinnears.

There was one thing I liked about law school, though. The Socratic
method.[5] This is the style of discourse Plato had Socrates use in his di-
alogues, I think, but what it means is just teaching something by asking
a lot of questions. It also meant that class lectures weren't just lectures,
they were improvised talk shows. At any given time, a professor could
turn his or her steely gaze upon you, and you had to sink or swim on
your own merits. I liked that part.

But mostly, I hated my life. I hated where I lived, I hated what I did
every day, I hated that I didn't have any good friends, I hated that I didn't
have any fun left in my life. As time went on, I also began to recognize that
my lack of enthusiasm for law school might mean I wouldn't love being a
lawyer enough to be good at it, and that scared me deeply. Spending my
life in a career I didn't love would be hard, but spending my life doing
something I'd be mediocre at . . . that was chilling. All of these hatreds
were melding together into a worldview devoid of joy; I was scared.

At the University of Minnesota Law School, the honor code man-
dates that you can use only study materials to which you contributed

---

[5] I'm sure this isn't the aspect of ancient Greek culture you expected to be most discussed in my coming-out story.

at least 25 percent. What this means is that everyone is in a four-member study group. It's cataclysmically important. This four-person team is your eyes and ears in class. They gossip, they research, they tell you when you need to get your shit together. And when study groups formed . . . I was left without a dance partner. First finals came, first grades came. Academically, I was doing fine but not amazing; emotionally, I was failing.

Look, let's not catastrophize. After first semester, there were a couple of key breakups that shattered social stability and left some of the best and brightest scraping to find new study groups. I landed in a great one. There was Tara, a savvy but grounded Wisconsinite who always knew the right thing to say; Bryan, a scruffy San Francisco bike messenger with two dogs and the coolest wife in America; and Rachel, a Minnesota Jewess (that means she's still half-Norwegian) with a keen mind and quality one-liners. I had found a little family, but I spent most of my time complaining to them.

A cloud was growing inside me. I had always experienced depression, I think, but no one in Sutter County in 1990 had been looking at a fourteen-year-old and saying, "Oh, yes, he satisfies five of the nine diagnostic categories for major depression." They would've just said . . . I guess they probably would've just said I was weird. I was weird enough that no one was really paying attention to how my mood drifted around in that weirdness.

The truth is that my brain has a likelihood to go into periods of depression when I stop being able to sleep, can't get things done, and obsess over external obstacles and internal inadequacies. I lose the ability to get happy. I get sad for no reason. I get sad when happy things happen. During the longest period of unbroken success in my life, when I was on *Chelsea Lately* and mildly famous and had great friends and went out a lot, on the very night I was celebrating getting hired to write a feature screenplay,[6] at this time when everything was

---

[6] That didn't work out, but we'll have to leave that for another book.

going right, I realized I was still slightly sad. I made myself remember that. "Even now, you are sad, Guy. The sadness is not a reflection of the world; it is in you."

That is what I know now. Then, I was a shithead. And I was sad; nothing gave me pleasure. I wasn't noticing the ways that this sadness was showing up in my physical life. Lack of energy. Lack of sleep. I didn't think about why they were happening, I was just mad at myself that they were true.

There's another ingredient to this story that we have to mention. A revolution more powerful than my little depression, a catalyst that would have forced these developments whether I liked them or not.

In 1986, Senator Al Gore invented a system of tubes we now refer to as "The Internet." Twelve years later, when the events of this chapter were taking place, said system of tubes had advanced to a point when one could, with patience and dial-up service, download a naked photo of a muscley guy over the course of about ten minutes, and steal a song with breezy efficiency in just under two hours.

Here's how old I am: I remember being in a physical anthropology class in my second year at Berkeley. A girl leaned over to another girl and explained that she was in this very cool class: "It's about the *information superhighway*," she said, stressing every syllable. I kind of knew what that meant. I had an email address and had learned how to check message boards for information about Janeane Garofalo's career.[7] It would be years before I thought to use the anonymity and access of the Internet to start probing the meaning of my attraction to men.

A big part of this was just our old friend denial. As I have said, my brain was split down the middle: It knew full well that I was only and exclusively and explosively attracted to men. It remembered that time I'd called a hot guy from student government and not said anything just so I could hear his voice and be in his life for a moment. It knew about

---

[7] I *deeply* cared about Janeane Garofalo during the nascent years of the Internet. We all did.

those muscle-magazine photos on the wall of the high school weight room and just how much they meant to me.[8] It was also, simultaneously, very certain I was not gay. *What gay is, that's not me. That's other people, weird people, bad people.*

Also, the Internet was terrible. I have already made a hack "dial-up was slow" joke, but I must underline the point for my younger viewers. The summer before I went to law school, I was living at my parents' house and had finally worked up the nerve to use the Internet to get naked photos of men. Some will rail against this broad presence of the salacious online, but I must respect it. The desire of people with dicks to look at the stuff that turns us on is a potent fuel that powered the Internet bubble that became Mark Zuckerberg's fortune and the precipitous rise and fall of Pets.com. Yeah, stealing music is cool, but online porn is the stack of cinder blocks that built our current culture.

And the thing is, in the long run, online porn is why I can get married in this country. It's why we have an openly gay U.S. senator and a whole slate of Ryan Murphy productions on FX. In a history department, they teach you that the printing press changed Europe for centuries afterward. The printing press made pamphleteering possible in a way that broke religion, economics, and politics and catapulted us into a world of protest and revolution. The printing press executed Marie Antoinette, shoved the Catholic Church out of Northern Europe, and set up Karl Marx and Adam Smith to fight for control of the globe. The Internet did the same in a number of ways, but noteworthy here is its effect on gayness. Basically, dial-up was the beginning of the end for the closet. Once gays could safely, anonymously dip our toes into gayness, we could learn to accept it within ourselves and be open, and for any

---

[8] The most truly, deeply handsome of these bodybuilder photos my coach had put up in the weight room was of a guy in saffron-colored trunks posing in front of some ornate European architecture. I thought, "This man is so perfect, he could never be gay." Turns out that photo was of Bob Paris, the first openly gay competitive bodybuilder. Please keep this in mind when you read the *Babette's Feast* chapter.

holdouts, the Internet was also full of the thing even the most closeted of gays was hankering for: porn.[9]

That night at my parents' place, I tried to download a photo. It was a black-and-white photo of these twins[10] frolicking with each other. The twins actually became medium-famous and were featured in some Old Navy commercials with Tia and Tamera, then I *think* they had the Internet scoured to remove all the photos of them with their dicks out. What I am sure of is that they were the sexiest thing I'd seen to that date, and it took a half hour for that photo to download just to the nipples-visible level. I gave up and came. I didn't have time to wait for dick.[11]

A year later, at the end of my first year in law school, I'd become even more adventuresome with my Interent explorations. As we will discuss later in the book, I regularly went into gay chat rooms on AOL. Yes, I know, I am old and un-tech-savvy. Half the people I went to college with became tech billionaires, and I was using an AOL CD to hit on guys in Australia. Also, I *always* went into said chat rooms with a fake identity. If I revealed even the smallest fact about myself, someone would clearly piece together my real identity and immediately call my mother to tell her that I wanted to fuck in the poop hole.

My depression was compounded by this hunger and had grown more concrete through exposure to chat with real gay guys. I wanted a whole life, but I knew I was too scared to take the step. Well, I didn't fully KNOW this tension was fucking with me, but the parts of my head that were broken apart from each other, the part that knew I liked sexy-twin nipples and the part that told me what my identity was, they were starting to grow back together.

---

[9] If Johannes Gutenberg had the forethought to print gay porn instead of bibles, the gay civil rights movement may have happened much, much sooner, and he definitely would have made more guilders.

[10] The Brewer twins.

[11] *Waiting for Dick* is, of course, the title of my erotically charged, all-nude adaptation of Samuel Beckett's classic *Waiting for Godot*.

Three events changed things.

The first is that I got a nice, stable job working for the Hennepin County Attorney's Office as a summer law clerk. It wasn't as glamorous or lucrative as what my friends were making as summer associates, but it did mean I had an income. I knew that if I ever said anything to my parents about My Secret Shame, they would leave my life to one extent or another. I am a child of the working class, I know the first thing you figure out is money.

The second event was a party. For the Fourth of July, my friend Mike invited a bunch of people from the law school to his parents' large and glorious home by the banks of Lake Minnetonka. I made guacamole, which in Minnesota in 1999 was considered a form of witchcraft. I drank beer and swam and had fun. Mike, our host, was shortish and athletic and attractive, so I was stealing memories of what he looked like to masturbate to later. The closeted homosexuals are a diligent and resourceful people. He was cuddling with his girlfriend, Mona, and sharply, searingly, I became aware that I would never have that.

Tearing something apart is supposed to hurt, but in this situation, it was the reverse. I was putting together that my life as I was leading it would mean I would never have a relationship, never have love, comfort, cuddling. It burned. My brain, already pushed by my life in Minnesota into the deeper end of depression, seized upon this truth. And I couldn't say a word about it to anyone. My best friends in Minnesota, Tara, Bryan, Rachel, were all there, but I couldn't say anything, because my very problem was that I couldn't say anything.

(For the record, Mike and Mona are still together, and whatever the state of their marriage may be, I am so glad to know that the relationship that triggered this, well, let's use it, epiphany in me was the real deal. Also, according to photos on Facebook, Mike has kept shit tight.)

That was not enough. I needed further knife-twisting. I needed a different character of motivation. If we know anything about Guy Branum by this point, it's that he does not learn things from experience. He learns things from books.

Every day at work, I had an hour for lunch. I would get food, then go to the one used bookstore in downtown Minneapolis and read. It's what lonely people did before we had phones with the Internet on them. I was, in July 1999, reading a book about the Bloomsbury Group, and I got to a section about E. M. Forster's sexuality. It recounted two things that were of particular note to me:

1. At one party, E. M. Forster left early because, he said, he needed to put his mother to bed. As he left, Virginia Woolf is quoted as quietly muttering to her sister, "The midlife of buggers is a thing not to be contemplated without some degree of horror."
2. It told the story of Forster losing his virginity at the age of thirty-eight to an Egyptian trolley car conductor.

"That will be me," I thought. "If I keep going like I'm going, more years will slip away. I'll keep doing what I'm supposed to be doing, and I'll do it so long that I will never have a life."

My life was miserable, and I didn't know how to fix it. I didn't know how I'd ask someone to help. Something had to change, so I resolved to change the one thing I knew had to change. July fourth was a Sunday. I called the following Sunday, July eleventh.

My mom cried. Moms always cry. Maybe not every mom, maybe there's some cool downtown Manhattan mom who throws up her arms in joy and suggests that her sixteen-year-old son date one of the twenty-nine-year-old gallerists she works with, but for just about everyone I know, their mom cried.[12] And when it's happening, you feel like ice. You know when Annie Lennox sings "Let the wind blow through me" in "Walking on Broken Glass"? That's what it felt like.

---

[12] However chill with Elio being gay she was, you know that professor mom from *Call Me By Your Name* cried. She's Jewish *and* Italian—of course she cried.

But now that I know all moms cry, I wonder if it's different. Maybe moms aren't crying because you're breaking their heart; they're just crying like they would cry at a wedding. They're crying because life has changed, and that needs to be acknowledged through prolactin and salt.

Nah, my mom was crying because I broke her heart.

*

First of all, I didn't tell them I was gay. I said I was bisexual, then twenty minutes later, I made clear that I had never really been turned on by women in any way.[13]

My mom said, "Are you trying to hurt me? Because if that's what you're trying to do, you've succeeded."

My dad said, "What? Did God make a mistake?" And I said, "No, you did." And my mom, to some extent, still believes that if my father had not rhetorically fumbled so hard at the beginning of this, they might have successfully argued me out of homosexuality.

That's what they tried to do. They tried to argue me out of being gay. They tried to shame me and threaten me. They let me know that they were no longer possible financial support, just as I'd suspected. For weeks and months afterward, my parents let me know that there was no compromise. If there was a me that was gay, they didn't want it. Finally, they resorted to the final tool. They stopped loving me as much.

Let us first address the fact that they could have just never spoken to me again. Lots of parents do that. My parents thought they were being bold and liberal for not doing that. Their generosity was continuing to speak to me until the point at which I said anything incorporating the idea that I might be gay or date guys. And yes, they needed these ideas to be separate, because they deeply, fundamentally believed that my homosexuality was an affectation I just wanted to bring up to hurt them

---

[13] There was one photo in *George* magazine of Cameron Diaz in a knit bikini that gave me a boner once in high school, but that may just have been a reaction to the idea of a knit bikini.

and seem cool at parties.[14] It could not have a practical meaning in my life. I had made so much of my life invisible to them for such a long time that any time I tried to make it visible, they were horrified.

And they *did* stop loving me as much. You can say, "*Guy!* They never stopped *loving* you." You don't fucking know. And I didn't say they stopped loving me. I'm saying they withdrew. They became cold. They hardened their hearts, like when God hardened Pharaoh's. Their sympathy was gone, their interest gone. As I was sliding into the hardest period of my life, the two people best positioned to be there for me let me know that wasn't an option.

There is little good art about coming out. Yes, it's the only story we've got, and we sure do put it in our one-man shows, but we can't represent it. The people who have experienced it cannot have enough distance to comment on it. Also, it is a moment of raw feelings. "Raw" doesn't capture what I'm trying to say. Rather, let us say it is an act of graphic emotional nudity with no poise or sophistication. It's snot-dripping-out-of-your nose emotions, and gay men don't like those. We like watching Viola Davis experience them, but only because we never let ourselves be that honest. We are creatures with the option of hiding, and even when we're trying to be frank about a moment like this, we'll always retreat to the safety of a bland smile and presumed normalcy.

There's an exception: Queen's "Bohemian Rhapsody." You know and are familiar with "Bohemian Rhapsody." You loved it in *Wayne's World.* You may say, "That's not what it's about!" or the gentler "Is that what it's about?" But you will skeptically hold to a construction of the song that is not about gayness. You know Freddie Mercury was gay, or you may insist he was bisexual, because he was married to a woman and no gay man has ever been married to a woman.[15]

---

[14] My mother told me I only thought I was gay because I was depressed and had fallen in with a band of homosexuals who treated me kindly to take advantage of me. I wish I had met such a band. I knew like two gay guys in Minnesota.

[15] Oscar Wilde, Vincente Minnelli, and Rock Hudson were all married to women.

Also, you have no idea what "Bohemian Rhapsody" is about. You don't have some rival theory, you just know that your nonreading is more valid than my reading (which we still haven't gotten to because I'm fighting with you about opinions you probably don't have) because I'm not allowed to just say something's gay when it isn't explicitly gay.

That's one of the magnificent things about "Bohemian Rhapsody." It couldn't be explicitly gay. Freddie Mercury, like all other gay guys, had this bundle of emotions that he could not let the world see directly, because if they saw, they would be horrified. He also needed to share them, just as much as I needed to share them in 1999, maybe as much as I need to share them now, so he created a puzzle with all the pieces a gay guy would need to create art that could soothe him but enough complexity to be plausibly deniable.

"Bohemian Rhapsody" is a breakup song for your mom. Let's do a close reading.[16]

The speaker in the song begins by asking if what he's experiencing is real or fantasy. He's talking about his sexual desires. He is fantasizing about men, but is it part of the real life of who he is, or just his brain playing a trick on him? Like me at any point before July 11, 1999. He, for the first of many times, identifies his sexual desire as something that has been thrust upon him. He cannot deny the landslide of emotions men give him, or the simple reality of what makes his dick hard. A line after speculating that this whole thing is fantasy, he admits it's not just reality but inescapable. Like me on July 11, 1999.

Okay, why is the person who's about to sing you "Bohemian Rhapsody," the most melodramatic song of all time, saying nothing really matters to him? Why is this person about to sing of pain telling you he needs no sympathy? This passage is all about the emotional displacement of closetedness. It's about the managed mind of the closet case that divests itself from an emotional world it can't participate in. He's

---

[16] For copyright reasons, I cannot reprint the lyrics. You are, however, free to listen to the song or google the lyrics to refresh your memory of the song.

telling himself he needs no sympathy, because there's going to be none for him if he asks for it. The singer in "Bohemian Rhapsody" is looking up at the sky for the same reason I spent my teen years studying for the SAT too much: the slim hope that there might be something else out there better than the life you're currently living. A place where you fit.

Now we get to the mama. He's telling her or longing to tell her. "But Guy," you say, "this isn't about sex. He says he has a gun, it's a *crime*. He's sad because he committed a *crime*." And I say, "Yes, he is sad that he committed a crime, because that's what gay sex was in Britain in the 1970s. His dick was as deadly a weapon as a pistol. It turned the other dude into a nonperson as his cum verified that dude's homosexuality."

I know it's not an easy or transparent reading, but one of the things I'm saying is that Mercury had to code this song to make it not obviously gay, or it would have destroyed him. Worse, revealed him.

The key is the word "my." He didn't pull "the" trigger, he pulled "my" trigger. It links him to the bullet/orgasm/ejaculation in an intimate way.

If he's talking about a literal murder, why does he seem to be saying he's thrown his life away? Again, one might say, "Because he committed a crime." The singer doesn't seem to be worried about being caught, though. It seems that whatever he's done to throw away his life was completed with the act committed by his "gun."

The preoccupation of this song is deadening emotions. The singer who has already expressed his ability to not be emotionally invested is now urging his mother to do the same. She's crying, and as we previously established, moms *always* cry. Whatever he's done means he needs to leave, and his mom needs to deaden her emotions around that fact.

Then we get to the spine shivers and body aching. This is how we know it's not a literal murder. Murders don't send shivers down your spine or make your body ache. That's what dicks do, that's what dicks in your butt do, that's what sexual desire does. The singer's sexual desire is the truth he must face, and after the brief refractory period since he "killed" that man with his "gun," the desire is back.

The singer does not want to die, but he also says he wishes he'd never been born. It's a strange paradox. One could say he fears the punishment of the state for the murder he previously committed, but you'd be the one bringing the state into this. The singer's words make clear that whatever death this is would be caused by nothing more than the actions he's already discussed. He is also unmade by the act of gay sex. As much as he is a murderer, he is a suicide.

Then the song changes. It lets go of gravity and depression and starts being fun. He sees a man's "little silhouetto."

A dick. I think it's a dick. It's a little silhouette of a hard dick inside pants. Is it his, is it someone else's? I don't care. After all the emotional hand-wringing of the song, finally, this kid has something to be positive about. In this portion of the song, Mercury is throwing a lot of proper nouns at us. Everyone likes all these cool-sounding words, but no one can ever give you a plausible reading for what they mean together. Because keeping his meaning opaque is really important to Mercury, I think he uses these words as a kind of collage to give us ideas of his construction of gay sexuality, but not a clear narrative.

Scaramouche, of course, is a commedia dell'arte character. He's a clown. Is the singer saying sexual desire makes us all clowns? Maybe. Scaramouche also showed up as a popular puppet in *Punch and Judy* shows. He was always getting beaten by Punch, which led to Scaramouche becoming a term for a type of puppet with an extendable neck. A thing that gets beaten and has an extendable neck, you say? Maybe the little clown he's speaking of is a dick, and I think we know what kind of fandango he'd want to do with that.

This person who keeps saying nothing matters to him is deeply frightened once the "thunderbolts and lightning" start. If the thunderbolts and lightning are the electric desire that comes from sex, the fear is what that sex might mean to the outside world. That is immediately followed by name-checking Galileo, a dude who was tried for heresy by the Catholic Church. Then he name-checks a famous comic lover. The forces that are working on the singer are making him a heretic and a fool.

Then the song shrinks again to describe his emotional impoverishment. The singer cycles from the empowered invocation of these figures back to his pathos. The forces that created the thunderbolts and lightning are a monstrosity that threaten him and his family. He's not indulging in it; he's begging to be saved.

Now the song approaches its apex. The singer has been kidnapped and spirited away by his desire. He's a damsel getting tied to the railroad tracks. He uses the word "bismillah," which is an Arabic word meaning "in the name of God." The forces that hold him are so demonic, it's going to take God to save him.

But God isn't strong enough to save him. The forces will not let him go, and Beelzebub, Satan himself, has identified him for torture. The singer is having to tell his mom that however much she might hope he could use self-discipline and self-hatred to manage his sexual desire, there is a devil of desire that will not release him.

Then we turn to the resolution, which is also the most delicious part of the song. He is indignant about the lack of empathy he's facing from the people around him. He references stoning, a biblical punishment, and spitting in his eye, an assault to personal dignity. His family and loved ones want the right to humiliate him for his desires. That's when the singer wants to "get out" of the situation and abandon his audience. Our singer finally lashes out at his mother. He's gone through a drama of self-hatred to illustrate his lack of control, but now he takes control enough to blame his mom for not being able to deal with the situation.

He's mad that she's doing this, but he still calls her baby. His injury and his love for the person who is injuring him are at war, so the only option is to leave and start suppressing a new set of emotions.

That's why we return to the cries of "nothing really matters." The gay man must return to suppressing his emotions to get through a new situation. Before he was hoping he could live without a lover; now he must accept that wanting a lover means he can't have a mom.

I didn't become "easy come, easy go." I struggled, I strove, I fought tooth and nail with my parents, and my depression got worse and worse.

There was one cute gay boy in my law school. He seemed impossibly tall and impossibly handsome and so very good at being sophisticated and gay. I got a crush on him; I'd never gotten a crush before, and it overwhelmed me. The thunderbolts and lightning from the song. And he was kind and patient with my loudness and obsession until he couldn't take it anymore and told me he'd never be into me.

I cracked, I crashed. I drank too much and sent a message of help to everyone in my email contacts list. It was a bad thing, but it also sent me to the campus health service for mental health care. I went to a therapist, and I went on Prozac.

Prozac helped me become easy come, easy go. It helped me make the emotions the right size so I could move past them.

But I wonder, like the singer in "Bohemian Rhapsody," did I go too far? Did I release my hope to protect my heart and, in the process, insulate myself too much?

There's only one way to find out. If you're an attractive, funny, resilient gay man, try making me fall in love with you. I'm sure I've got some fandango left in me.

THE DISCO ROUND

WE DO NOT MAKE nice stories about nightlife. It seems like almost a ridiculous idea. If there is nightlife in a story, that story must end poorly. People must be punished and learn lessons about frivolity, drug abuse, and who your real friends really are. Oh, bars can be nice. Bars can be so homey that we put them in TV shows—sitcoms, even. But a place with dancing, with low lights, where everyone doesn't know your name . . . that's reserved for a very particular kind of film.[1]

As we have previously addressed in this book, I am a very good dancer. Further, I like dancing, but that is not the point we should lead with. I, on a dance floor, am like a pig in a deep slop, contented beyond reason and doing precisely the thing I was born to do. Unfortunately, institutionally promoted dancing ends with high school, unless you go

---

[1] They can almost never be effectively evoked on episodic television. Clubs require too many extras and too much thumping music. A rare exception was the third episode of *The Mindy Project*, "In The Club," which wasn't the most realistic representation of a nightclub, but at least felt sexy and fun. It's when I fell in love with *Mindy*, a show for which I eventually wrote.

to some corny adorable school in the Midwest or belong to a fraternity or sorority. For nice middle- or lower-class kids who go to a state school, after prom, no one is going to make you dance unless your cousin is getting married.

When I was in college, I missed dancing. And dancing, I was reasonably sure, missed me. Tragically, the only dancing that existed for persons in their late teens and early twenties existed at clubs, and clubs, I knew, were dark and dangerous places meant for people far cooler than I.

This paranoia was certainly rooted in my practiced asexuality of the time. I wasn't gay, so I wasn't going to gay bars. I wasn't dating a girl whom I had to sate by taking her dancing. Plus, it was Berkeley in the 1990s, a structureless sit-in of a school where everyone was just coming home from class, reading some Maxine Hong Kingston, then doing heroin until they passed out. It wasn't a social scene in which trying was prioritized.

But let us not declare that my situation was entirely the product of my personal failings. The fungus floating at the rim of said personal failings was our culture's representations of nightlife, a quietly accepted construction of dance clubs as bad, soulless, and dangerous that is still with us today.

The club isn't the best place to find a lover
So the bar is where I go

This lyric is from Ed Sheeran's "Shape of You," which no one is saying isn't a bop. It is *clearly* a bop, but it is also representative of a crusty social bias that annoys me.

Why is Ed Sheeran so certain that the club isn't the best place to find a lover? He doesn't even defend his thesis; he simply takes it as self-evident. In that line, he builds upon every *Boogie Nights* or *54*, every cautionary *Growing Pains* where Mike went into the city on a school night, and we therefore accept as fact the idea that dance clubs are inherently loci of turpitude or at least deceit.

"But GUY!" you cry out. "Ed references dancing to Van Morrison mere lines after this passage."

Really? Van Morrison? What kind of midwestern family wedding in 1987 is this where they're dancing to "Brown Eyed Girl"? Ed Sheeran wants to massage you through the safety of what he's doing. This isn't *sexy* dancing. It's *affable, wholesome* dancing. It's Ally McBeal bouncing around while Vonda Shepard croons a lifeless rendition of a Motown standard. It is dancing that leads to a nice Presbyterian wedding and 2.4 wanted children.

Pop culture knows you want to go to clubs, but it also demands that you know you're doing something *bad* by going to clubs. The moment you get that thrilling, exciting tracking shot of the wonders and delights of the club in *Party Monster* or *24 Hour Party People* or *The Last Days of Disco*, you know that it's only a matter of time before the venality, shallowness, and otherness of the club consumes itself and is destroyed. Supporting characters will die of overdoses and be arrested for cooking the books. Pleasure is sin, and sin must be punished. Only our protagonist, probably white, probably male, will escape undestroyed.

Even *Party Girl*, one of my favorite films of all time, and one deeply rooted in club culture, assents to this view of clubs as corrupt. Mary, the titular Party Girl, played by Parker Posey, has a rich world of friends and fun in the club: Her friend Leo is a DJ, her friend Rene owns the club, and there is a parade of fabulous others ready to dance with her. Despite this normalized, human representation of nightlife, the film insists that the only way to find true, meaningful love is to give up drugs and dancing and become a librarian.

A key tool in establishing this order for representations of clubs in film is the emphasis of racial and sexual otherness in the space. Those shots of the club show beautiful people dancing, but they also show drugs, they show various kinds of queer sex, and they show racially diverse spaces. We are asked to assume that no place so diverse can be wholesome. In the film *54*, this otherness is embodied in Disco Dottie, an elderly woman in slutty sequins who frequents the eponymous club. We're supposed to be unsettled by her contribution to the carnivalesque atmosphere—shouldn't this grandma be at home, baking blondies? Then we transition to pathos as she dies of an overdose on the dance floor in the arms of our white, male, heterosexual protagonist. This is propaganda.

Disco Dottie was based on an actual patron of Studio 54, seventy-seven-year-old attorney Sally Lippman. "Disco Sally," as she was known, found the club not long after her husband's death and began frequenting it. A beloved fixture, celebrities waited turns to dance with her, and she found a new boyfriend, a twenty-six-year-old she called her "Greek god." Sally didn't die tragically of an overdose; she wasn't a symptom of necrotic decadence. She was a cool, powerful lady who found fun and acceptance in a diverse and happy, if libertine, world. Movies can't tell you that story, because the only story about pleasure we want to tell is "The Ant and the Grasshopper."

Since all I knew of clubs was what pop culture told me, I was scared of them. I was pretty certain there was no place for me there. Still, they fascinated me. They were representative of the wide swath of life I'd declared off-limits. Who would I be at a club? I wasn't hot. Could there be not-hot people at clubs? Movies like *54* were *always* showing us our hot protagonist getting into the club while his or her not-hot friends, whom our protagonist should *really* be more loyal to, weren't. I expected that inevitable fate. I was waiting for this cold, hateful den of shallowness and drugs to reject me. To say that there was no place for me.

Also, all of those movies about how shallow clubs were? None of them *ever* seemed to be about the people who couldn't get into the club. The movie was judging the club for letting only the hot one in, but the movie itself was letting only the hot one be central. Who's shallow now, movie?

✳

There were two periods in my life when I went to clubs a lot. The first was in Minneapolis, in the wake of my coming out.[2]

---

[2] The second, which I did not get to in this book, was during the delicious period when I was on *Chelsea Lately* for the first time. Suffice it to say that being on a

When you come out of the closet, you have this interesting moment in which you might reset your life. It's like when Adam and Eve ate of the fruit of knowledge of good and evil and finally saw their nakedness. I saw my nakedness and was, of course, horrified. After all, everyone is supposed to be horrified by their nakedness. We don't like clubs for the same reason we don't like people who like their own nakedness. Acceptance of yourself on the terms by which you exist *now* seems as arrogant, unambitious, and un-American as going to a place that is entirely about having fun in the present. Righteous, God-fearing citizens are too self-conscious to enjoy dancing or removing their clothes.

So, while you're accepting that significant chunks of your closet-years self were bald lies, you get to shed other parts of yourself alongside those lies. I determined that I would put personal attention into what I wore.[3] I decided that my fatness was simply a reflection of the fact that I had denied my body and sexuality. My fatness was going to end. And my being a person who sat at home on Fridays was going to end. This was my makeover montage. And we know I love a makeover montage.

I followed that line of thinking after I came out. I was going to have a whole new life. Yet I had no idea how I was going to pull it off. I did a lot of whining in my head about how figuring out a new, gay life had to be much easier for boys who'd been tempted from the closet by some dashing suitor. But whining wasn't going to yield results. After a few months of moping around law school, I finally located a spot on the Internet[4] where the gay men of Minneapolis congregated to relax and

---

dumb, silly pop culture show that is primarily watched by gay porn stars in their twenties is a very nice life.

[3] Until I was the age of twenty-three, my mother purchased every piece of clothing I wore. That's the kind of shit you let happen when your desires are walled off from the rest of your brain. My mother was deeply proud of her capacity to acquire clothing at below its original retail cost, and if you'd seen me in any of those outfits, I can trust you would have thought "I hope no one paid anything close to the original retail cost for that outfit."

[4] I've previously referenced going into gay chatrooms on AOL. You might wonder why this didn't satisfy the need to meet gays in Minneapolis. The answer is that AOL chatrooms at the time were not regionally specific. It's hard to find anonymous tail

find strangers to have sex with. In its way, Gay.com, the most lamely named, now defunct website in an era of lamely named, now defunct websites, was the first club I entered. (In many ways, it was also the cruelest. However, such stories are not visual nor dynamic, so let us move forward the plot.) I found friends. Through sharp wit and strong takes, I won over some gay guys in the chat room, and we started hanging out in real life. There was Kevvy, the sweet one; Matt, the cool, sexy one; and Steve, the cautious, introspective one who was—*GASP*—over thirty. Essentially, Kevvy was the Charlotte; Matt was the Samantha; Steve was, fittingly, the Miranda; and since I am currently typing reflections on my laptop, let's say I was the Carrie, even though all of you reading this should, by this point in the book, realize that I was a Miranda who slowly, over time, evolved into a Samantha.[5]

No one teaches you how to be gay. I know you're going to say, "No one teaches you how to be straight," but if you were in front of me and said that, I'd slap you and say, "Society teaches you how to be straight. Your parents taught you how to be straight. Every movie you ever saw taught you how to be straight. That's why all those rapes in 1980s sex comedies fucked up society for years to come." And you're probably thinking, "Yeah, but you wouldn't really have slapped me." But back then, in 2000, in Minnesota, fresh from the rage and depression of coming out, I would have slapped the shit out of you. I was fucking crazy, deal with it.

I had to learn from these guys how to be gay. I used to spend a great deal of time fantasizing how much easier it'd be if I were regular and cute and had a boyfriend who was teaching me the lay of the land. But I had no such Virgil to delineate the rings of this underworld. There weren't even YouTube videos to teach you how to clean your butt for sex back then. You had to learn from word of mouth,[6] and these guys'

---

when everyone you're chatting with is on another continent. Figuring out how the Internet could properly facilitate gay male anon sex was a process of trial and error. The course of true love never did run smooth.

[5] In 2018, we call that a Molly from *Insecure*.

[6] And, occasionally, ass-to-mouth.

mouths were the ones I had. Kevvy showed me *Into the Woods* for the first time and gave me a basic primer on sex hole sanitation. Steve taught me how to dote on a boyfriend, how to pine after an ex-boyfriend, and how to get blown in the back room of a club.[7] And Matt, he taught me the best lessons: how to drink, how to be promiscuous, how to have swagger, and, most important, how to go to a club.

I was scared shitless of going to a club for *all* the culturally defined reasons cataloged above. Furthermore, it was a *gay club*; visiting it would mean all my desires would be laid bare before me. I couldn't sneak a look at a cute boy, then run and hide behind the pretense of heterosexuality. I was going to play the real game. But mostly, my fear was rooted in the fact that my body was abnormal. I'd be showing up there *fat*. Fat in the way that gay men and people at clubs are not supposed to be. My essential fear was that someone would say, "You should go; this place is not for you."

I have gone to great lengths to argue that we do not tell positive stories about clubs in TV or film, but there is an area of American culture where club life is celebrated as paradise: popular music. 50 Cent drinks Bacardi like it's his birthday in the club, Nicki Minaj steps up in that party like her name is "That Bitch," Destiny's Child leaves their man at home because the club is full of ballers, Beyoncé even skips to the front of the line. And these songs encourage people to do exactly the destructive things that curse the supporting characters in our nightclub movies: sex, drugs, and living in the moment. Pitbull insists you give everything tonight, because we might not get a tomorrow. Nicki Minaj blows off all her money and she don't give two shits. One reason songs celebrate the culture of clubs is obvious: They are played in them. Dance music and clubs have a commensal need to romanticize the other; they, with alcohol, cocaine, and genitals, are vested stakeholders in the thriving concern of nightlife fun.

---

[7] I understand that the ramp-up of this paragraph would be better if I left all the sexy club-related stuff to Matt, but Steve's capacity to go from Miranda to sex felon in under two drinks was truly dazzling.

Now you may point out that the first document I cited to prove our popular disdain for nightlife was a song. This leads us to the second reason clubs are positively referenced in songs. Yes, "Shape of You" shits on clubs, but who sings "Shape of You"? A white guy. A significant aspect of the demonization of clubs rests on the diversity of the clientele. In *Cocktail*, Tom Cruise[8] goes from his white, middle-class suburban family bar in New Jersey to a Manhattan club full of drugs, rich people, black people (there aren't many, but that's still a lot for a Tom Cruise movie in 1988), and maybe even gays. In *54*, Ryan Phillippe makes the same journey from New Jersey to a place with even more queers and people of color. The reason pop music is able to be enthusiastic about clubs is because, unlike films or TV, it's often made by queers and people of color.

Mainstream films cost millions of dollars to make and release; television, until recently, took nearly as much money and the cooperation of a major TV network. This meant control of such ventures usually rested in the hands of white, cisgender, heterosexual men. Making a song is way more democratic, and it means queers and people of color have been able to make music for ourselves for decades. Twenty years ago when gay characters[9] weren't even allowed a chaste peck in a mainstream movie, German electronic music group Interactive made a dance song that was just the word "dildo" repeated over and over again.[10] Part of the reason nightlife movies are showing you diverse club-goers is because those clubs are powered by music from LGBT people and people of color. A nice guy like Ed Sheeran might be focused on meeting a nice girl he can settle down with at the bar, but for a gay kid without the protection of his family or society, giving everything tonight because he might not have a tomorrow makes more sense. Film had spent my entire life telling me that clubs were sordid and dangerous. What I didn't

---

[8] No one knows his character's name. It's been lost to history.

[9] By which I mean straight actors playing gay characters.

[10] Aptly, the song is called "Dildo."

realize was the reason it thought they were so "dangerous" was because they were full of people like me.

I went, on a Thursday, to the Saloon. This was the crown jewel of the gay week in Minneapolis—nay, the entire upper Midwest. Guys came from as far as Duluth and Eau Claire to partake of this Lutheran bacchanal. And it wasn't just *any* Thursday; this was the Thursday of Pride Weekend, the formal beginning of the most decadent four days Minneapolis could contain. The Bud Light flowed like water.

On a Thursday one year before, I was working at one of the large law firms in Minneapolis, and one of our file clerks, an exceedingly gay one, perfunctorily informed his supervisor that he'd be back on Tuesday. When I asked her why, she said, "Oh, he takes off for Pride every year . . . plus one day for recovery." This, to a closeted me, was the height of glamour. I wanted to be that gay guy.[11] Now I was that gay guy.

The Saloon in Minneapolis was what midwestern gay bars have long been: a black, windowless club that protected the privacy of patrons who may not have been out in every aspect of their life. It also carried the midwestern responsibility of being as many types of bars as possible under one roof. In a town where you didn't have too many gay options, you needed a space that could be a dance club, a video bar, a bingo parlor, and a barbecue. I think at this point in time, the Saloon even had four PCs in one of the bars so you could troll for sex and/or check your eBay auctions. (The first tech bubble was great.) The Saloon was and is a magical, sexy place. Yes, it was full of midwestern practicality, but it was the kind of strong, attractive, well-educated practicality that made

---

[11] To this day, I consider treatment of Pride and Halloween as the gay High Holidays to be central to rectitudinous homosexual observance. This is but a small example of the way a tiny dose of gay behavioral modeling is invaluable to budding homosexuals. (I do not say "young" because I think I was older than that clerk was.) But suffice to say that when I saw that guy taking off for Pride, I thought, "His eyebrows are so well manicured, he must know what he's doing!" And both of us were right.

That said, no one should need to take off Monday for hangover recovery. The glory of getting day-drunk for a Pride parade is that you should fall asleep by nine p.m. and wake up fresh and new for work the next day. Also, on the gay High Holidays you don't blow a ram's horn, you blow a man's horn.

Minnesota homosexuals so valuable as Broadway chorus boys or Disney Cruise Herculeses.

I entered, shaken. My body was raw to the experience of being perceived by strangers as gay. Not just strangers. *Hot* strangers. It prickled. They *knew* me. They knew what I wanted. If seeing my own nakedness was bad, this was excoriating. I'm sure I made that dumb "look at this" face Ryan Phillippe made when he first went into the club in *54*. Luckily, I had my friends—guides who could pull me out of panic and into the back-room bar.

I got drunk. Matt told me to order a Malibu and pineapple.[12] It was delicious, and after months of starving myself into a new identity I'd never achieve, the decadent run of simple sugars into my system was as intoxicating as the alcohol. Finally, I understood why all my high school classmates had been so thirsty while trying to flirt with each other.

Sliding into the warm onesie of tipsiness, I took in what was around me. Boys dressed smartly in a way I never could. Cheekbones. Abs. Rough and confident bartenders. Comfort. Prowess.

Then I noticed that something was off. The guys in this bar were bad dancers. I thought that gay guys were supposed to be good dancers. It was early in the evening, and the dance floor was pretty sparse. I couldn't tell if what I was seeing was an insight about the homosexuals of Minneapolis or just errata. It was, however, just the cruel judgement I needed to feel a little less exposed.[13]

I was to learn over the course of the following year that what I was seeing was solid, representative data about the dancing skills of Minneapolis. I'm not saying they're all terrible dancers; like I mentioned before, many of them go on to be highly successful Flying Monkeys in

---

[12] Were we ever that young?

[13] If you are jarred by this honest admission that looking down on someone else made me feel better, go fuck yourself. We are not always generous; we are not always our best selves; and your pretense to perfection is emotional dishonesty of the highest order. Why did you buy this book? And could you buy another copy for a friend, as penance?

touring productions of *Wicked*, or the previously referenced Disney Cruise Herculeses. I'm just saying that a combination of bulky winter wear, Norwegian emotional distance, closeted-gay alienation from one's own physicality, and fierce cultural isolation make the gay men of Minnesota, Iowa, and the Dakotas not the most amazing at isolated hip motion.

That evening at the Saloon, I went wild. I talked to strangers. I danced. I grabbed guys' butts. I know we're not supposed to grab strangers' butts anymore, but I would kindly ask you how I was supposed to know that then. Had I seen gay men socializing on TV or in movies? Had anyone talked to me about it? "Well," you would say, "you should just know that's not proper behavior." I would respond by asking you if consensual gay sex is proper behavior, because the sequence we are discussing is taking place in a state that had[14] a perfectly valid sodomy law on the books. As a law student, I could tell you that what each and every person was doing in that bar was, technically, conspiracy to commit sodomy, thus a felony. Should I have just known what was right, acceptable behavior? In a place that my parents and culture had spent my life telling me was morally wrong and corrupt, was I supposed to instinctively know right from wrong? Was it so simply evident? Later, on the dance floor, when a gentleman slid his hand down Matt's pants and started giving him a hand job without saying a word, was that a wrong that this man was supposed to have intuited, or was it fucking great?[15]

What cultural context I did have was from those movies we discussed before, the movies that said there was no safe or moral way to be a person in a club. In for a penny, in for a pound. Once you start barbacking at a club, you're just a few montages away from doing cocaine, making out

---

[14] Criminal laws punishing sodomy were declared unconstitutional by the 2003 Supreme Court case *Lawrence v. Texas*. Minnesota's sodomy law was declared unconstitutional in 2001 from a State Supreme Court ruling on several merged cases, *Doe et al. v. Ventura*. I co-wrote the Minnesota Civil Liberties Union's initial motion to dismiss in the Doe case, about a dude who got blown by a lady in a bar after hours. (The security cameras were on.)

[15] It was fucking great.

with a person of the same sex, making out with someone who *is not hot* (the greatest indignity) but from whom you want something, and then, finally, eventually, selling your baby for crystal meth. I had abandoned the propriety I knew. Like Don John in *Much Ado About Nothing*, my pretenses to propriety were gone, and all that remained were my desires. *I must be sad when I have cause, eat when I have stomach, sleep when I am drowsy and laugh when I am merry. It must not be denied, but I am a plain-dealing villain.*

I grabbed butts. It was Pride Weekend. People were having a good time and seemed pretty comfortable facilitating the good time of others in whatever way they could. Some let me know they weren't interested with a simple facial expression, so I left them alone. I'd started homosexuality far too late to waste too much time with people who were less interested in fun than I was. My point is that I did it: I had a good time at a gay bar, and if you're looking to lecture people about transgressive and exploitative sexual behavior, maybe focus on the sexual orientation that systematically dehumanizes and disempowers half of their participants. Gay guys are different, our system works differently, and I don't necessarily need straight men and women to tell me how my community is supposed to mirror theirs. After twenty-three years of longing, I got to touch some butts and some pectorals. It was pretty great.

Though I had been dropped into very cold water, I learned to swim. Minneapolis was just the right size to have a different place to go every night of the week, but never *two* places to go on any night. I met guys, and while I lusted after some, I befriended others.

Underneath the very real fun, though, was an ever-present fear: Eventually, someone was going to tell me that I was too fat to be there.

One of the first times[16] I was at the Saloon, I saw The Most Beau-

---

[16] I mean, it might have actually been the first time. I *think* Pride was the first time, but you know how in *Midnight's Children* Saleem insists that, in his memory, Gandhi died on a different day from what the history books say? Well, under similar rules, I'm just going to say these were both my first time at the Saloon. I was new, just know that. I was new.

tiful Boy in Minneapolis.[17] I recognized him from online. His Gay.com username was LukeMichael, and he was a six-foot-eight-inch dancer who went to college in Iowa. He had perfect abs and golden hair and a beautiful face and was generally the kind of muscular, trim, goyische golden beauty that I had always dreamed of being or touching. He was dressed exactly as a gay man was supposed to dress in 2000: powder blue T-shirt, male capris, male slides with a SMALL heel, and an upside-down turned-around visor. I was young and simple and *knew* that if I were someone like him, I would have no problems. I just wanted to know what all that absence of problems smelled like.[18]

We were out on the patio of the Saloon, relatively early in the evening. I was sitting down, waiting for my friends to show, and LukeMichael came out with his small court of attendant almost-but-not-quite-as-hot guys. I heard him say something about Gay.com, and I went in hot. Going in hot would eventually become my signature move: Storm into a stranger's conversation, co-opt it, and make them fall in love with me in the process.[19] It's my favorite sport. Unfortunately, at this point in

---

[17] I'd go on to declare at least forty people to be The Most Beautiful Boy in Minneapolis before I left. I don't think I've declared that many in Los Angeles, and I've lived here seven times as long as I was gay in Minnesota. Everyone knows that gay guys in L.A. are way, way hotter than anywhere else on the planet. Maybe not an actual runway in Paris or Milan, but comparing cities to cities, Los Angeles is doing aiight. Now I am jaded to such attractions, but in Minneapolis, fresh from the closet, I was very new to the game, and every attraction seemed cataclysmic.

[18] I have learned in the intervening years that the problem-free life of beautiful dancers in the early 2000s smelled mostly like Abercrombie & Fitch's Fierce.

[19] I'm sure many of you think interrupting a stranger's conversation is an act of transgression nearly on par with touching a stranger's butt. I would write another screed informing you of the conservatism and limitations of this opinion, but I run the risk of this chapter simply turning into a diatribe on my part about the dangers of heterosexual dating mores being applied to gays. Thus, I will be brief:

1. You show up to gay bars to talk to people you don't know. If you just wanted to talk to your friends, you'd meet up at home or a place with mozzarella sticks.
2. The precept that initiating conversation with strangers who might not be interested is wrong is looksist. My primary appeals are not visual. If I play my entire game waiting for someone to look at me and be enchanted by that alone, I will probably wait a long time. If I give myself a chance to be delightful, charming, and smart, things go a lot better.

time, I had no idea what I was doing, so I stammered out some line about how LukeMichael was out for a lovely evening and should stop focusing on the virtual experience of online chat. Even the take was hack. LukeMichael simply turned his head away. His eyes didn't need to suffer my unpleasant countenance. Another guy, his grand vizier, chief among his almost-as-hot friends, turned to manage me. "Ummm . . . Hi, sorry, but we don't come here to meet new people. We just want to talk to our friends."

I retreated and sulked. Soon my friends were there, and my mood brightened. The moral of the interaction was clear, though: I should know my place. There were some people I wasn't good enough to talk to. There would be guys at gay bars who'd dismiss me on looks alone. It wasn't nearly being told "You're too fat, leave," but it was close enough for my serotonin-deprived little brain to cling to.[20]

Coming out as a homosexual—and not "coming out" in a telling-my-parents-and-friends "coming out of the closet" sense, but "coming out" in a debutante-ball sense—had released me into an ecosystem full of highly adapted predators and prey. They had powers, skills, weapons: adaptations to the requirements of gay. I had none, like that giant rabbit from prehistoric Minorca[21] that had no predators and went extinct the moment it got ecological competition.[22] Basically, I had the social skills

---

[20] Once, during that *Chelsea Lately* fame–fueled second period of club frequenting around 2010, a door guy did tell me I was too fat to come in. He let my friend in, but not me. My friend, who was actually a photographer upon whom I had a soul-rending crush, asked, "Why did I get in and not him?" The bouncer said, "Because you're cute and he's fat." Exactly, precisely the thing I most feared happening happened. And then like three minutes later the club promoter told him to let me in. And ten minutes after that I had a vodka soda, and twenty minutes after that I was making out with a boy who is hotter than any person currently living in Minneapolis. I kept waiting for myself to cry, but I was too busy making out with that boy. Sometimes the thing you fear most in the world isn't that bad.

[21] It's called Nuralagus. It was a giant rabbit that lived on the island of Minorca and didn't evolve any natural defenses because it was isolated from competitors or predators. Basically, me in 1999.

[22] From the weird Majorcan mouse-goat Myotragus. It's a tiny goat with eyes in the front of its head so it can see eagles that might try to kill it. Its evolutionary advantages made it way better at eating bark and shrubs than Nuralagus, so when the

of someone who knows a lot about extinct giant rabbits. I was power-less. I was reasonably certain I'd spend the rest of my life being battered around by emotions I'd unleashed by entering this stupid, sexy world.

As LukeMichael went back to college in Iowa, I continued to learn about being gay. I kissed a boy for the first time. I blew and got blown. I had full-on real sex with a flight attendant with a barbed-wire arm tattoo whom I knew only by his AOL instant messenger name.[23] Real romance.

And then, during the holidays, LukeMichael returned to my laptop screen. He was back in town, visiting his parents again, and that sense of powerlessness and hopelessness returned. Then I remembered that I was a goddess.

If the months between LukeMichael's minor condescending dis-missal of me and his reemergence had not taught me much about the tax or family law I should have been studying, they had taught me scads about how to fraudulently acquire men's nude photos on the Internet. I quickly summoned up one of my classic fake profiles. Long before we had such terms as "catfishing," I had delved into the dark arts of pre-tending to be someone else for fun and profit. Mostly, as I said above, my profit was the naked photos of guys who didn't think I was hot. By this point in time, I had a few personas in regular rotation. My favorite was a junior bisexual wrestler from Augsburg College whose roommate was always disturbing the privacy he needed to have sex with men while still closeted. His name was CollegeJock24. This was a time so new and simple, names as blandly sexy as CollegeJock24 were readily available. Why I didn't use some small bit of this creative energy to capitalize on the ripe, lucrative, untapped territories of tech in 2001 is a thing for which I still have not forgiven myself.

In my time posing as men far more attractive than I was, I'd learned

---

Myotragus made its way to Minorca, Nuralagus went extinct. So, in this metaphor, every other gay guy in Minneapolis. Seriously, you guys need to spend more time researching island-isolated species.

[23] Flyboy69.

some confidence. CollegeJock24 was far more capable than I was of weathering a silence and demanding what he was worth. I told the story of my sexy bisexuality and my deep hope that no one would find out I was into men. With the benefit of his nipple ring and perfect abs, I sold a story of purest masculinity. LukeMichael was like wet sauerkraut in my hands. He sent me his shirtless photos and a dick pic.[24] I was elated in a way that's hard to express. I was seeing what people as fat as I was didn't get to see. I was getting to experience what life was like for the sexy classes.

LukeMichael kept asking for my address. He really wanted to come over and mutually masturbate with the explicitly self-hating masc-musc wrestler I was purporting to be.[25] A horrible, delicious thought came into my mind. I told LukeMichael that he couldn't come to my door because if my roommate saw him, he'd suspect I was gay. I told him to come to the parking lot of the Perkins[26] across the street from my apartment and to wait there.

Forty minutes later, a Range Rover pulled into the empty, snow-dusted parking lot just visible from my balcony. I looked out, delighted that I'd managed to hijack the evening of a hot guy the way his sexy magic had co-opted hours of my life. I'd felt so out of control since I'd come out of the closet, and my depressed brain had convinced me that I was taking something back.[27] Eventually, about fifteen minutes later, LukeMichael pulled out and drove back to the upper-middle-class western suburb where his parents lived.

I went back online, giddy from the success of my little prank. You can imagine how surprised I was when LukeMichael showed up back online

---

[24] Still got 'em!

[25] He said he wasn't interested in anything more sexually invasive because he was a "safe boi." This was an era when "boi" was a deeply meaningful and useful term.

[26] If you don't know what a Perkins is, it's a Denny's that was properly loved by its mother.

[27] I also went through a *real* shoplifting phase then. I only now realized these two horrid behaviors might have similar psychological antecedents.

forty-five or so minutes later. He was very upset that my perfect abs and not-visible-in-the-photo face had not come out to greet his perfect abs and heavenly face while he waited in the Perkins parking lot. I did what any sensitive person would. I suggested he return to the parking lot because my fictitious roommate had finally gone to sleep.

Improbably, another forty-five minutes later, that Range Rover was sitting in the dark parking lot again, acquiring a light dusting of snow. Again, I peered with glee. Again, he waited about ten minutes, then left.

What a ridiculous scam I'd run, what a rambunctious swindle, what a . . . wait, what? He was online again? Deeply frustrated that my hot pretend self had not yet drained his body of its erotic juices, he again questioned my commitment. I had to. I told him he could return. This time he insisted I give him my specific address and apartment number. I assented.

What a strange three quarters of an hour ensued. I was thrilled and terrified. My swindle had swindled above its weight class. I had co-opted a hot guy's evening and made him suffer the way hot guys' indifference had made *me* suffer, and *what the fuck was I going to do when he actually showed up?*

Soon enough, there was a knock at the door. I steeled myself and opened it. All six feet eight inches of LukeMichael's frame were situated very deliberately, leaning on the doorframe. When he saw me, he was obviously shocked. I said, "You can leave now." He did.

This isn't a noble story. I don't think what I did was right. I was a scared, confused, depressed man firing a shot across the bow of the forces he thought were oppressing him. Lashing out is rarely a good choice, but when you're feeling powerless, you just hunger to feel like there's anything you can control.

This story did a terrible job of making the point I wanted to make, which is essentially that clubs can be very nice. They're full of fun, optimistic people who want to have a good time, and you can make really great friends there. But this story isn't about clubs at all. It's just about me harassing a guy who was once vaguely indifferent to me at a club one time. Okay, that's the part that makes it about clubs. I guess my story is mostly just an exploration of the idea that you can't be at home somewhere you fear, and my magnificent trolling of LukeMichael was a resolution to stop being afraid. It would be more atmospheric if it all happened in a gay bar, and we will definitely take that note into account before we adapt this chapter into a screenplay that will go unproduced.

So, I made friends, I started going out five nights a week, and I stopped being a responsible law student in every way. I went from having an abject fear of gay clubs to being a person who was oddly soothed by the smell of stale beer and too much cologne. I stopped being scared of the people at the club—because I was now one of the people at the club.

BABETTE CAN COOK

I DO NOT KNOW when I first asked my mother to teach me to cook, but I know what she said when I did: "Sit there." She pointed to the bar overlooking our stove. She cooked. I watched. She talked, she joked, she riffed, she entertained for her audience of one. Periodically, I would push: "Can I help?" "Watch," she'd reply.

There are many ways you can lead life as a working-class family in a farm town in a part of America that no one knows exists. My mother was firmly committed to making one that was as wonderful as it could be. She sincerely believed that wit, ingenuity, and a positive outlook could get the most out of the life you could afford. Nowhere was this truer than in her kitchen. She toyed with pomelos and bulgogi marinades while the moms down the road cranked out another Hamburger Helper. She knew we deserved better, and maybe she herself deserved better, too. If she was going to mix ground beef with sauce and noodles, *she* would decide what they were, not some anthropomorphic oven mitt. Sitting, watching my mom create, were some of the most magical times of my life.

The worst years of my life were my time in law school in Minnesota.

This has already been established in this book, but a very real and concrete issue is what one is supposed to do when the worst time in one's
life is over. My answer was to pack my bags and return to the last place
I could remember being happy: Berkeley, California.

Building your life up from smoking ruins is terrifying and great.
Like, you could do *anything*! Am I still a lawyer? Maybe not, maybe
I'm professionally spelunking now, and everything I once loved will be
forgotten, and I'll spend the rest of my life hunting through caves. I'll
spend most of my time in Chile, I'll speak heavily accented Spanish, I'll
develop hypersensitivity to daylight and become primarily nocturnal.
I'll be known as "El Gordo De Las Cuevas" and all my friends will be
bats. Maybe that? Which makes you understand the terrifying part:
losing the groundwork you've done in your life up until that point and
knowing you might be making another terrible choice.

I didn't completely start anew. Like I said, I moved back to my college
town and pretended that August 1998 to May 2001 had not happened. I
also figured I'd eventually put that law degree to work, but since I hadn't
participated in the highly ritualized system of finding first jobs for lawyers, I'd have to figure that out later. In the meantime, I had to survive.
That terrified me deeply. Even though I'd worked construction for my
dad, delivered pizzas, worked at a movie theater, and held various other
jobs during law school, I knew I could not survive. My parents had made
this very clear to me during most of my childhood. I was disorganized,
lazy, and liked nice things. I couldn't possibly just find a job and survive,
I *needed* my parents, but since my coming out, they had made clear that
their willingness to help me financially or emotionally was mostly gone.

I moved into a dilapidated house on the Oakland-Berkeley border, a
transitional territory where Berkeley grads getting ready for their first
kids were gentrifying out older black families. The house was one of the
few remaining holdouts of six to ten recent college grads sharing a home
the landlords were unwilling to develop into something they could make
more money from. We were surrounded by twenty-eight-year-old professional couples with craftsman bungalows and three-year-olds, and
working-class older black couples who spent a lot of time working on

cars. There were lots of cats named after jazz legends in our neighbor-hood. That's what you need to know.

My viability was a continuing question. I'd survived Minnesota, I hadn't killed myself, but could I survive surviving? Were my smarts and skills as useless as I'd been told? I hunted as aggressively as I could for a job, knowing full well that few persons were as unemployable as a J.D. without a bar membership. Any job I'd want would require me to be a real lawyer; any job I could get would know I'd quit as soon as I passed. I remember praying, begging the universe to give me a chance to make an income so I could have a life of my own.

I got one, of course. I worked at a small legal publication we'll call *Litigation Compendium*. It basically went through all the civil litigation decisions in California and published them for other lawyers to consult when demanding damages. If this sounds technical and unrelatable, let me put it more simply: For about six months, my job was to keep track of how much a dead baby was worth in California. Look, for parents, a dead baby is a horrifying pain that will never truly be healed, but for the attorney they hire to sue whoever killed that baby, things have to be a bit more clinical. Thus I learned that, in 2001, the time of my employment at *Litigation Compendium*, a dead newborn baby was worth about $800,000, declined for the first six months, then grew in value as its viability increased, to a peak of around $1.1 million at around age four or five. The value then steadily decreased through the teenage years, when we understand that a tortious homicide is really as much a favor to the parents as a tragedy. You could back over a sixteen-year-old in your Chevy Tahoe for like $600K in the early 2000s.

Being an editorial assistant at *Litigation Compendium* barely paid better than working at a movie theater. I was mad at myself for not making more money. I was educated, but I certainly wasn't important. Finally, I managed to land a job as a glorified paralegal at an insurance defense law firm in Oakland. It paid much better, and I was excited to jump into something less morbid. It could not have been further from the truth.

In my tiny, windowless office in a midsize high-rise in Oakland, there sat across from me binders that read "Breast," "Bladder," "Brain," "Multiple Myeloma," "Leukemia," "Lymphoma." It was all of the cancers of the people who were suing our client, the company who insured a tech manufacturer in Silicon Valley. I was one of the bad people in *Erin Brockovitch*. Not one of the lawyers you see, but one of the army of lawyers behind them that does terrible things to help large companies keep their millions. The workers at the tech manufacturer, almost entirely women, were saying that exposure to toxic metals had given them cancer. Our job was to get them to settle for as small a sum as possible. My job, particularly, was to come up with legal theories to make their most embarrassing medical facts admissible in court, and by "most embarrassing medical facts," I think you know what I mean. We, as a law firm, were trying to shame as many women—mostly Catholic, mostly Latina—about the abortions they'd had, to get them to stop saying our client's client had negligently caused their cancer. I had jumped out of the dead-baby frying pan and into the aborted-fetus fire.

Needless to say, this was the grossest job I've ever had. Grosser than writing for *Punk'd*. My protest was to be as bad at my job as humanly possible. I goofed off, I wasted time, I wrote jokes. The worst part was the end of the day, when I had to bill for my time. See, lawyers bill their clients by the hour, so every law firm has a draconian system that tracks your time in six-minute increments. Every day, in detail, I had to account for the uses of my time by the tenth of an hour. Filling out the billing software honestly would have been onerous enough if I'd actually been doing my job, but how was I supposed to explain what had happened during that hour I was writing jokes about the Hebrew calendar?[1]

---

[1] I will make you read an actual joke I actually wrote at that actual job about the Hebrew calendar: There are twelve months in the Hebrew calendar, usually, but since we have a lunar calendar, we have to periodically find a way to catch up with you kids on the solar calendar. We accomplish this through a leap month seven out of every nineteen years. A leap month seven out of nineteen years: My religion is a bad episode of *Star Trek*. The coolest part of this leap month is its name. It comes right after the month of Adar, so the rabbis, in their infinite wisdom, named it Adar II. You really have to be impressed when the calendar is so successful it gets a sequel. I just think it needs a subtitle. Like *Breakin' 2: Electric Boogaloo* or *Mannequin 2:*

The last hour of every day at work became a short fiction seminar when I attempted to come up with plausible lies for what had filled my day. It was during this dark period of my life that I discovered the cost of my soul was twenty dollars an hour, plus benefits.

During this time, I started doing stand-up. The whole time I was in law school, I'd kept thinking that when it was all over, I'd go back to a place full of interesting people with interesting opinions: I'd go be a stand-up in San Francisco. I was scared but enchanted. When I actually returned, I let my fears rule me, particularly those that centered on my capacity to exist and support myself. It wasn't until the financial stability of moral prostitution was present that I felt like I was allowed to cross the bay and start dipping my toe into the world of open-mic comedy.

I was soon fired from my job. I was truly, magnificently irresponsible at it. I was worried that said irresponsibility might affect my application for the California bar. There's a thing called a Character and Fitness application you have to submit, to show that you're honest and responsible. I was certain that my bad performance at the legal job, combined with my truly execrable credit score, would lead the state of California to reject my application. This is ridiculous; the law is a profession rife with criminals, and no one cared about my stupid little problems. I was probably just creating barriers to guide me away from a life in the law. Fundamentally, I knew I did not love it enough to be really good at it.

When I got fired, I should have been scared, right? I was, but not scared like I'd been when I first moved back. The successful acquisition of two jobs and the ensuing ten months of job-having had sort of taught me I was capable of survival. But more than that, doing stand-up meant I was happy, and despite my cynical thoughts to the contrary, part of me was certain that following what made me happy would be the right path.

I got a semi-bullshit job selling high-end tech solutions over the

---

On the Move. I think it should be called "Adar 2: Enter the Boredom of Discussing the Hebrew Calendar."

phone. It was basically tech-boom telemarketing. It didn't matter. I had decided to stop worrying about what my career and path were and focus on making a life that seemed rewarding. Plus there were two sassy ladies who worked there who liked to get chips 'n' margs after work.

For the better part of a year, that was my life. I did stand-up nearly every night. I did a job I didn't care about every day, and it never gave me any problems. Finally—for the first time in this book, maybe—I was just being me. There were problems, failures, and bounced checks, yes, but it was living.

Then, in April 2003, two separate people asked me if I was going to have a Passover Seder. One was my roommate Alice, one of the original founding hipsters of the East Bay. Before we had a word for hipsters, she was drinking PBR and having bluebirds tattooed on her shoulder blades. She also had a graduate degree in medieval Irish history, a deep love of Catholicism, and a passion for ritualized religion of any sort. The other person was my friend Ryan, my editor from the *Daily Cal*, who was then a scrappy young tech journalist. He was neither Jewish nor obsessed with religious ritual, so his motivations will remain a mystery. I said no to both of them, then decided if I had been asked twice, I should consent to whatever force was attempting to nudge me in that direction.

What is Passover? you may ask. Passover is a Jewish holiday, which, like all Jewish holidays, commemorates an occasion when a genocide against the Jewish people only mostly succeeded. Hanukkah, Purim, the story is always the same: People tried to kill us, they only mostly succeeded, so now we eat, we don't eat, or we eat in a weird way.

In the case of Passover, it was Egyptians who attempted to kill us; various miracles that managed to save us and transport us to the land of Israel; and the weird way we eat is a removal of leavened bread from our diet for a week.[2]

---

[2] In a classically Jewish bit of hyperlegality, it is celebrated for eight days in all places outside of Israel just to make sure you celebrate all seven days that occur IN Israel.

And what is a seder? you ask. A seder is the highly ritualized dinner party that is the core of Passover celebrations. Like Thanksgiving but with a script and props and elements of a talk show.

I did not grow up having fabulous seders. My mom's deeply closeted Arkansas approach to Judaism precluded splashy celebrations. For the most part, we just waited for the supermarket to put up an end-of-the-aisle display that included all the items from the Jewish section, not just matzo but mourning candles and bean soup mixes, everything remotely Jewish out at the end of the aisle for everyone to see. My mother would clandestinely buy a few boxes of matzo and possibly kosher-for-Passover breakfast cereal and try to check out without anyone noticing. At dinner, we'd have matzo, and she'd explain to us that we really needed to remember that we were brought out of Egypt and that we were once slaves. I loved it, though I did have a hard time remembering which one was matzo and which one was pita. The breads of the Mediterranean were a blur to me as a third-grader.

However, I did grow up with feasts. Once every few months, sometimes for a holiday, sometimes not, my mother would take it upon herself to work miracles. She would start with an onion or some peaches off the tree, then reimagine them. Sure, there were ancient and traditional recipes—she deemed my paternal grandmother's cobbler[3] better than her mother's and never looked back. Most of the time, she was riffing, improvising, improving. She'd buy seeds for something she'd never heard of, plant it in the garden, and sixty days later we were discovering what snow peas were. There was also meticulous planning. She was a

---

[3] Cobbler: Pre-heat oven to 350. Place a stick of butter in a cast iron skillet or Pyrex 8-by-12 dish. Put the dish in the oven. Combine 1 cup all-purpose flour, 1 cup heavy whipping cream, 1 cup sugar, 1½ teaspoons baking powder, ¼ teaspoon salt, and 1 teaspoon vanilla extract in a bowl until it forms a stiff batter. In a separate bowl, combine 3 cups blackberries (fresh or frozen) or peaches (fresh, don't fuck with me) with ½ cup sugar. When the butter in the dish begins to brown, pull the dish out. There should be a good-size pool of butter at the bottom of the dish. Pour the batter into the butter pool. It will try to rise above the batter, coating the outside of the dish. Pour the fruit over the batter. Bake until done. What? You don't know what done is? Get your shit together.

cafeteria manager: Every feast was a series of tasks to be accomplished, surmounted. She always aimed a little too high, but the results were always delicious. When I was around the age of twelve, she let me cross the bar. I was her foot soldier. I chopped onions, I snapped peas and peeled peaches. If I did a shoddy job, she yelled at me;[4] if I did a good job, she just kept joking and talking and cooking.

Let's return to 2003. Having a seder of my own seemed like a fun lark. I researched some compelling Sephardic dishes, put together a menu,[5] and bought some groceries. Then I realized I needed a Haggadah. A Haggadah is the script-thing you read at a seder. My mom would buy them for me and give them to me when I was growing up,[6] so I could imagine what real Judaism was like. I considered asking Berkeley Hillel to loan me some, then the answer hit me: I should write my own Haggadah.

So my first Passover seder was just me and four friends around our kitchen table, eating artichokes I had not properly cleaned and which were thus exceedingly fibrous. We drank too much kosher wine and laughed at the silly jokes I'd made in my version of the Haggadah, and the years of sadness and uncertainty seemed gone. If my childhood had been a knife fight to maintain my identity, if my coming out had been a wrestling match with depression, in that moment in 2003, a couple of weeks after the U.S. invaded Iraq, I, if I alone, felt at peace.

The next year, I knew I had to do it again. Bigger. I borrowed a table from a nearby elementary school and got some folding chairs from a church. I invited eight people, including some of the cool people from my new writing job. To impress them I had to write a longer, more joke-

---

[4] You cannot believe the side-eye I received when I referred to one such job as "a rustic chop."

[5] The entrée at my first seder was an Italian Jewish salmon with artichoke sauce. I also started my habit of making *huevos haminados* for the boiled eggs. It's a Sephardic recipe where you leave eggs in simmering water with onion skins and coffee beans overnight and they turn brown and delicious. *Try it.* You will thank me.

[6] "Hey, asshole, I got you something." Then she'd throw it at me.

heavy Haggadah. The 2004 menu centered on a dish of tuna steaks with bitter lettuces that no one really appreciated. It didn't matter—it was a gleeful success.

This ritual became part of me. When I moved to L.A., I brought it with me. It got bigger and bigger by the year. I started ordering custom kippot[7] in springy, pastel colors with little slogans stamped in them like "Guy's Seder '09: You Don't Deserve to Be Here" or "Guy Branum's Seder 2017: You'll Never Feel This Alive Again." I added games, like the ritualized asking of a moderately invasive question of someone at the table you don't know,[8] or a fun round of anti-Semitic Password.

When I could afford it and couldn't afford it, I'd rent tables. I'd buy racks of lamb. I'd spend weeks planning and preparing when I should have been writing spec scripts and doing comedy shows. I spend too much time, money, and labor on a religious dinner party that no one cares about. It is, perhaps, the most important thing you can know about me.

To understand why, we must go to the 1987 Danish film *Babette's Feast*.

Babette's Feast is one of those well-reputed foreign films from before your time that you've never seen but people have told you to watch. It sounds vaguely boring and inoffensive, and while you're not sure, there may be Nazis involved. Everything but that last part is true. It is, in actuality, an adaptation of a short story by Karen Blixen, the lady Meryl Streep played in *Out of Africa*. That's how deep the 1980s prestige movie cred of *Babette's Feast* goes: It was written by a Meryl Streep character.

The story seems insanely dry. Two old sisters live in a community of Lutheran ascetics founded by their dad. Each has a chance at romance, one with a dashing army officer, the other with a French opera star.

---

[7] This is the Hebrew word for yarmulke. I don't say yarmulke because I'm from California, and California Jews don't fuck with Yiddish.

[8] *Talk Show the Game Show* lead judge Casey Schreiner's query of "How much money do you have in your primary checking account right now?" is still the benchmark for what "moderately invasive" really means.

They both turn down this secular glamour to assist in their father's work. Then, one dark and stormy night, a woman appears at their door. She's Babette, a friend of the French opera star who's fled the purges of the Paris Commune and seeks employment as a maid. The old sisters grudgingly agree, and they find that somehow Babette manages to make their meager income go further and their lives feel better.

Then Babette wins the lottery and makes dinner for the religious community.

That's the movie. Drained of its life and presented as a series of events, it's certainly a lot less compelling than *Inception*. *Babette's Feast* isn't about plot points or set pieces, though. It is, fundamentally, about art and generosity.

See, Babette had a friend in Paris who bought a lottery ticket for her every year: her only connection to her life before she became a refugee. When she wins, the sisters assume Babette will be leaving them, but Babette asks for the chance to cook a meal for the hundredth anniversary of the women's father's birth. They agree.

Babette then begins a long process of purchasing strange ingredients and fancy table service from France. The old, ascetic Danes have only ever eaten salt cod and a porridge made from beer and bread. Babette brings in a turtle, quails, truffles, and Veuve Clicquot. The Danes are scared—they do not know what kind of witch's Sabbath this foreigner is making—but they love her, so they vow to go to the meal and consume it without making any judgmental comments.

We see Babette cooking, not like a breezy Nancy Meyers heroine or a luscious Nigella but like a seasoned field marshal. Like Debbie Branum. This bitch knows some shit. We've seen glimpses of it in the rest of the movie, but here, fully equipped, she summons the fullness of her powers. Blinis Demidoff, turtle soup, tiny quails stuffed with truffles and pâté and then baked in puff pastry. The dashing soldier happens to be in town; now a widowed general, he accompanies his aunt to the meal and is able to identify what they're eating: "Cailles en Sarcophages," the specialty of the greatest chef in Paris. That this decadence is happening in a windswept village on the Jutland coast seems miraculous.

Miraculous, too, is its effect on the little community. Old and poor, they have seen their lives and relationships turn to bitterness and regret, but full of champagne and amontillado, they change, they soften, they remember that the world is a beautiful place full of beautiful things to love.

A friend of mine, one of the smartest I know, read the short story "Babette's Feast" at my recommendation. He was confused. When he read it, he could make sense of it only as a Christian allegory. People who lived lives of service were rewarded with treasures in the "afterlife" by the Christlike Babette. There's a line from the general in which he evokes the afterlife: "Everything we have chosen has been granted to us. And everything we rejected has also been granted." It feels impossible and antinomian, a nice idea for an afterlife but meaningless to a person who does not believe in that messiah or afterlife. It's a perfectly valid reading, but it's not my reading.

In the wake of the magical, transformative feast, the two aged sisters, Philippa and Martine, ask when Babette will be leaving with the rest of her lottery winnings. Babette says she has spent the entirety of the ten thousand francs on the meal. The sisters are perplexed. "Now you will be poor the rest of your life," one says. "An artist is never poor," Babette responds.

The Last Supper is, of course, the image evoked by *Babette's Feast*. Christ offering his blood and flesh to sustain his fellow Christians. And the Last Supper was, of course, a Passover seder, a meal and a ritual where we consider the horrible fate that should have destroyed us but did not. I have had my seder in good years and bad years, when my career was going great and when it was in the tank. It is, if nothing else, a reminder to myself that my worth is not what I receive, or what I have saved away, but what I can make and give.

Before the dinner, Babette never refers to herself as an artist. She's a maid. She's a functionary. She's good at her job, but the job she does is the job that's instructed. As she carves and sautés and simmers and tastes, sweat rolls down her face, and she begins to glow. She remembers the powerful creature she once was; she remembers that she's a goddess.

She does not eat the meal, she never enters the dining room when the meal is being eaten. No one tells her it is good. That's not what matters. What matters is she got to do the thing she is capable of doing. She got to use the fullness of herself. Babette never talks about cooking before this meal, and cooking is a strange thing to think of as a creative art form. When the meal is served, however, we are all aware her creative powers are legion. She may then reference her artistry as self-evident. "Throughout the world sounds one long cry from the heart of the artist: Give me the chance to do my very best."

That is why you do not know me unless you've been to my Passover seder. It is my chance to be my very best. It is a chance to give my love and attention to food and words and my friends, to create one night when life in my little apartment touches the divine not in spite of the physical world but through it.

The first time I had my seder, it was a benchmark, a moment to say, "You're fine, bad things have happened in the past, but you made it through." Each year I get to remind myself of that. I am a fat, gay, bald, depressive man with no husband who will probably never have a long-term relationship. I live in a world that hates me for a lot of reasons. It'd be very simple to sour in these things, but I am consistently dazzled by the extent to which everything I have chosen has been granted to me, and everything I have rejected has also been granted. This creation is rich with possibilities and opportunities. I have friends who are funnier and smarter than I ever could have imagined. I make a living writing jokes. I get to dust quail with za'atar, grill it, hand it to someone I love, and have him see the world a little bit differently afterward.

When Babette presents Martine and Philippa with her letter of introduction from the famous opera star, the final line of the letter is the simple, magnificent understatement "Babette can cook." Our world is a constant, glorious understatement of miracles we did everything and nothing to earn. One evening every spring, I remind myself to notice them.

THE RULES OF ENCHANTMENT

IF YOU WERE BORN after the year 1980, you cannot possibly understand how my household was changed by the advent of the videocassette recorder. Sure, VCRs existed in the 1970s, I guess people had them, but no one I knew. The VHS recorder, and its short-lived brethren the videodisc player and Betamax, really overtook America in 1983. It was quite a year for me.

The winter of '82/'83 was the greatest depth of the Carter/Reagan recession. Unemployment was at 10.8 percent, and my dad's industry, construction, was one of the fields most reactive to economic slowdown. Construction is a sketchy field in the winter, anyway. Rain means no work, and no work means no money. No money means fighting. On so many gray mornings, I would wake up to find my dad still at home. That was never good. It meant anger was in the air. I knew the word "recession," and it meant I needed to play quietly.

Then came the spring of '83. Maybe it was Reagan's tax cut on the rich, maybe it was global oil supplies stabilizing, maybe it was just Friedrich Hayek's cycles of boom and bust, but the economy started moving again. This was the beginning of the glory days of 1980s prosperity and consumerism that would crash so miserably in the 1990s. Concretely, for me, a seven-year-old, it meant my life started getting better.

Uncle Ray's family acquired a VCR before we did. This was part of an ongoing cold war between our families, which, unlike the actual Cold War, would not end with a peaceable breakdown of tension and dismantling of walls. No—wall construction or, rather, fence construction, would serve a major role in the late stages of this conflict, as my uncle Ray was, by profession, a fencing contractor.

Uncle Ray was and is my mom's brother. My family represented the following philosophies:

1. Personal discipline
2. Domesticity
3. Observant religion (Jewish and Christian)
4. Good cooking
5. Waterfowl hunting
6. Financial responsibility
7. Book learning

His family represented the following philosophies:

1. Drinking
2. Masculinity
3. Godlessness
4. Good times
5. Deer hunting
6. Conspicuous consumption
7. Stupidity

Ray was a beer-swilling, gun-toting, pickup-driving redneck of the highest order. The sort of man who bragged because he'd never read a book in his life. The sort of man who couldn't read a book because he was pretty dyslexic. The kind of man who bragged about things he once was ridiculed for. The kind of man who bragged and fought and blustered his fears away until it seemed they became too strong and it took beer or bourbon or something stronger to make them go away. Such was Ray. He *hated* me.

Ray and his wife, Dinah (who my mother would like you to know is an inferior-quality cook), had purchased a plot of land in the orchard from my paternal grandparents and built a house on it. Ray, like my dad, worked construction, so, like my dad, he built the house himself on weekends with the help of friends. Unlike my father, Ray drank a lot, so he had famously designed his house with a sunken living room and then forgotten to sink the thing during the construction process. My parents found this *hilarious* and brought it up frequently, much to my aunt and uncle's consternation. No one is saying my parents didn't fully participate in the escalation of tensions.

Ray and Dinah's house was directly back from ours through the orchard. Their attempts to directly mirror my parents' lives were further cemented by their production of an older daughter, Tori, and a younger son, Robby. These were the primary playmates of my childhood. On summer days, my sister and I would trek through the magic and danger of the orchard to Tori and Robby's house or, more dazzlingly, for a party or event, traverse the distance in the night, when bats or a random dog could present real or imagined threat.

These were the early days of the cold war, when it was still barely forming, but as in any cold war, proxy wars were being fought. In our case, the puppet states were dogs. Neither Ray's property nor ours had fences at this time, so our dogs ranged the orchard unchecked. Our dog was a German shepherd/Chesapeake Bay retriever mix named Charlie, after my mom's other brother, I believe as a slow-burn shade in which my mom implied his wife was a bitch. Ray's dog was a yellow Lab named Seger, I believe after Bob Seger, though possibly it was Seeger after Pete Seeger. I do not care about heterosexual men's music enough to know the difference.

Charlie would accompany me on my many treks through the orchard, mostly occasions when I would find a stick, decide it was my staff, wand, or sword, then engage in something midway between creative play and *Lord of the Rings* fan fiction. At some point, Seger would arrive, and the dogs, coached by their masters to be territorial and hate each other, would growl and snarl and, about half of the time, end up getting in a fight.

Managing dog fights was like 30 percent of my childhood. In our yard or Ray's, it was a basic game: You got the hose and turned it on them. In the orchard, plumbing was but a memory. I was instructed to flee such situations but also understood that turning one's back to a dog and running would indicate I was prey. Thus, I spent a great chunk of my childhood slowly backing away while Charlie tore Seger's neck open. A key design flaw in the yellow Lab is this very floppy, poorly defended neck which Charlie opened up like a Sprite every time he got near Seger. It was a major point of pride for my father that Ray had paid hundreds of dollars to vets to have that neck stitched up. Everyone here was an asshole.

This has been rather a long digression to explain my most 1983 memory of all time. I have a memory of being at Ray and Dinah's house on a weekend morning. I was eating C-3PO's cereal, a promotional tie-in for *Return of the Jedi* that is, to this day, the single finest cereal I have ever experienced. My sister, cousins, and I were watching *Gandhi* on a top-loading VCR. Many of you barely know what VCRs are, let alone top-loading ones. A lot of you don't understand why four children, all twelve years of age or younger, would be watching a three-hour epic about Indian independence. You don't understand the resounding sensation that *Gandhi* was. It was in the press so much that we all thought we needed to be watching it a *lot*. And you can never then put together the intensely dated experience of using this anachronistic technology to watch this zeitgeisty Oscar movie, eating a cereal that existed for less than a year while hanging out with people I'd essentially never speak to after 1986. I call it *my* most 1983 memory out of a sense of humility and discretion, but I understand that it is truly the most 1983 memory possible for *any human being*.

Except for, like, Mr. T. He had a really big year in 1983. I'm sure he has some more 1983-ish memories than that.

We got a VCR in 1984. It was a really important step in ending re-source dependence on Ray and Dinah. These moments when conduits of culture got added to our house were strangely empowering to my mom. I was an idiot playing with He-Man when the VCR came, but I remember my mother's ecstasy when she first discovered cable TV was coming out to where we lived. It would be the 1990s before that happened. I do not remember her reaction to the VCR, just her steadily growing power. She and my dad would bring home videocassettes, and videocassettes were art, which enriched her. Sure, some of them were nice broad-market comedy that my dad could get behind, a *Caddyshack* here, a *Police Academy 3: Back in Training* there, but all entertainment was, to some extent, anathema to him. It was wasted time.

And oh, the wasted time she brought into our house! Movies we never would have seen at the theaters, movies that never would have played in theaters within two hours of us. I never asked to see *A Room with a View* or *Hope and Glory*; Roger Ebert and Gene Siskel just told us to watch them, and my mother complied.

Our Saturday nights got better. *Diff'rent Strokes* was great, but now we had the option of major motion pictures, each funnier, cooler, and more explosive than the last. And then there were those Sunday-afternoon movies, ones my mom would watch after the lion's share of the work was done. Merchant Ivory. Jessica Lange feeling too much. Holocaust survivors in a dark but lovely sex comedy? My dad didn't always watch; he didn't have to. My mom was working a job now, and she deserved some little bit of relaxation in her week.

Soon my mother's hunger for culture had run through the backlog of film offerings at the video store, and she started ranging further afield. Having mowed through blockbusters, also-rans, British movies we didn't realize were British until we got them home, and *Eddie and the Cruisers*, she finally, on one fateful day, brought her hand to rest on a video that wasn't a movie at all. It was a moment that continues to echo in my life.

I feel like the first one was George Carlin, though one can hardly be certain. The point is that the stand-up boom that was bringing monologuizing men in sweater-vests to strip malls, cable stations, and network sitcoms all across the country had found its way into my house, and I was rapt. Stand-up was more laughs per minute than anything I'd ever seen. I loved to laugh, I loved being entertained, but stand-up was something more. It was perspective and philosophy. Could someone with as many punch lines as George Carlin really be wrong about *anything*?[1]

This is all my highly circuitous way of saying that in the mid-1980s, in a living room in the Sacramento Valley, during the hottest part of the middle of the day, after my mother had drawn the curtains to keep us as cool as possible as cheaply as possible, we watched a video and I fell in love with stand-up comedy, the thing I make my living from today.

*

The stand-up comedy special that had the biggest impact on me was undoubtedly *Eddie Murphy: Delirious*. Before I'd even seen it, I'd heard my uncle (ten years older) and sister (five years older) detailing its coolness. When the video entered our home, it was with a tinge of awe. Finally, we were going to get to see this. My early-thirties parents, made conservative by parenthood, often felt the need to guard us from or caution us away from racy content, especially when said content came from "urban"[2] voices. Not this time; they were as excited to see the special as we were.

For sixty-nine minutes, Eddie strutted onstage in a red leather suit and told the world how it was. He danced back and forth between biography and cultural commentary, simultaneously tracing a story of his very specific life and analyzing universal touchstones to assure his audience that he wasn't so unlike them. I wanted to be like that.

---

[1] Okay, Carlin's joke about global warming not being real kept me skeptical on the subject for far longer than is defensible.

[2] Black.

The most powerful force in *Eddie Murphy: Delirious* is his certainty. Eddie's intellect, sex appeal, and wit are all palpably present, but they draft behind the powerful force of his certainty. Eddie isn't asking permission, and he's not calling out for collaboration or validation from his audience. He is laying out a worldview and communicating it with merciless brutality. In the decade and a half that would transpire between my first blush of love for stand-up and me actually trying it, I consumed vast amounts of stand-up from numerous sources. Women, men, deadpan, prop, absurdist, and one-liner. I watched it all and loved almost all of it, but I always understood that what Eddie Murphy had done was most powerful.

My freshman year at Berkeley, my friend Lorelei laughed at something I said in conversation and said, "You're so funny, we need to get you to an open mic sometime." It was a simple aside, a throwaway compliment, but I took that compliment and treasured it in my head for years. I polished and contemplated that compliment, but I did nothing with it.

Because you guys should probably understand by this point in the book that I had and have no business being a stand-up comedian. For my entire life, my ability to communicate my perspective to the people around me has been a constant struggle suffused with folly. My use of "suffused with folly" is the best example of said folly. Why would I use that phrasing? Whose understanding is it clarifying? My life has been this weird uncostumed cosplay in which I'm trying to be a rural eight-year-old's best estimation of what a Victorian cabinet member's life should be while the people around me squint in confusion. I wasn't a class clown. Most of the jokes I had growing up were just for *me*. If I wanted to be that, why not go into one of those self-congratulatory fields where the abstruse would be a merit? Why didn't I become a person who writes for "Shouts and Murmurs" or *McSweeney's*?

My column for the *Daily Cal* was the first verified proof that people, lots of people, could enjoy things I wrote. I remember walking into the main library on campus, and the person who looked at my ID[3] said, "Oh, hey, you're funny." Though at that age I had never had wine,[4] I drank that line up like wine. I know Berkeley isn't exactly the unwashed masses, but it is a broad, diverse populace. I think I was mostly surprised and excited that I was doing, in a tiny way, the thing I thought I'd never be able to do.

My final semester at Berkeley, I started going across the Bay to watch comedy in San Francisco. In the early days of the Internet, figuring out when and how to go to these indie shows was complex, and I was terrible at doing things outside of my regular little routine, but I loved it. Going to those shows felt sexy and dangerous.

Around the comedy scene in San Francisco back then, you'd see ads for this guy who called himself "The Comedy Coach." I should have been immediately aware of the inadequacy of his comedy skills by the fact that he did not spell it "The Komedy Koach." K's are just funnier. His name was Neil Lieberman, and he had a very bad ponytail, and he assured you that he had the keys to the kingdom of the comedy world. Another point I should have considered: If he understood comedy so well, why wasn't he a famous comic? I wasn't thinking that critically; all I knew was I very much liked the world of stand-up comedy, and I'm a person who needs to do a lot of research before I can try something.

His services were eight hundred dollars for eight weeks of coaching. This sum was unimaginable to me. However, Neil was having an introductory three-hour class at the Punch Line Comedy Club in San

---

[3] In the 1990s, a human being looked at your ID when you entered the campus library, not some robot or automated eye. Why does no one ever talk about the deleterious effect of automation on the careers of state college students with a ten-hour-a-week work-study requirement?

[4] My parents, both from Arkansas, have a deep cultural aversion to wine. My father's family, Baptists, do not drink at all. My mother's family, a mix of Jews and alcoholic bootleggers, drink heavily. More heavily than probably any Jews you've ever experienced unless you knew Amy Winehouse during the end times. They drink only beer and hard liquor. I have tried really hard to find some academic work explaining the forces that so distanced my ancestors from wine culture, but all I end up finding are websites for shitty wineries in southern Missouri.

Francisco for fifty dollars. I could barely afford BART fare to go to comedy shows; fifty dollars was a lot, and it certainly wasn't a sum I could imagine asking my parents to give me. They would have considered it a waste of money to pursue a different waste of money.

I scraped the cash together and I went, and at that class, I got up and "did stand-up" for the first time. It was not a real audience; it was other comics who'd paid to be there. This was not stand-up comedy. It was a baby step. I did my very long, thinky bit about how there weren't enough roles for older actresses, so we should make them go into professional wrestling because they could make it seem less fake. The entire time, my leg was shaking in fear.

Neil Lieberman laid out a few clear rules: Leave the mic in the stand, stand in one place, write three jokes each on four topics: this will be your first five minutes. These were valuable lessons, but the biggest lesson I learned from the class was "you shouldn't take classes to learn to do stand-up." The only way to pursue it, it seemed, was to do it.

Finally, one Friday afternoon in the spring, I steeled my nerves, marched down to the BART station, crossed the Bay, and showed up at a small, unassuming coffee shop in the Western Addition.[5] I signed up on the list, lower than I would have liked, waited through the comics before me, then, terrified, took the stage. It was wonderful, it was everything I'd hoped it would be. It was a balm for my soul, it was a give-and-take with the audience.[6] It was sublime. This is not *really* the first time I did stand-up comedy.

The reason for that is that it was not the event that transformed me from a human being to a stand-up comic. I saw the guys around me, guys[7] who lived and breathed stand-up. They were real. They might get

---

[5] This is a neighborhood of San Francisco which is neither nice nor not nice.

[6] The audience was nine aspiring stand-up comedians and a woman trying to drink her coffee.

[7] The scene was 80-plus percent male comics, and the paradigm of "person whose life is consumed by stand-up" was uniformly male in the popular imagination of the scene.

to be famous. I could not be one of them. There were a number of reasons, mostly that I had to go do responsible, important things. By this point in time, I'd already been accepted to law school. I was going to be a lawyer. Another reason I couldn't be a stand-up was that my mom wouldn't let me. I also fundamentally doubted my ability to commit to something. I lived my life in ruts. I had rituals and habits, and in my experience, attempts to shift those habits (lose weight, brush my teeth thrice a day, keep my apartment clean) never worked. One summer, I was delivering pizzas instead of working for my dad, so I asked my mom if I could get a gym membership for the summer. I was going to try to lose weight and be healthier. My mother said, "It is a waste of money, you will never go." Any time I had a hope or aspiration that required an investment, my mom would assure me I wouldn't stick with it, and I rarely did.[8] I believed this about myself, and believed I did not have the tenacity to really, really be a stand-up comic. I believed I did not have the power to change things.

The summer before I went to law school, I was again living at home, working for my dad. It was a small project at some local schools, and I was assisting him as construction inspector by taking notes and keeping records. One Saturday, I asked if I could go to San Francisco and do comedy. My mother said no. Gas was too expensive. It was a waste of money. It was a waste of time. I made the gentle argument that I was working for my dad without getting paid, and my dad got very angry. "Oh, we owe *you* money, huh?"

But I loved stand-up, so I gently persisted. Some people, twenty-two-year-old adults, would have just gone and done it. I was not one of those adults. I was a twenty-two-year-old child. A very obedient one at whom my parents still managed to be very angry all the time.

A few times over that summer, I went. I drove the two and a half hours to San Francisco blaring disco music, electrified that I would get

---

[8] Look, the lady's great in a *lot* of ways. Let's not behave as though people are only heroes or villains. Life is complex.

to perform. I cannot remember the drives back because I was so, well, delirious with pleasure that I may have technically been intoxicated.

Then I moved to Minnesota and did not get on a stage for three years.

Why didn't I do a *little* stand-up in Minnesota? Why didn't I dip my feet in the water? When your parents forbid you from marrying the woman you love, you don't periodically smell her hair to be reminded just how deep your longing is. You forget about it, you shut it away, you let it live with the other unrealized desires in the chamber of your heart where they hide.

Then I came out, and a storm of depression and reevaluation followed, as we discussed previously. With a great deal of help, I picked myself up, pulled myself together, learned how to be gay, finished law school while doing nothing to get myself a permanent job, and managed to be a semifunctional human being by the time law school was over.

Through the smoggy night of depression, I had fixed my mind on one thing, the memory of a happiness that felt real. I remembered those nights doing stand-up. "When I am done here, I will do stand-up in San Francisco," I told myself. "When I no longer have to be around these law students, I will go every night to a place full of people who are, if nothing else, interesting."

It took nearly six months after my return for me to get on a stage. Part of me expected respectability to leap out from behind a bush and capture me, forcing me into a good job that would pay for the suits I had to wear to the office, and all of it would make my mom happy. This is what I'd been moving toward for so long; could it really be avoided?

Its avoidance was unavoidable. I didn't care nearly enough about being fancy or making a hundred thousand dollars a year. When I ran into Berkeley friends and they asked me what firm I was at, I was filled with shame, but not enough shame to change me. Shame isn't good at changing me. Love changes me.

One night in the latter part of 2001, after 9/11 but before my twenty-sixth birthday, I went to an open mic in the Mission District of San Francisco with a word-for-word printout of my set in hand.[9] I got up, the room responded, and I felt alive in a way I hadn't since I'd gone to Minnesota.

That is also not the first time I did stand-up. After the show, an established comic said to me, "You seem like you'd make a really good writer." Lots of people would say this to me over the course of the following month or two. I got mad. They seemed to be saying that I didn't seem like a real performer. They were right. Part of me had been fearing

---

[9] For your records, here is the content of the first set I performed in my ongoing comedy career. Please note the complete absence of setups or punch lines.

Good evening, ladies and gentlemen, my name is Guy Branum. Before I begin, I'd just like to say that I'm not here to entertain you; I'm not here for any sense of self-actualization. I'm here because I need to keep my personal monologue skills honed in case I'm ever on a reality television program.

Now, I know you're probably saying to yourself, "Guy, if the skill you're looking to practice is simply talking about yourself incessantly in the fashion of a mid-nineties *Real World* cast member . . . Isn't that what coffee dates are for?"

Tragically, I am allergic to boring, which makes dating most people quite difficult.

I've come to the opinion that between digital cable and online pornography, it's possible that we, as a species, have simply evolved past dating. Scoff if you will, but the three p.m. showing of *Private Benjamin* on the USA Network is never going to tell me it finds me really interesting but just isn't attracted to me.

It's difficult, try as I might, to wean myself from the milky teat of American popular culture; I just can't break the cycle of dependence. I'll spend weeks, months only watching independent films, only having sex with actual human beings, then BAM, I spend nine hours watching VH1 count down the hundred most sextastic moments in music video history. J-Lo, oh, how I missed you.

I was still swept up in the . . . mediocrity of it all when three attractive women came on the screen and apprised me of the fact that I may not be ready for that "jelly." I was confused but concerned. Ladies and gentlemen, what if I'm not ready for that jelly? What if their vibe is too vibalicious for AMERICA?

I immediately started researching the subject and discovered that the women in question were actually the singing group Destiny's Child, which is apparently French for En Vogue.

I then decided that I needed to go down to my local Target, buy the *Survivor* CD, and confront them in one single, climactic, dare I say Tolkienesque battle. This did not occur, as Destiny's Child is simply a bad pop group and not a dark lord of Mordor.

such a response. Part of me knew I was fat and not-hot and my job was to be behind the scenes and not onstage. What the rest of me wasn't thinking was that I was essentially just reciting very long, dense sentences onstage very, very quickly so I wouldn't go over my time. I hadn't thought about how an audience consumes ideas; I hadn't thought about how listener cognition works or when laughs come. I was trying to make my material dense so it would seem like smart-people comedy. Like all those years in school, I was making jokes for myself. I still didn't know how to meet my audience halfway.

The one thing I did was keep at it. The Internet was less sophisticated in those times, so I worked from a rumpled printout of all the open mics and booked shows in the city. I got up once a night, every night, except for Sunday. Sunday was when the showcase for Real Comics was at the Punch Line. Every comic in San Francisco went to the club and hoped they'd get put up. New comics had to go every week for six months to get asked. I didn't think I was ready to even start waiting. As the Lord intended, on Sunday, I rested.

The thing is, I changed. I stuck with something. I took a thing outside of myself and made it part of myself, and I was really proud of that. Every set taught me a new lesson. It was a roller coaster of emotions, sometimes the purest highs but often crushing anger at myself for some stupid mistake. And I kept it all inside. None of my friends knew I was doing stand-up. I loved it, but I was embarrassed, too.

About three or four months into doing stand-up, I went back to that

---

Luckily, I enjoy bad pop, so I continued to listen to the CD as I went about my errands. . . . Then I heard the question: "Kelly, can you handle this?" I knew the answer was "No." "Michelle, can you handle this?" Slightly better chance? Again, probably not. "Beyoncé, can you handle this?" And I knew, ladies and gentlemen, with a certainty rare in this crazy, mixed-up world, that if anyone could handle those fine mocha asses, it was Beyoncé. Simultaneously, somehow, I BECAME Beyoncé: my coppery-gold extensions flowing in the wind-machine-provided breeze, two entirely disposable backup singers by my side . . . and an ass more powerful than God MYself.

Then I realized I was frightening the other shoppers at Trader Joe's, so I stopped listening to Destiny's Child.

open mic in the Mission where I'd started back up. It was at a black-box theater called the Marsh. They had a little annex with a tiny stage called the Mock Café because it *seemed* like a little art café but it didn't serve coffee. It seated about thirty people, but it always had a good audience, because two or three times a year, Robin Williams would come there and perform.[10] People showed up all year long on the outside hope that this would be one of those nights. Most shitty coffeehouse or bar open mics barely had an audience, so the Mock Café always seemed like a jewel in the week. I showed up with the material I was trying to hone into a tight five, certain that this audience would give solid data for how to improve it. While I sat waiting, a heterosexual couple in their late twenties walked in. They were beautiful and exquisitely dressed, and so much of my soul just wanted to talk to them and find out what their deal was.

When my appointed time came and I got up onstage, I did that. I talked to them, they talked back, and I improvised jokes in response. The energy in the room changed. Because I was talking about what was going on in that very room, everyone was engaged. My energy changed. It wasn't a recitation. There was threat and danger, but I kept it alive. I kept it funny. I told the man his shoes were more expensive than my truck; I told them I wanted them to have a baby so if I were successful in entertainment, it could be my trophy husband in twenty-five years. I was flirty and kind and cutting and mean, and they loved it. When I got offstage, I was changed. That is the first time I really did stand-up.

I do not mean for you to think that when I "just got onstage and talked from my heart," that's when it happened. No, no one wants to see that. People at open mics do it all the time, and it's crap. What I mean is that when I was able to unify the lessons I'd learned from four

---

[10] Eventually, I was there for one of those nights. Mr. Williams stood politely in the back with his son Zak, and watched every comic on the list. At the end, he got up and did a frenetic forty-five minutes of workout material. It was exactly what you'd expect from him. He did take a moment to talk about a few of the comics from the evening, and he said of me, "I never knew Jesse Ventura and Liza Minnelli had a child." It felt pretty good.

months of stand-up[11] and merge them with what was actually going on around me[12] and turn it into real, immediate entertainment, I loved it, and I knew that I had found something I loved enough to be good at. I hoped quite desperately that maybe, just maybe, this could be my profession.

*

Eddie Murphy: Delirious begins with the exhortation "Faggots are not allowed to look at my ass while I am onstage." This gets an applause break. It is a joke in and of itself. What follows are four minutes of exhaustive detail about everything that is gross about gay men. He declares that he has nightmares about gay people; he does impressions of popular celebrities, imagining how ridiculous it would be if they were gay. He expresses concern that his girlfriend will "carry AIDS home with her" after a tennis date with a gay man.

I did not remember this. In my head, *Eddie Murphy: Delirious* was the special that made me fall in love with stand-up, that taught me the language of the art form, and stood as the paragon of what confidence in comedy can and should be. When I naively decided to rewatch *Eddie Murphy: Delirious* a few years ago, to let its greatness wash over me, I was stunned to discover its beginning was this unrelenting tirade against the ridiculous putrescence of the gays.

I thought back to me, lying on a carpet at nine years old, consuming this work wholly, lapping up Murphy's every word, intoxicated by the power and humor behind it. I thought about the way I had also consumed ideas that would poison my understanding of myself before I knew they were about me.

I had to confront the very confusing reality that this special that was one of the building blocks of my love of stand-up, that contributed to my understanding of the language of the thing I do professionally, also

---

[11] Audience control, pressure for punch lines, clarity of thought.

[12] Hot people.

taught me the building blocks of the homophobia that would keep me closeted and self-hating into my twenties. I was forced to accept that as deeply as my love of stand-up comedy was baked into me, Murphy's disgusted view of gay men was as deeply in my bones. These things cannot be extricated from each other, and I cannot wholly dismiss or reject *Eddie Murphy: Delirious* any more than I can wholly dismiss or reject my father. Both of them did things that scarred, abused, created, and nurtured me.

In the special, Murphy says, "I kid the homosexuals a lot, because they homosexuals." The audience laughs: Faggots deserve what they get, they seem to say. Then he says, "I fuck with everybody, I don't give a fuck." This is a common refrain among comics who don't want to be criticized. The implication is that everyone is a fair target, so everyone gets mocked equally. But do they? Does Murphy take aim at Kazakhs or Methodists or white men or people with over a 750 credit rating? Would he think to? Would he have the capacity to dehumanize these people in the cultural landscape of 1983? Can you ever reduce a white, cisgender, heterosexual man to nonexistence with the completeness that a word like "faggot" so simply, elegantly achieves?

When I was nine, I was pretty certain I was a person, and Eddie Murphy was powerfully, resoundingly telling me that faggots weren't people. For over a decade afterward, I would solve that equation with the clear answer that I was unequal to the word "faggot." To quote the West End musical *Everybody's Talking About Jamie*, I built a wall in my head. It took years of experiencing my own life as a gay guy to question these terms that had been defined for me.

When I started doing stand-up comedy, I didn't realize there were no gay men who were nationally headlining comedians. I didn't think about it. I was used to living in a world without gay people, or where gay people were confined to the cultural spaces defined for them. I never noticed.

As I sat at open mics, I heard comics, mostly straight men, some straight women, using "fag" and "gay" as shorthand, defining themselves away from the danger and disgust of these characters. That's the thing:

Faggots in these comics' acts were characters, cartoonish caricatures without a soul or identity outside their faggishness. I realized this bogeyman of a fag was able to persist only because it was a space where no fags were actually talking. In stand-up comedy, fags were constantly discussed but never discussing. It became my obsession; my only desire, to get up onstage after one of those perfunctory, half-hearted open-mic fag bashings.

San Francisco was one of the rarest, best places to be a gay stand-up comic in the early 2000s. There were a number of regular shows that catered specifically to gay performers and audiences, an entire separate circuit just for gay comics. In no other city in America could I have done gay comedy for gay audiences with such frequency, but there was a distinct difference from the mainstream comedy scene. There was nowhere for anyone to go. No one succeeded. No one got the big chance. No big names from out of town came, with the exception of a few drag queens and midlevel lesbians.

I wanted to succeed on the big stage, so I worked hard at the mainstream shows and the Punch Line. As my class of comics started getting better, the more established comics from the club started taking them on the road. An absurdist comic took an absurdist comic under his wing, a Latino comic took a Latino comic under his wing, black comic with black comic, dirty comic with dirty comic, but there was essentially no one more established than me doing what I did. The few established gay comics on the San Francisco scene were hitting the ceiling of what was possible for their careers. There was no demand for gay comics in Hollywood or New York—the fame and success they had in San Francisco was all they were going to get. Thus they were territorial about their place in the city, and tended to see new gay comics as threats rather than colleagues. As I looked at stand-up, I saw no clear place for me to go.

There is one good academic work on stand-up comedy. It's called *Stand-Up Comedy in Theory, or, Abjection in America*, by John Limon. In it, Limon uses Julia Kristeva's concept of the abject to explain the role of stand-up as an art. He basically says comics are engaged in a dance of exploration of and distancing from the abject, the aspects of ourselves that remind us of our "corporeal reality." In Kristeva's terms, the abject is stuff like poop or cum or even hair clippings that remind you that you are not so far from being a dead object. More broadly, it's a dance with the things you are potentially most disgusted with in yourself.

In Limon's work, he repeatedly points to icons of comedy—Richard Pryor, Mel Brooks, Lenny Bruce—and identifies the abjection they're toying with as being deeply rooted in the fear of the effeminate and homosexual. He then writes an essay on Paula Poundstone and Ellen DeGeneres that centers on their cagey refusals to engage with their sexual identities onstage. In many ways, his arguments about why the past sixty years of stand-up comedy were successful are because no one like me was there.

Let me put this in more immediate terms. In late 2017, the *New York Times* published an article wherein five women discussed sexual harassment and assault from Louis C.K., and threats of retribution they'd received when they discussed it publicly. I was contacted by *New York* magazine to write my thoughts on the subject, and I wrote an essay arguing that uniformly portraying heterosexual men as the highest icons of comedy contributed to a culture and power structure of comedy that made exploitation of women easy and common. I used media representations of the comics' table at the Comedy Cellar, frequently used on the TV show *Louie*, as a representative image. A lot of people, rightfully so, made the point that this misrepresented the actual comics' table, at which some women and a few gays are welcome.

What matters is the Comedy Cellar asked me to do their podcast to discuss the article, mostly to tell me that I was wrong and didn't get it. During the podcast, I talked about the nonpresence of gay men among touring headliners, and Noam Dworman, the owner of the Comedy Cellar, compared me to his experience of seeing John Leguizamo with his wife. Basically, he said that he could never enjoy Leguizamo as much as his wife, because she is Puerto Rican. He said, "Is it possible that if gay men are ten percent or five percent of the population . . . that if you want to have an act about that . . . it's hard to appeal to the other ninety-five percent who can't really identify with that." In a sentence, he academically speculated that my chosen life's work might be a false premise. Maybe I can never be the comic I hope to be. Maybe there's no space for that comic to exist. It is a fear that comes to visit me very regularly, even when other people aren't saying it.

There's a Margaret Atwood poem in which she describes her daughter playing with plastic letters, "learning how to spell / how to make spells." She talks about women of the past who ignored domestic life to "mainline words," and punctuates it with "A word after a word after a word is power."

There are not currently A-list out-of-the-closet gay male stand-up comedians. This is an absence, and it is more. Stand-up comedy is laid thick with spells, spells about faggots and women and Asians and Muslims and airplane food. They are spells that define people as subjects and objects, heroes and monsters, and we cannot, in a field in which the spellcasters are overwhelmingly male and straight, behave as though these spells bind everyone equally or similarly. "I make fun of everyone" doesn't exonerate anyone, because the issue in the sentence isn't the object; it's not "I make fun of homosexuals" or "I make fun of everyone." The issue is the subject. Who gets to be "I"?

※

I know this chapter is already too long. I know those first couple of pages about the advent of the VCR in my home were self-indulgent nonsense. I know we've already discussed my starting stand-up, Eddie Murphy's career, a close reading of some Atwood, and some cheeky but thoroughly unacademic winks at the work of Bruno Bettelheim. I know you're tired, but for me to wrap this up, I'm going to need to go somewhere else. If this chapter is going to shake its defeatist nihilism, we're going to need some help. I'm going to have to explain to you that you like Ruth Bader Ginsburg for the wrong reasons.

I get it. You like her. She's liberal. She does the right thing on the Supreme Court. They made that meme. Kate McKinnon gives her a cartoon mouse voice, and it's funny to think of this very small woman with a severe bun and a doily around her neck taking on the powerful men of the right. You have reasons to like her. That is not why you should like her.

In 1970, the laws of the United States freely discriminated against women. From infancy to retirement, from Maine to Hawaii, the codes of American law treated women as fundamentally different from men, and it was all perfectly constitutional. Over the course of eight years, that changed, and while millions of women contributed to the social change that powered that revolution, the immediate technical work of making women in this country legally equal to men was disproportionately done by a small woman from Brooklyn whose friends call her "Kiki," but whom we should probably call Ruth.

But before we go any further than that, we need to establish that Ruth Bader Ginsburg does not sound like a cartoon mouse. She sounds like a furrier's daughter from Brooklyn who's trying to sound like a fancy lady. She sounds like a girl from the city who went to one of the two Ivy League schools that admitted women and didn't have restrictive quotas on Jewish students. Mostly, she sounds like a person who knows exactly what she wants to say at all times.

She was not always this. When she started at Harvard Law School, the dean invited the nine women in the 1L class to his home. He asked them why they deserved a spot that could have gone to a man. Ginsburg, flustered, stood up to answer and dropped an ashtray on the ground. After cleaning it up, she said she was in law school to understand her future husband's career better. Ruth was not always brave and correct; there was a time when she hid.

She hid in school. When her husband graduated a year before her and took a job in New York, she asked Harvard to let her finish her classes at Columbia and still get a Harvard degree. She was ranked first in her class. Harvard refused. She didn't make a stink; she put her head down and accepted her fate and graduated with a degree from Columbia. She was first in her class there, too.

She hid in her work. When she graduated from law school, she couldn't get a job at any firm, so she did academic work, the tiniest, most niche, most nitpicky thing she could find, because that's the only place a woman would be able to survive, right? She studied comparative civil procedure, with an emphasis on Swedish civil procedure. It's the closest she could come to being a librarian without just being a law librarian.

Then, one day, Ruth was in a courtroom in Sweden doing research for a book she was writing. The judge came in, and the judge was eight months pregnant. Kiki hadn't known that could happen; she had never imagined a pregnant woman being in a courtroom, let alone running a courtroom. She realized those tiny ways she was defining herself out of professional importance without even realizing it.

She came back and taught at Rutgers. She learned that the male faculty members doing the same job she was were making significantly more money. She and the other female faculty asked for raises and, when they didn't get them, went on strike. Female students saw this young female professor getting militant about feminist issues and asked her to teach a class on gender in the law. Ginsburg realized there was no book that addressed gender issues in the law. No one thought of the disparate treatment of women as an issue, just as a fact.

Then, in 1970, the ACLU asked her to head their women's rights program, and she took the job and had one clear goal. In 1970, the Equal Protection Clause of the Fourteenth Amendment did not include women. The amendment was written in the wake of the Civil War and was clearly intended to protect freed slaves from discrimination. When it was written, women were not allowed to vote, hold office, create contracts, or own property. The law that made people equal in the United States didn't think women were people. Ruth was going to change that.

It wouldn't be the first time that law was changed. For eighty years, the Equal Protection Clause was considered to allow for "separate but equal" treatment of the races through Jim Crow laws. Starting in the 1930s, the NAACP Legal Defense Fund had used a highly organized, targeted strategy of litigation to challenge "separate but equal" in practice, then as an entire concept. Ruth was going to try to do the same thing, but for a group of people the law pretty clearly wasn't intended to protect. She studied the work that NAACP attorneys like Thurgood Marshall and Constance Baker Motley had done to fight racial discrimination, and she used it as the framework for an attack on gender discrimination.

Between 1973 and 1979, Ruth Bader Ginsburg argued six cases before the Supreme Court. In six years, in six cases, she changed America.

When she was done, legally discriminating on the basis of gender was all but illegal. She took a constitution written by men who kept some women as figurative property and some as literal property, and she forced it to evolve to embrace people it didn't imagine. That's why you should love Ruth Bader Ginsburg.

There are audio recordings of her oral arguments. I listen to them sometimes. The first case she had before the Supreme Court, *Reed v. Reed*,[13] she didn't even argue, she just wrote a brief. She won. Then came *Frontiero v. Richardson*,[14] and she showed up at the Supreme Court for the first time. The case was in the afternoon, and she didn't eat all day long because she was scared she might vomit in the Supreme Court. She argued only after a male co-counsel made the bulk of the argument, and she was tentative and overly cautious. She didn't believe in herself. She won.

By the time *Kahn v. Shevin*[15] came along, she knew what she was doing. She was confident, and she was aggressive in that Supreme Court chamber. She had every answer before the justices asked the question. The justices, all men, didn't care for it. This was her single loss at the Supreme Court.

But Ginsburg is about results, and she learned from that setback. In her remaining appearances before the court, *Edwards v. Healy*,[16]

---

[13] 404 U.S. 71 (1971): Idaho law presumed that, all things being equal, courts should prefer that men act as executors for the estates of the deceased. Teenager Richard Lynn Reed killed himself while in the abusive custody of his father. Both his father and mother applied to be executors, and the state was forced to prefer the father by law. Sally Reed challenged on the basis of the Equal Protection Clause of the Fourteenth Amendment.

[14] 411 U.S. 677 (1973): Male Air Force officers were allowed to claim their wives as dependents for purposes of housing benefits, but female officers were allowed to only if they contributed over half of their husband's support. Sharron Frontiero challenged on behalf of her husband, Joseph.

[15] 416 U.S. 351 (1974): Florida gave certain property tax deductions to widows that were not granted to widowers. Kahn, a widower, challenged.

[16] 421 U.S. 722 (1974): Challenging Louisiana's presumptive exclusion of women from jury pools.

Weinberger v. Wiesenfeld,[17] *Califano v. Goldfarb*,[18] and *Duren v. Missouri*,[19] she was resplendent. Confident, precise in her wording, and constantly positioning the questions to make it impossible for the justices to find gender discrimination benign. But she was deferential. She never let them feel threatened. She won all of them.

You may say, "She shouldn't have to be deferential." She shouldn't. But she did. She needed results, so she did what it took to get them, and the law evolved. After staring down Ruth Bader Ginsburg six times, the Supreme Court could no longer define women as second-class citizens because they'd been so resoundingly reminded that this woman was a sharper legal mind than any of them.

Eventually, years later, Ruth would join the court, and when that court saw its first major gender discrimination case with Ginsburg as a member, *U.S. v. Virginia*,[20] Justice Stevens, the ranking justice, tapped Ruth to write the decision. She got to write the gender equal protection decision she'd been asking for all those years.

That's why you should love Ruth Bader Ginsburg.

❊

You should listen to those recordings of Ruth Bader Ginsburg's oral arguments. Her voice is full of clarity, understanding, authority, and urgency. She knows what she needs, and she's fighting for it with every

---

[17] 420 U.S. 636 (1975): Social security provided additional support to widows who did not work because they provided care to dependent children, but not to widowers who did the same. Stephen Wiesenfeld, a freelance computer engineer, was primarily supported by his wife. When his wife died in labor, Wiesenfeld continued with his plan to be a stay-at-home dad and filed for survivor childcare benefits. He was refused.

[18] 430 U.S. 199 (1977): Surviving widows were allowed to apply for survivor's social security benefits for a deceased husband, but widowers were allowed to apply only if they met a means test for dependency. Widower Leon Goldfarb challenged.

[19] 439 U.S. 357 (1979): Challenging Missouri's law that offered women an automatic exemption from jury pools.

[20] 518 U.S. 515 (1996): Challenging the Virginia Military Academy's male-only admissions policy.

fiber of her being. I like listening to the cases because most of them have a good outcome that aligns with my politics and all that bullshit, but mostly, I listen because she is powerful. Powerful like Eddie Murphy in *Delirious*. She's casting spells that changed America.

Ruth Bader Ginsburg could have looked at the U.S. Constitution as a dead document. As a pile of chains intended to bind black Americans, Native Americans, women, and others into ignominy and slavery. She would have been right. She could have looked at a Fourteenth Amendment that no one thought protected her and agreed. She didn't. She saw the potential in the rules and ideals that our nation's founders so imperfectly built into the governing documents of the country. She imagined herself into the Constitution, then she made it real.

A lot of people say the Constitution and the Declaration of Independence are lies. I agree with them. Ideas like equal protection, freedom of speech, and life, liberty, and the pursuit of happiness have never been real. I also think the best thing about America is its lies. Like a declaration of intention, like a New Year's resolution, those lies don't describe the country as it is; they contemplate a future of what we wish could be. Those lies are words after words after words, and they are powerful.

So in my much lowlier, much lesser, much more frivolous situation, I could dismiss Eddie Murphy as a bigot and a homophobe. I could say stand-up comedy doesn't want me and has never needed me. I could accept that many spells have been cast in this world of comedy to ensure that I am always the object of a joke, not a subject. But I won't.

Of all the things Eddie Murphy taught me, the power of my own perspective is the most important. The substance of his material may be dehumanizing to me, but the structures he used taught me to liberate myself from other people's narratives. When Margaret Cho got her first comedy special in 1994, she came onstage in a leather suit, just like Eddie Murphy. His material may have been grossly misogynistic, homophobic, and dehumanizing to Asians. The Notorious C.H.O. didn't care about that. She used the powers she learned from Eddie Murphy—perspective, swagger, and leather suits—to weave her female, Asian, queer narrative into stand-up. I learned that power from her.

Gay men are terrified of our own perspective. We love perspective, other people's perspectives, rarely our own. We write for other people, we act and use other people's words, we lip-synch and use other people's voices. We fear using our own perspective because it endangers us. It lays our desires and weaknesses bare. Camouflage is our defense. But defense isn't enough. It is survival, nothing more. It is managing your status as an object. Perspective is power.

That's why I will continue to love *Eddie Murphy: Delirious*, and why I will continue to do stand-up comedy. To keep casting spells, to use the tools I learned from Eddie Murphy and Margaret Atwood and Ruth Bader Ginsburg to add my perspective to this art form, and maybe teach straight people to look through my eyes on occasion. I'm not doing it because it's noble. I'm doing it because it's fun. I'm doing it because I've wanted since childhood to feel the kind of confidence and certainty that Eddie Murphy slathered across that stage, the kind of precision and acuity Ginsburg had behind that podium at the Supreme Court. I'm doing it because I've always wanted to be a hero, and a hero's got to have a monster to fight.

THREE WOMEN AND A
MULTINATIONAL CORPORATION

IN THE EARLIEST DAYS of 2004, I wanted a thing more intensely than I had ever wanted a thing before, more intensely than I have wanted a thing since. Impossible intangibles that I have desired—to be beautiful, to be immortal, perfect abs, the complete spiritual love of 2009 Chris Pine, telekinetic powers—however impossible these things are and however much I have futilely hoped for them, none was as deep as the longing of 2004.

Let us step back to the middle of 2003. Two new comics had shown up on the San Francisco scene. They were attractive young women, so all the male comics descended upon them like hyenas on an impala carcass. I intervened and graciously extended an offering of my support and guidance to these callow new comedians. They gently humored me for a bit and then explained that they were experienced Los Angeles comedians who'd moved up to San Francisco to work for a small cable network. I, obviously, felt like an idiot.

A few weeks later, one of the women, Laura Swisher, asked me to be in a video she was making for the show she hosted. The network was TechTV, a cable network about technology that some guy who founded Microsoft but wasn't Bill Gates started when he wasn't busy owning the world's largest yacht. The show was a late-night talk show about random bits of magic from the Internet; it was called *Unscrewed with Martin Sargent*. It was basically like *Tosh.0* or *Web Soup* but eight years too early and three times less funny. Laura was doing a video about the new, dazzling trend of flash mobs, and she needed one sad man to be a flash mob of his own. I drove in to San Francisco, danced around for an afternoon in a tutu, then watched myself a few days later on what was *barely* television. I was proud of myself.

By this point in my career, I'd gotten fired from that one legal job, then I'd gotten hired by a company that telemarketed for high-end tech clients. I *briefly* quit that job to be campaign manager for a woman running for Oakland City Council, then realized that she expected the job to be something more akin to a body servant than a political consultant, so I quit her campaign and begged the telemarketing place to take me back. They did. She won her campaign and became one of Oakland's least successful mayors.[1] I stayed at the telemarketing job over a year after that, but eventually, I realized, I had to face my real life. I convinced the HR manager at the telemarketing place to include me in a bout of layoffs[2] so I could receive unemployment, and I started aggressively applying for jobs as a lawyer.

It was in these circumstances that I performed said dance in said tutu for Ms. Swisher, and you can imagine my reaction when Ms. Swisher called me a few weeks later to tell me that her show would be

---

[1] When Mayor Jean Quan ran for reelection in 2014, she got 15 percent of the vote. As an incumbent. This was largely the result of her handling of the 2011 Occupy Oakland protests, where she visited and supported the protestors, then authorized use of tear gas, rubber bullets, and flash grenades to disperse the protestors. She wasn't great at her job.

[2] Look, if I'd gotten fired, I would tell you.

needing a new online-content writer. The job was amazing, with full benefits and a very respectable salary. It would also mean that I'd get to be a writer—better yet, that I didn't have to be a lawyer.

The show sent me the writing packet, and it had a very tight turn-around. I stayed up all night working on it and, a few days later, got called in for an interview. Then another interview. Then an assurance that I would find out in two to three days. For nearly a week, I stared at a phone—a landline, no less—waiting for it to ring. Fearing it would and fearing it wouldn't. Fearing I wouldn't be home to get it. Knowing that the thing I wanted was a thing I wanted so bad there was no way that phone could ever ring and deliver me from the drudgery of the law to the broad, sunny uplands of a career as a professional comedy writer. There was no way that phone could ring.

It rang. I was there to answer it.

Dick

I have previously expressed that *The Dick Van Dyke Show* occupied an important place in my childhood. It provided me with an idyllic vision of suburban domesticity, but it was also the first place I saw a creative workplace represented. The premise of *The Dick Van Dyke Show* is that Rob Petrie is a nice suburban dad who is the head writer of a variety show in New York. It's two shows, really: a suburban family sitcom and an urban workplace sitcom. Actually it was three shows, because the cast was constantly pulling out vaudeville skills like singing, dancing, and stand-up comedy, so it was sort of a variety show, too. However many shows it was, it seemed like the best possible life a human could live.

The Dick Van Dyke Show was originally based on Carl Reiner's real life as a writer for *Your Show of Shows*. Yes, Richie Petrie is Rob Reiner and Laura Petrie is that woman who says "I'll have what she's having" in *When Harry Met Sally*. It was also not the only attempt to mythologize the magic of the *Your Show of Shows* writers' room. *Laughter on the*

23rd Floor is a Neil Simon play about his time working there; *My Favorite Year* was a play Mel Brooks produced about his time there. Why are these guys spending so much time writing about a workplace almost no one has experienced firsthand?

One answer is that they're lazy. A writers' room is where they work—they just want to write about their own lives.

One answer is that it cuts out a middleman. Workplace sitcom writers' rooms are full of people writing jokes to put into the mouths of the employees of some fictitious business. In a show about a writers' room, the business is jokes. There's no clean-up on aisle three like on *Superstore* or app to launch like on *Silicon Valley*—it's just jokes on jokes on jokes.

But the real answer is people want dish. We want to know how the sausage gets made. You didn't come here for all this rhapsodizing about life as a writer. You've slogged through hundreds of pages of my turgid, self-congratulatory cultural "analysis," and now you finally get what you came for: me telling you which famous people I worked with are fun-crazy and which are batshit-crazy.

Comcast[3]

In January 2004, I began my professional writing career as an Associate Online Producer at TechTV. If two things defined the viewership of TechTV, it was that, one, they were extremely technically knowledgeable about the subjects that were discussed on the network, and, two, they were male. Five months into my employment, TechTV was purchased by G4, I was moved down to Los Angeles, and these facts became even truer. My faggy, political, video game–ignorant comedic voice wasn't an obvious fit for these Axe body spray–saturated networks. The people

---

[3] This section is for a very small subset of people who care what TechTV and/or G4 actually were. If you're not a committed nerd who really wants to know what Olivia Munn smelled like, just skip to the next section.

who hired me loved me and thought I was funny, but that didn't assuage my fear. On my first day of the job, as on my first day at every writing job since, I've understood exactly why I wasn't a perfect writer for the show, then tried to do everything I could to try to turn myself into that.

Here are the biggest lessons I learned from my four years writing for a network for straight guys:

1. Find the parts of your voice that overlap with the show's voice, and let those parts grow.
2. If you're writing a joke about a thing you don't know about, make sure it's not just factually correct but tonally correct.
3. Fall in love with the people you write for. If you can appreciate their strengths, you'll write to them.

Eventually, I also learned:

4. If you're authoritative and funny, you can make teenage boys be fascinated by anything.[4]
5. When you can tell your show is about to be canceled, start stealing office supplies. Everyone else is losing their job, too, so they won't notice.

I learned to be a functional, competent little writer at G4. My last job there was as head writer of *X-Play*, a video game review show that had sketches in it. The hosts, Adam Sessler and Morgan Webb, were funny, kind, and knew more about video games than nearly anyone on the staff. The fanboys of G4, who would grow up to become the trolls who gave us Gamergate, cut their teeth challenging the "real gamer" status of Adam and Morgan. This was ridiculous. I was the one who knew nothing about video games. They were, if anything, the last line of editorial defense against my ignorance. If I'd gotten something wrong, I

---

[4] Adam Sessler once insisted on including a Betty Friedan joke on *X-Play*.

knew that in the read-through. Adam or Morgan would just say "That's not right." It extended beyond just video games. In once script I wrote a line that began "Gravity is strong . . ." Morgan just said, "No it isn't, it's the weakest of the four fundamental forces." That's the kind of TV hosts I was working with there: ones who'd lovingly school you on anything from *Disgaea* to modern feminism to physics. It was quiz bowl as a workplace. It was pretty great.

I worked on that show for two years, and I might have stayed longer if it hadn't become clear that I was no longer welcome on-camera.

See, the whole time I was at G4, I was doing bit parts in sketches. It was fun and meant I occasionally got recognized by nerds on the street. Over time, the nice bosses who'd hired me went away and were replaced by men in their fifties desperately trying to pander to men in their early twenties. They wanted boobs and dudes wearing leather wrist cuffs. To them, having a bald fat gay guy on-camera seemed somewhat at odds with G4's purpose. I stopped getting cast in stuff. I felt a little shallow for being mad that I wasn't getting to be on-camera, but fundamentally, I felt like the executives didn't trust me anymore. I'd guided the show's voice for two relatively successful years, but now they seemed to think my instincts weren't "male" enough for the show.

That's when I learned the importance of workplace whining.

G4 was part of Comcast, which meant that for the last few years, we shared offices with E! Entertainment Television. That meant that the guy whose desk was directly opposite mine was a very thin, very attractive, very catty gay guy, Jesse. On my first day in the office, I laughed loudly, as I do, and Jesse leaned into the cubicle next to his and stage-whispered to the muscular accountant next to him, "If I have to listen to that laugh every day, I'm going to hang myself."

We were soon the dearest of frenemies.

So I was DM-bitching to Jesse about the growing lack of respect I was feeling from the G4 higher-ups. Normally, Jesse would tell me to stop complaining so he could go back to talking about the hot guy he'd almost-fucked in Laguna Beach the previous weekend, but this time he just asked, "Would you want another job?"

I said yes. He gave me writing packet guidelines for one of the shows that his boss oversaw, *Chelsea Lately*. The deadline was the next day, and I stayed up all night writing it. I submitted, and a week later, I had the job.

Oh, and to answer your question, Olivia Munn smells like expensive hair products and the Nietzschean Will to Power.

Chelsea

Chelsea Lately paid me roughly three times what I'd made at G4. That's important. For you to properly understand the fear echoing in my brain from the moment I got that job, you really have to get that fact. In the most fundamental of ways, I didn't think I deserved it.

Even at my interview, I was, to some extent, apologizing for my inadequacy. I referenced one of the jokes in my packet and said it was a pretty obvious joke. Sue Murphy, the senior writer on the show and a comic I'd admired for years, leaned in and said, "Yes, it's obvious, but someone in the room has to say it." That's what being a comedy writer is: someone who says all the jokes, then figures out which ones are actually funny.

At G4, we'd written everything on our own. We'd have read-throughs, and maybe do a bit of group punch-up here or there, but our work was primarily done alone at a desk. That's not how a late-night show works. At *Chelsea Lately*, we went into a room at nine every morning, we brought up all the important pop culture news from the night before, and we did our best to say all the jokes, then figure out which ones are funny before eleven a.m. There was nowhere to hide.

The first day, I went into the writers' room at nine sharp. No one else was there. When someone finally did enter—my office-mate, Heather McDonald—she told me I couldn't sit where I was sitting. Everyone had an assigned seat, so I had to sit where the writer I was replacing sat. Since then, any time I've started work on a show, I discreetly ask one of the experienced writers where I should sit. They always have a clear answer.

The writers filed in, then Chelsea. This was back when she was somewhat famous, before she became extremely famous in 2010, then settled back down to quite famous around 2016. She was bright and enthusiastic and personable. By the time we went into the writers' room, she'd already been up for three or four hours, working out and engaging in the innumerable wellness and restorative rituals of Los Angeles ladies, so she always arrived in workout clothes, slightly sweaty. She was usually chomping on a breakfast that would be unidentifiable to a midwesterner: a box of arugula, eighteen ounces of lean turkey, a beet and turmeric juice. Since it was my first day, she opened up with a brief interrogation. "Where are you from?" "Do you have any brothers or sisters?" "When were you last penetrated?" It was polite hazing that did the work of making me uncomfortable so I could settle in and get comfortable. After a few more, she shoved her arugula aside and we got to the business of jokes.

Pitching in a room is like Double Dutch: You have to see the rhythm of how it's working, then jump in at exactly the right time so you're not interrupting or getting interrupted. I had pitched jokes, yes, but this was my first time in the room of a daily show. My best friend, Ryan,[5] had reminded me that on your first day at a job, you're allowed to just observe and learn.

Here's the thing, though: You can't be scared of pitching. You can be cautious, you can self-censor to ensure quality. However, if you're keeping quiet, you're fundamentally assuming that if they hear the joke you really want to pitch, they're not going to like it. I have totally seen people try to be quiet and stay under the radar and not offend. In the long run, it will not work, and on a late-night show, or a cable show with a small staff, it's impossible. They hire people to make jokes. Give them your best, and if they don't like your best, the show's not a good fit for you. Or the profession isn't.

Finally, on that first day, I reached the moment when I had a joke

---

[5] Yet another of the plethora of gay Ryans in my life.

that was too good to not add. I tossed it in. I learned the rhythm. I became part of the show. I started feeling like I'd earned that money.[6]

It was fun to be writing for a woman's voice. Getting to pitch jokes about my pussy or my period was a change. Plus, it was a show with a woman in charge, with a writing staff that was half women. From eyebrow threading to unwanted sexual attention from your dad's male friends, women's experiences weren't novelties, they were the backbone of the show.

My voice wasn't perfect for the show, though. In my first weeks, a couple of my jokes that Chelsea attempted to use fell flat. In each case, the joke relied on a specific word order. She doesn't work like that; she can never be certain to deliver a phrase exactly the way it was written. I adapted: I stopped pitching jokes that hinged on word order and followed her comedic lead. Chelsea's jokes are about perspective. She doesn't need funny phrasing, she needs an opinion. If you can help her find that, she'll figure out how to make it funny.

Chelsea was astoundingly kind and generous along the way. She was always giving women handbags or shoes, periodically pulling money from her purse to shove at someone. One day a few weeks into my tenure, she stalked through the office, asking people if they were under thirty. If they said yes, she handed them a hundred-dollar bill. She always got us extravagant birthday presents, and since she could never figure out how to shop for me, mine was usually just five hundred dollars. We could say it's because she could never really understand me, that I was too dorky or complex for her to grasp. Really, it was like your grandma giving you a check for your birthday—it may be impersonal, but it's way better than the aunt who buys you a sweatshirt that doesn't fit.

She wasn't just financially generous—she was a level of emotionally aware that I've never experienced in a male boss. The best example

---

[6] Okay, the joke wasn't that great. If I remember correctly, we were discussing Britney Spears getting probation for driving without a license, and I said, "If Britney goes to jail, who's going to neglect Sean Preston and Jayden James?" This was before her conservatorship made such jokes in bad taste.

happened when I'd been working there almost a year. A newer writer, Jen Kirkman, had been hired after I was, and one day when we were trying to figure out new female comics to have on the roundtable, Jen said with polite self-confidence, "I'd like to do it." I felt silly. I wanted to do the roundtable so badly, but I'd been scared to say anything. The people at work barely knew that I did stand-up. I was mad at myself for not having Jen's basic level of professional self-confidence.

That evening, I emailed Chelsea personally and said that while I wasn't a female comic, I would appreciate a chance to do the roundtable. She was polite but dismissed the request.

A few months later, we were at the morning meeting. It was that magical time before the work had started and when everyone was drinking coffee and talking about what they did the night before. Jen mentioned that she was going to be doing her first late-night set on *The Late Late Show with Craig Ferguson*. My heart immediately sank as I was once again reminded that people who pursued their stand-up careers more aggressively than I—like Jen—got opportunities. I was mad at myself for being lazy. That was a moment, a flash in the eyes, before I put on a responsible smile and told Jen how proud and impressed I was.

Later, when we went back to our offices to write up the jokes that had been pitched,[7] I asked my office-mate, Heather, if she'd noticed me being glum when Jen revealed her news. Heather assured me that it was all in my head and no one had noticed.

Two hours later, Chelsea Handler was in my office, asking me if I was ready to do the roundtable.

That's the kind of person she is. She notices people, and she cares.

I got a lot out of the show. Once I was on the roundtable, I started to become famous; managers wanted to represent me, then agents. I started opening for Chelsea, and then the comedians from the roundtable started touring together. It was the biggest, longest, best oppor-

---

[7] That's how low-rent and cable the show was. Our writers' assistant didn't type up the jokes, we did.

tunity I've had in my career. Most importantly, Chelsea did everything humanly possible to get me laid as much as possible. Three years at that show changed my life.

And there were bad things. All the bags and shoes and money and trips meant we were in a constant state of competition. When I first got there, the key issue was that there were only seven seats in the private jet that Chelsea took on her quasi-monthly trips to Mexico, so everyone was jockeying to be one of her six favorite people in time to get asked along on the trip. My strategy was just to ignore it and do my job, but Chelsea didn't want that. She came from a large family, and she liked the push and pull of sibling squabbles. She wanted us to be fighting for her love, though not too hard.

It got worse as the rewards got bigger. Opening for her stand-up tour could net one of us twelve thousand dollars in a weekend. Spots on the roundtable fueled our solo touring and facilitated getting other jobs. We became buzzy—each of us had a manager in our ear telling us how we were going to be the breakout star of the show—and we were all, in our way, clamoring for more.

Things got bad when one of the other writers decided I was a threat to his position. He was very close to Chelsea and had reduced his work-load on the show to half-time so he could act as one of the executives of her production company. And I suspect he didn't like the idea that she trusted and respected my taste, so he did a lot of talking about how full of myself and irresponsible I was. Some of it was true: I was working on a lot of outside projects, and I was periodically a few minutes late to work. He mentioned that a lot.

I should have responded. I should have talked shit at him or crit-icized him behind his back. If I'd played the game, perhaps Chelsea would have understood me better. My strategy was to keep my head down, do my job well, and try to get one of my other projects off the ground. It didn't work.

Chelsea came to me and said she was going to be hosting the MTV Video Music Awards. She wanted me and this other guy to write for her. I told her I was working on another project that was due, and I was sorry, but I couldn't do it. She walked out of the room and didn't speak to me for a month.

It was bad. I was worried about how much my new, glamorous life depended on her good graces. She'd given me so much, and so much could be taken away just as easily. I worked harder on getting something else, another job, selling a show. I needed something stable in case she really stopped liking me.

And the dude, that unnamed writer, he redoubled his efforts. Heather dutifully reported all the stuff he said when I was out of earshot. It was mostly about how disloyal I was. I was. I was scared of the emotional complexity of the workplace, and I was trying to figure out an exit strategy. That's pretty disloyal.

We all ended up writing the VMAs together, and they were quite bad. In the end, Chelsea seemed to spend more time focused on how she'd look in her dress than how funny the monologue would be. Being a female celebrity is a mindfuck I will never understand, and Chelsea, nearing the peak of her success, was tormented by the constant scrutiny of her appearance. It was hard to watch, although not as hard to watch as those VMAs.

As a reward, Chelsea took us all to Mexico, and it seemed like things were healed. She and I were talking again. Maybe we'd learned a lesson about working with each other.

Of course, we hadn't. A month later, MTV wanted to buy a TV show I'd created. Chelsea had previously optioned the script, but the option had lapsed. Now my managers were going to be the producers, and they assured me that if I stayed with Chelsea, she'd insist on being a producer, too, and that would ruin everything.[8] They told me it was time for me to quit *Chelsea Lately*.

I was freaked out. I called my agent for advice. He said I shouldn't do anything rash, then our connection cut out as I went under an overpass.

---

[8] It wouldn't have ruined everything. It would have made my show infinitely more sellable and producible. It just meant they'd make marginally less money. I was too old and too law-schooled to not see this conflict of interest, but I didn't.

I didn't call him back. I figured if I didn't do anything rash, it wouldn't be a big deal.

I didn't do anything rash. Instead, I did something stupid. The Sunday of that weekend was Halloween, which you will remember I consider a gay High Holiday. The following day, we were supposed to be at work early to accommodate one of Chelsea's movie shoots.[9] When I came home on Halloween night, drunk and dressed as Suzanne Sugarbaker from *Designing Women*, my press-on nail accidentally hit the wrong button on my alarm clock. That meant my alarm didn't go off at six. That meant I woke up in makeup and a dress ten minutes before I was supposed to be at work. That meant when I finally made it to work, Chelsea was pissed.

She had already been pissed. See, at that point in time, Chelsea and I were repped by the same agency, and when my agent had gotten off the phone with me, the first thing he'd done was tell his boss's boss, who was Chelsea's agent, that I was considering leaving. Chelsea and Tom, the showrunner, were having none of it. This lateness was but the last in a line of treacheries I'd committed. When I showed up, Tom told me to just leave and come back the next day.

I left, chilled. I wrote an apology to Chelsea, then wondered if it was the right thing to do, then didn't send it. The next day I returned to the office and quietly did one responsible day of work. Chelsea was gone shooting a movie, so I stayed at my desk, avoiding eye contact. At the end of the day, Tom called me into his office. He told me to take the week off and come back able to say that *Chelsea Lately* was my singular priority. No more screenwriting work, no more meetings, no more auditions. *Chelsea Lately* and nothing else. I couldn't. The show was great and had given me so much money and popularity, I didn't know how I'd live without it. That scared me. I got scared that if I stayed at the show, I'd be too happy to push myself to do something more substantial. Mostly, I was mad that Tom and Chelsea didn't respect my actual contribution

---

[9] *This Means War.*

to the jokes on the show. I did my job and I did it well; if they wanted something else out of an employee, it shouldn't be me.

I simmered on these questions for a few days, and the issue I couldn't let go of was that I was good at my job. I wrote more good jokes every day than most of the people in that office. I did my work quickly and responsibly. That didn't matter to Tom and Chelsea, and at a workplace where that didn't matter, I'd never really feel safe. On Wednesday of that week, Tom and I talked on the phone. I told him it was probably time for me to leave. I immediately regretted it.

Chelsea didn't like this. We were a family, and families fight, but families stick together. She emailed me and told me she was going to talk to me and figure it out. I was terrified, all of this stuff terrified me, but I felt like maybe the situation could be healed. Maybe there was professional respect that would shine through. She was in Vancouver shooting *This Means War*. She told me she would call me on Saturday.

That particular Saturday was the weekend before my birthday, and my friends and I had scheduled to go to Palm Springs to celebrate. I spent the entire morning by the pool at the Ace Hotel, sick to my stomach and not drinking so I could be clearheaded for the telephone call that was supposed to unfuck my life. Fifteen minutes before it was supposed to happen, I scurried away to my darkened room and waited for the call. And waited. And waited. Eventually, Chelsea's assistant called to tell me she was going to dinner with Reese Witherspoon and she'd talk to me the following morning.

The upset stomach stayed. And the fear. The hope and the doubt. The following morning, while my friends were at breakfast, I sat in my car, waiting, waiting. This time it was a text, or an email, or a call. Another hour. We sat by the pool, they drank, I waited. It got late, and we drove back to Los Angeles. My weekend and birthday consumed.

Finally, she called. It was night, I'd dropped off my friends and was sitting in my car on Santa Monica Boulevard. She wanted an apology. She wouldn't say it, but that was all she wanted, it was clear. She wanted to berate me and for me to fall prostrate and beg forgiveness. All she wanted was theater. It wasn't that much, and I had fucked up in a number of ways, but I didn't apologize. Maybe I couldn't. After two days of waiting and fearing and not being her priority, after months of her weighing that asshole writer's backstabbing as more valuable than the jokes I contributed to her show, I was done. I just remember I kept saying, "It's probably for the best if I go."

Joan

What followed were the roughest eighteen months of my life. I couldn't find work, my agents (who were Chelsea's agents, to remind you) dropped me, and my managers were semi-aware they'd fucked up. No one related to *Chelsea Lately* would work with me; few would talk with me.

I had savings, I had a tour of college shows booked, but that was it. My managers represented mostly scripted TV writers, so they never knew when late-night shows were hiring. They just kept sending me on endless development meetings where I'd get homework to create a show, then get notes, then more notes, then more notes, then finally get to pitch it, then finally have it not sell.

I was running out of money. A friend recommended me for a job as a "producer" for *Punk'd* at Ashton Kutcher's production company. It was a terrible job, it paid terribly, and it wasn't writing, it was figuring out creative ways to demolish the cars of supporting cast members of the *Twilight* franchise.

I was *really* regretting not just apologizing to Chelsea.

Then I got the following DM on Twitter: "Sweetheart, not sure how superbusy you are/aren't, but any interest in writing bitchy jokes for Joan Rivers? I need to hire a couple damaged souls for the upcoming awards specials. Interested?"

It was from Tony Tripoli, a gay comic I'd performed with a couple of times but didn't know well. The message was like water to a parched man in the desert. I'd gone a full year without writing jokes profession-ally, and I needed it, bad. A few emails later, Tony was explaining to me that I'd be coming to Melissa Rivers's house in Malibu to watch the Golden Globes with Joan Rivers. It wasn't just a job. It was my childhood dream.

Of course, I showed up slightly late. As this had been one of the key issues in ruining my relationship with Chelsea, I was torturing myself about how Joan might react to this. I hadn't calculated the long drive to Malibu, or the fact that there would be traffic in Beverly Hills because the Golden Globes were happening there, so I arrived a few minutes after red-carpet arrivals had begun. No one cared. A maid greeted me and took me to the TV room where Joan Rivers sat in a house dress with her grandson, Cooper; Tony, the head writer of *Fashion Police*; and the legendary drag queen Jackie Beat. It turned out to be Jackie's first day writing for *Fashion Police*. I was a huge fan of Jackie's, but I was so busy trying to rationalize how I was in the same room with Joan that I didn't have time to be intimidated by Jackie.

Joan gestured to a huge array of deli sandwiches and told Jackie and me to help ourselves. I figured I'd wait until everyone else showed up to eat a sandwich, failing to realize that everyone had shown up. Joan had simply purchased three dozen sandwiches to feed the six of us (Melissa was also there, in a tennis dress).

So it was intimidating, it was awe-inspiring. It was what I'd dreamed of since watching Joan guest-host *The Tonight Show* in the 1980s. My job, however, was to be funny. Tony was at a laptop, and we were supposed to be coming up with material for the show. The rest of the writers were watching the awards at the E! offices, but Joan always had a few writers in her living room with her because their riffs could get hers going.

I didn't make jokes in that room in spite of being intimidated. I didn't fight through the fear. I made jokes *because* I was intimidated. I was so scared and so awestruck that I had to do *something* to prove my worth. I made jokes, I laughed at Joan's and Tony's and Jackie's, and pretty soon I felt like I was watching an awards show and ridiculing celebrities with my mom.

Afterward, Tony, Jackie, and I drove back to the E! building to join the other writers. Joan was getting a few hours' rest. We wrote all night, then at four thirty the following morning, Joan arrived for us to pitch jokes to her. What I'm saying is I saw 2012 Joan Rivers with no makeup. It is an image I shall not soon forget.

That's me being catty. Here's me being reverent: A seventy-eight-year-old woman working on three hours' sleep sat for two hours, processing and evaluating jokes about celebrities most people haven't heard of. She was pitiless and exacting in narrowing the jokes down to the ones she thought were strongest, then she was whisked off to hair and makeup. After sixteen hours of continuous work, the writers were exhausted but sipped coffee because we still had to go to the taping at ten.

I watched, anxious. Would one of my jokes make it on? Would I prove my worth? At *Chelsea*, I'd never counted how many jokes I got on—I'd known I did good work—but here, after a year in the wilderness, I needed it. I wanted it. And it came. She used one,[10] then another,[11] then another.[12] At one point, Giuliana Rancic made a comment about Heidi Klum's Native American–inspired outfit that perfectly set up one of the jokes I'd written, one that Joan hadn't picked to go on tele-prompter for the show. She effortlessly recalled the joke and lobbed it out to beautiful effect. "It's interesting that Heidi Klum is dressed as a Native American because I've always had reservations about her career." It was exciting to think that doing something you love could keep you that intellectually spry into your late seventies.

Fashion Police was a part-time job. I had to do it while I was still working at *Punk'd*. At one point I had to sneak away from a prank we were playing on Drake to print out jokes so I could drive to Joan's house immediately after filming. It was a lot of work without much pay, but

---

[10] On Lea Michele in a silver dress: "She looks like a filling."

[11] On Channing Tatum and Jenna Dewan: "I'm so glad Channing's wife could get the night off at Cheesecake Factory."

[12] On Zooey Deschanel: "You know Zooey just started a website to encourage women to do comedy. I just started a website to discourage Zooey from doing comedy."

getting to write actual jokes meant a lot to me, as did learning from Joan. I was driving from Drake to Joan Rivers. Life wasn't so bad.

Here's the biggest lesson I learned from Joan Rivers. Our writers' meetings weren't pitch meetings like we had at *Chelsea*; they weren't everyone riffing jokes together. We all wrote jokes on our own, then read them to Joan, who decided which she wanted to use. At one meeting, I had a joke that referenced kombucha. Everyone at the table laughed, including Joan. Tony then took Joan to the makeup room and, when he returned, told us that as soon as they'd left the room, Joan had taken his arm and asked what kombucha was. She then had him explain it thoroughly, and how it worked in the context of the joke.[13] Other people would have dismissed it, said, "I don't get it," and moved along. That's not what Joan did; she learned. If a joke got a good laugh, she wanted to know why and to be able to use that power.

She also did some terrible things. Joan was obsessed with having the best, strongest writers she could get (for cheap). Every week, you didn't know whether you'd be coming back to *Fashion Police*. You had to be asked back every time. It was like a mechanical bull. A lot of people got thrown off after a week. Some would last four to six weeks, then meet their fate. A few, like me and Jackie, managed to stay on the bull long enough to be able to take it for granted.

Eventually, I got a real job, writing for *Awkward.* on MTV. After I left *Fashion Police*, the Writers Guild of America tried to unionize the show and get decent wages and conditions for the writers. Joan was scared of that: Unionization would have meant going from twelve or so part-time writers to five or six full-time writers like on *Chelsea*. Joan wanted to feel like she was getting the best that a roomful of people had to offer; she just didn't consider whether those people were making enough money to pay rent. I was sad that a show which had been such a lovely lifeline for me had turned into something sad and ugly. However, it made sense:

---

[13] I'm sorry I don't have the joke. It may not have been kombucha. It may have been Google Glass or Justin Bieber's fragrance, Someday. All I remember is that it was something very 2012.

Joan Rivers had to fight tooth and nail for everything she achieved, and she didn't know when to stop fighting. Eliza Skinner, an astounding comic and writer who worked with me on the show and was one of the leaders of the strike, put it best: "Joan Rivers is a bag of knives. Why are we surprised that she's cutting us now?"

Also, I once wrote a joke that Joan Rivers thought was too mean to tell, and I'm really proud of that.[14]

An Interlude

I started this chapter with the expectation of making it primarily about the experience of writing for women, of sharing women's voices, along with telling the story of why I left *Chelsea Lately*. People often want to know that. I planned to exclude my time writing for *Totally Biased with W. Kamau Bell* and *Billy on the Street*, but that's foolish. That's me, as a gay man, treating situations as more engaging because they are female. Yes, Mindy, Chelsea, and Joan are fabulous divas, but let us take a moment to consider the time I spent working for men.

The most distinctive aspect of working on *Totally Biased* was that it talked about race a lot. Kamau loves diversity, and he always wanted a writers' room with lots of voices, and he did a great job of putting those voices on the show. But most of the show was Kamau talking about the stuff he was interested in, and sometimes that meant movies or tax hikes, and sometimes it meant racial slurs I have no business having opinions about.

One day Aparna Nancherla, one of the other writers, and I were assigned to write a bit about the use of a certain racial slur in *Django Unchained*. Working from notes of what Kamau wanted to say, I was

---

[14] It was from the 2012 Grammys episode. Adele won five Grammys, and I said, "Usually, when Adele leaves with five of something, it comes with coleslaw and some biscuits." Joan thought it was very funny but didn't want to make fun of a woman for being fat. I had no business making fun of a woman for being fat, either.

typing it up. Aparna looked over my shoulder and said, "You can't just keep typing 'N*.' This has to go into the teleprompter." I told her I wasn't comfortable typing the word, and maybe she, a person of color, should do it. Aparna said, "Guy, I don't think me doing your job for you will make it less racist." That is why I love Aparna.

Working on *Totally Biased* was tough fun. Everyone was really excited about making comedy that came from a different perspective than most people were used to. But joking about politics, race, and gender can be hard. A white guy is going to make mistakes, and I am a white guy. When I inevitably ended up saying stupid stuff, people just told me I was wrong, I dusted myself off, and I kept pitching.

If *Totally Biased* was a lesson in learning to deal with a diverse group of writers tackling big problems, *Billy on the Street* was the opposite. It was a writers' room I was too similar to, tackling issues that were deliciously small. It presented its own problems.

The *Billy on the Street* writers' room is a think tank of queens (or, in some years, twink tank). Five to seven men and women with authoritative knowledge of all popular culture and the critical skills necessary to shade giants. I have never felt more understood by a writer's room, I've never felt more delighted by what a writer's room produced, I've never felt more redundant. Frankly, I was used to being the only gay in the room, and sitting in a room with younger, prettier ones (your Johns Early, your Joels Kim Booster, your sundry Virtels) who were just as funny as I was made me wonder what I was offering.

Billy Eichner, however, is one of the best creative managers I've ever dealt with. When he liked our material, he laughed, and he told us why it was great. When he rejected our material, he laughed even more. He always let us know he wished we could do something that mean or ridiculous or absurdist or frivolous. When I didn't know what I was bringing to the room at *Billy*, he did, and he reminded me regularly and generously.

I know, I wish I had more bitchy dish on these people, too.

Mindy

In the process of swinging from job to job, you sometimes have to swing to crap. In 2015, I'd been in New York working on *Billy on the Street*, and my landlord had figured out I was subletting and evicted me. Work on a season of *Billy* only lasted six months or so, so I was back in L.A. with no apartment, working a very shitty job at the VMAs. I mean, it's not the shittiest—I got to watch Nicki Minaj and Justin Bieber run through their dress rehearsals. But we weren't writing jokes for the host; we were just writing stupid, bland, boring host copy. Look, I'm thankful for any job, but more thankful for some than others.

So you can imagine my surprise when I was slogging through a gently-amusing-but-definitely-not-funny intro for Bruno Mars and I got a DM from a certified American icon, Mindy Kaling: "Guy, are you available for staffing right now by any chance? Hi!"

I'd met Mindy when we were in the movie *No Strings Attached*[15] together, but I didn't really know her beyond that. The offer came out of nowhere, like manna, or Taylor Swift dating Tom Hiddleston. As somebody who watched *The Mindy Project* religiously, I was thrilled.

I got the job. There were lots of jobs I didn't get, and I haven't told you about those. I have written hundreds of packets and sent hundreds of emails and hoped hundreds of hopes. That's not what this chapter is about. This chapter is about vacuous professional advice no one will actually pay attention to, and juicy stories about the famous ladies whom I've worked with.

Chelsea was a force of nature, and Joan Rivers was a legend, but Mindy Kaling was something even more daunting: She was a writer. Chelsea and Joan needed writers; they depended on them. Mindy is an exquisitely talented writer, trained at *The Office* with one of the stron-

---

[15] The one with Natalie Portman and Ashton Kutcher. The one with Mila Kunis and Justin Timberlake was called *Friends With Benefits*. We've discussed this before.

gest, smartest writing staffs ever assembled. At this point, I'd written on two sitcoms, and both of them were smallish cable operations with a lot of inexperienced staff. I'd been helpful there but didn't know how much I had to offer on a real network show.

One of the cool things was that I started midway through the season, so Mindy was already acting on the show. That meant I could get the feel of the room while she was on-set, and maybe be a bit more comfortable before I had to pitch in front of her.

Her writers' room was hardly less intimidating. Everyone there had written on *The Office*[16] or *The Simpsons*[17] or *30 Rock*,[18] except[19] my friend Chris Schleicher, who'd started at *The Mindy Project* straight out of college, and if you hear me saying someone got a sitcom writing job straight out of college, I think you can assume that college was Harvard and he was on the *Lampoon*. In Chris's case, that would be accurate. He was the first openly gay president of the *Harvard Lampoon*. Like I said, that room is intimidating.

A sitcom writers' room is a deeply hierarchical place. Everyone has a very specific title that doesn't indicate a specialization in work but, rather, a rank.[20] While I'd never been in one of these real, networky writers' rooms, I knew how the vibe was supposed to work. As my friend Christy Stratton Mann[21] had often told me, "In my day, being a staff writer meant you were supposed to talk once a day and expect that not a word you wrote would make it into the final draft of your script."

---

[16] Emmy winner Charlie Grandy.

[17] Emmy winner Matt Warburton.

[18] Emmy winner Tracey Wigfield and non–Emmy winning *underachiever* Lang Fisher.

[19] This is not entirely true. There are two other writers who didn't work for those shows, Ike Barinholtz and Dave Stassen, but they are both really hot, so intimidating in other ways.

[20] In descending order: executive producer, co–executive producer, consulting producer, supervising producer, producer, co-producer, executive story editor, story editor, staff writer.

[21] Go Gators!

That makes it hard, because you need to show deference, but you also have to prove that you're an asset to the writers' room. Figuring out the right moment to make a contribution, and making sure it's a good one that meets the tone of the room, takes finesse. I'm not great at finesse.

Luckily, it wasn't that bad. Since I was starting midway through the season, the room was in the middle of punching up a script that was already written. If we'd been at the beginning of the season, the room would have been breaking the story arcs for the episodes, and my contributions wouldn't have been particularly welcome or helpful. A staff writer isn't there to make major plot decisions; he or she is there to write jokes. I showed up when they needed jokes, and Double-Dutch-style, I managed to hop in and start playing along.

I found myself in a professional environment where I was appreciated, challenged, and the thing we've learned is super-important to me, respected. Mindy Kaling knows what shitty work looks like, and she will not accept it. She knows what good work is, and she loves people who work hard to share their talents with her projects. To say that at *The Mindy Project* I found the kind of professional environment where I work best doesn't mean I was a luminary in the room. I wasn't. I was surrounded every day by people who were funnier and better at writing TV than I was, and that forced me to be better. It was Berkeley quiz bowl all over again.

Joan Rivers was a legend, but even after I spent nearly a year working for her, I don't know that she knew my name.

Chelsea Handler is my family. People ask me if I like her. I always say, "I love her." That is different. One does not subsume the other. She gave me more than nearly anyone else has; she's also been cold to me in ways that only a family member would think to be. My relationship with her, and everyone I worked with at *Chelsea Lately*, is deep, probably deeper than my relationships with the folks at *The Mindy Project*, but that's only because we shared a crazy, chaotic, rewarding, and damaging experience together. The folks at *Mindy* and I just shared lunch and some laughs.

The bedrock of Mindy Kaling's friendships is respect. She wants respect and she demands it, and on the occasions when I gave less to the show than I could, she let me know, with respect. But she also gives a shit-ton of respect. The people around her know she doesn't just like them, she values their contributions.

And this is where I'm supposed to tie together my personal stories about Chelsea, Joan, Mindy, and Comcast's cable possessions with my analysis of *The Dick Van Dyke Show* to show you something new. I could make this seem like an insightful attempt to explore how writing for others has changed my own voice, or maybe some bullshit about gay ventriloquism through these three powerful ladies. Or I could admit that there are no great life lessons in this chapter, just some midlevel dish about why I left *Chelsea Lately*, professional advice on par with what you'd get at a South by Southwest diversity panel, and a fat joke about Adele. But maybe the life lesson is that we don't need life lessons. Maybe our lives are enriched enough by fat jokes about Adele.

IT NEVER RAINS IN SOUTHERN CALIFORNIA

MOVING TO LOS ANGELES is never going to be fun. It's tempting to imagine the terms on which it just *works*, like you're cast in some blockbuster movie or you're nominated for an Academy Award and you're beautiful and rich and beloved. You're moving into some glorious manse in the Bird Streets section of the West Hollywood Hills that you've seen on numerous episodes of *Million Dollar Listing: Los Angeles*. You could spend your life fictionalizing a story that involves you having enough money, power, beauty, sex appeal, and fame to move to Los Angeles like a queen. Even then, when you drove down a block of Sunset, you'd see thirty people who were so much hotter than you, and you'd feel like shooting yourself.

L.A. is a wonderful place. TV shows and movies and songs—mostly songs—will try to convince you that it's shallow and intellectually barren. This is rubbish. Los Angeles is a city populated by dreamers, and the minds of said dreamers are quick and powerful. It's paradise, a place more beautiful and full of possibility than you think real.

That's why coming here is terrible. It means confronting the extent to which you'll never be able to actualize all the potential in front of you. That's your problem—not Los Angeles's.

I moved to Los Angeles late in the summer of 2004. I have previously explained to you the events that liberated me from the indignities of life in the legal field and led me into America's creative classes. I've also told you that eight months after my hire, the network that had hired me was purchased by Comcast and two thirds of the employees were fired. I was one of said employees. I was then at an impasse. Did I accept my time in a creative job as errata on my plodding path into a boring life as a lawyer, or did I behave as though being a real, full-time comic was something I was able to do?

It would be cute if I'd gathered together my belongings and gotten in a car headed toward the Hollywood sign, but I didn't. The actual truth is that during my last two months at TechTV, the aforementioned dying cable company, I had, every morning, called a production company in New York that made some VH1 show I enjoyed, and left a message saying I'd like to work for them. It seemed like exactly the story of spunk you heard from people about how they'd managed to best the entertainment industry. After six weeks of calling, then a polite two-week cessation while the guy I was calling was on vacation, he called me back and told me I could come in and meet with them.

Thus, my journey to Los Angeles occurred by way of Manhattan. I officially went for the interview, but really I wanted to try my hand at stand-up in a bigger, realer city. It was depleting my limited severance pay, but it was also a first tiny gesture of belief that I might have the potential to make a career out of comedy. I didn't get the job, however.[1] What I got was a call from my former employers at TechTV, telling me that if I could be in L.A. by the first of August, I would have a job as a full, real writer for the show I'd been working for.

_____

[1] Why am I trying to milk this for dramatic tension when I just spent the last chapter detailing all the sweet writing gigs I've had?

The lesson of this story, children, is that the appearance of popularity matters. It is a very Los Angeles lesson. I did a moderate amount of buzzing about my rich job prospects on the Hudson, and those lovely, wonderful chumps at TechTV/G4 took the bait. God or The Universe or Lakshmi or *The Secret* had heard my gesture of belief in myself and had given me a chance at living a life based on commodified frivolity. All I had to do was move to Los Angeles.

One of my big theoretical points here is that no one moves to Los Angeles without an agenda. Occasionally, at parties, I will probe strangers by asking, "So, what's your Hollywood dream?" Usually, this involves a small bit of choreography, so it's really "So" (snap with both fingers) "What's your Hollywood Dream?" (point with both fingers). People *hate* this. They almost invariably begin by telling me that they do not have a Hollywood Dream, then, about five minutes later, explain that they originally moved to L.A. to be a screenwriter but now they're doing a lot of branded Snapchat content. There are certainly lawyers[2] and epidemiologists[3] who end up in the greater Los Angeles area for random "It's a big city" reasons, but for most of the people living in Los Angeles, the move was a specific and concrete declaration that they believed in their capacity to be a professional entertainer.[4]

I will often dismiss this idea of believing in my Hollywood Dream when it comes to my move. I will say that the job at G4 *forced* my move, and if I hadn't gotten it, I probably wouldn't have made the journey. Both of these statements are probably true, but they ignore the extent to which upending my life and moving to a place where I knew no one was a gesture of resolute self-confidence. Perhaps it was a gesture I didn't realize at the time, and God knows I love telling stories about how I lack the type of self-belief possessed by scrappy dreamers with

[2] My friends Kevin and Ryan! (This is a different gay Ryan.)

[3] My friend Sam!

[4] It's hard to believe *La La Land* didn't win.

better cheekbones than mine, but my move, no less than any other, was a declaration of "I can do this."

In Los Angeles, I rented a room in West Hollywood that was slightly too expensive. It was surrounded by gay guys who were all slightly too attractive. Meanwhile, I was surrounded by comics who were slightly too successful. Turned out that Los Angeles's overripe offerings were too much for me.

Three months later, I hid myself in a hole in West L.A. that was less expensive, less challenging, and less fun. I proceeded to hide from L.A. for the following two years.

✳

I distinctly remember sitting in my room in that too-expensive apartment in too-sexy West Hollywood and watching television. I was watching *Pilot Season* on Trio, a cable network about pop culture that has since died but gave us its only begotten son, Andy Cohen. I was very aware that there were too many shows in which Hollywood contemplated itself. At that point, we had *Pilot Season, Entourage, Curb Your Enthusiasm,* and *Greg the Bunny,* and within a year, they'd be joined by *The Comeback, Fat Actress, The Minor Accomplishments of Jackie Woodman,* and an almost forgotten film called *The TV Set.* I was oddly sickened by this need for an industry to mythologize itself, and I was terrified of how I might fit in to this story I'd decided to enter.

The two most important stories of Los Angeles from this mid-2000s crop are *Entourage* and *The Comeback.* Both have a central celebrity who's trying to ascend to the next level of success. In nearly every other way, they are different. *Entourage* is a fantasy of the Hollywood we wish existed for us, an attempt to purify happiness and success into an easily main-linable form. *The Comeback* is an autopsy, a forensic inquiry into the ways we tell ourselves what happiness is.

Entourage, for those of you who've managed to avoid its cultural presence for the past two decades, is the story of Vinnie Chase, a sexy young movie star on the verge of greatness, and the three buddies who

fill out his posse: his failed-actor brother, Johnny Drama; his manager, E.; and his chubby, pathetic friend, Turtle. The plot of every episode is the same. Vinnie's big chance at making it to the big time is put
in jeopardy, the boys put their devotion to one another above all other
things, and somehow their masculine solidarity catapults Vinnie on to
even more success. Jeremy Piven's hair plugs co-star.

Entourage is a comedy in the purest sense: In the end, things are
always fine. In Shakespeare, a tragedy ends with a death; a comedy
ends with lovers coming together and providing the specter of happy
heterosexual reproduction. *Entourage* didn't make many babies, but the
boys certainly did try a lot. In no other way is it a comedy: There aren't
really jokes on *Entourage*. Some of Ari's insults may qualify as such,
as might the stupid things Turtle says, but this show isn't about quips
or wordplay. *Entourage* is about excess. In the end, Vinnie always gets
more—more roles, more accolades, more women, more weed—and he
shares that largesse with his buddies. In the absence of wit, it is only this
untrammeled optimism and the thirty-minute running time that lets us
know *Entourage* is a comedy.

The presiding figure of Vinnie and the Boys' world is Ari, Vinnie's
agent, played by Piven. It's Ari's job to state the rules of the world and
introduce what passes for conflict in the plot. He must also berate his
gay assistant and his needy wife with condescension and glee. The terms
of the plot conflict do not matter. Oh, does E. need to get a director to
do Vinnie's movie? Does Vinnie need to pick the superhero movie over
the indie that a girl wants him to do? It doesn't matter, because the good
thing always happens. Ari's real role is to remind us of the moral code
of this world: Power is the goal, and power is achieved through loyalty
to your boys.

The Los Angeles of plenty that is imagined by *Entourage* is one created not by heterosexual procreation but from homosocial solidarity.
In *Entourage*, women are, at best, treasure, objects that are part of the
bounty that has been won by the boys for their correct performance of
masculinity. The most significant female character on the show, Ari's

wife, is, for the entire run of the series, known only by this title. She has no name. She is an appendage. A trophy and a whining burden.

Similarly, Ari's assistant for most of the series is a gay Asian man, Lloyd, who serves primarily as a sharpening stone for Ari's masculine power. Lloyd exists in trembling fear of Ari's berating tirades. He serves with selfless fidelity and deference. As a gay Asian man, Lloyd is representative of the identities that the jokes of 2005 categorized as least masculine. Rex Lee, a gifted performer, finds subversions in the performance, but the character as written is a sexless whipping boy. For in the world of *Entourage*, power makes masculinity and masculinity makes power.

So *Entourage* is a tight network of men whose mutual support leads to the seamless ascent of all. By the time of the *Entourage* movie, Ari is the head of a studio; Vinnie stars in and directs a hit film; Turtle has his own tequila line; E. has 10 percent of whatever Vinnie makes, as well as a beautiful wife and daughter; and Johnny Drama wins a Golden Globe. One suspects if this linear ascent were allowed to persist for a few more movies, Ari Gold would be a six-term president of the United States, and Vinnie Chase would be *The Young Pope*.

A key question in any comedy is "What is being ignored?" Comedy is a narrative form that attempts to see the world positively; to some extent, it must always be obscuring some aspect of the full human experience in order to maintain that positivity. Mel Brooks said, "Tragedy is when I cut my thumb; comedy is when you fall into an open sewer and die." When it's *your* thumb, you feel even the smallest of injuries, but when it's some other guy, you have the distance to see the charm in even egregious injury. Brooks doesn't make this poor schmuck break his leg. He kills him. Comedy is the joy of not having to feel all the pain.

What *Entourage* is ignoring is that no one's life is as good as Vinnie Chase's. No one always wins. Adrian Grenier, who is exactly as hot as Vinnie Chase, who is a movie star and a millionaire, who won at Hollywood—even he has not been in a movie you'd want to see since *The Devil Wears Prada* in 2005. Real people, even the most beautiful and successful, have failures. Vinnie Chase does not. Vinnie Chase—and thereby his boys—is playing through life with the cheat codes on. He cannot be defeated. He gets everything. That's not a real thing. It's as fantastical as Hobbits.

It may be easy to interpret my reading of *Entourage* as simple derision. Shitting on *Entourage* is easy, but it's not my goal. While *Entourage*'s storytelling is grossly unrealistic, I'd argue it is the story that powers Los Angeles. In *Entourage*, the show's creator, Doug Ellin, was able to essentialize the Hollywood Dream: eternal youth, beauty, and winning. Authors from Nathanael West to Billy Wilder to Randy Newman have tried to encapsulate precisely what makes L.A. tick, but most became enamored of the seedy underside of the story. They wanted to show you the rot created by the myth. *Entourage* is a magical land where that rot never touches our blessed boys. Vinnie may have occasional specters of failure, but they are always erased. Los Angeles is the hope that every day can be sunny, and *Entourage* lets you believe that so long as you are an attractive, heterosexual, not-too-short or too-fat or too-old white male, those sunny days can be yours.

The Comeback is set in this same land of plenty but makes very different choices about what it shows and obscures. I would say if *The Comeback* is about anything, it's about genre. In 2005, right at the time multicam sitcoms were losing prominence to single-cam sitcoms and reality TV, *The Comeback* analyzed how each of these genres created comedy through what they show and obscure. The questions at the core of the show are "What kind of laugh are you looking for?" and "Who's laughing?"

The Comeback tells the story of Valerie Cherish, an L.A. comic actress who had a successful five-season run on a multicam sitcom in the early 1990s. Her success was moderate, though. Her original series, *I'm It*, ended just short of the hundred episodes required for sitcom syndication and eternal money and glory. Valerie gets a chance at a comeback, however: She is cast in a multicam pilot, but she must agree to do a reality show about her comeback at the same time. Thus, we are presented with three rival renderings of comedy in three different genres.

The multicam sitcom-within-a-show on *The Comeback* is *Room and*

Bored, a sexy romp of the sort churned out in the late 1990s that aims to emulate Lisa Kudrow's original star vehicle, *Friends*. *Room and Bored* is set on the beach, presumably in Southern California, and features the low-stakes, simple-resolution conflict of a show like *Three's Company*. The jokes are hack. The writers all came from Harvard or Yale, but to sell out, they're cranking out pabulum we've all seen before. The director is the legendary James Burrows, but he's coasting by as the genre he helped create dies. The fact that Valerie Cherish takes her job slinging these jokes seriously in fact reduces her value in the estimation of the writer/producers. *Room and Bored* and, by extension, multicam comedy, is a bad, moribund genre of show made by exquisitely sharp and capable professionals servicing a backward-looking industry.

Yet the single-camera sitcom that we're watching, *The Comeback*, is an attempt to more closely echo the reality of what life is like for an aging actress in Hollywood. There's no laugh track; the characters are more rounded; our heroine faces actual emotional danger; and not everything works out great. We understand that Valerie Cherish's life has some similarities to Lisa Kudrow's, but that she has been sculpted into a heightened comic character. Single-cam comedy attempts to resuscitate TV comedy by asking us to see more of our character's reality and use pain to make joy more well-earned.

The reality show being shot about Valerie, confusingly also titled *The Comeback*, provides us with all the raw footage from behind the scenes of filming *Room and Bored*, but it is not seen by anyone in the show until the last episode of the first season. That is, this version exists according to the new rules being created for how we watch reality comedy shows. If *Room and Bored* is echoing *Friends*, then the reality-show-within-a-show *The Comeback* is being watched in the way we watched *The Osbornes* or *Here Comes Honey Boo Boo*. Through coercive editing of "real" events, it creates sharp, clear, simple reactions from viewers. The genre distances us enough to laugh at the tragedies befalling real people. It asks us to accept that no injury suffered by anyone on-camera can be that bad, because they're all famous people on TV.

The three competing approaches to comedy are placed in direct contrast in the last two episodes of *The Comeback*'s first season. After pressure from the network, the producers of *Room and Bored* finally give Valerie Cherish a big slapstick moment on the show. The multicam slapstick moment, a pratfall in a giant cupcake costume, is presented as hack and silly. No sophisticated viewer in 2005 is laughing at this.

But on the single-cam sitcom, we see the context: Valerie striving to perfect the pratfall despite her scoliosis; the callous producer, Paulie G, ignoring her hard work; Valerie reaching a boiling point and hitting the producer in the stomach; Paulie G vomiting; Valerie vomiting. Here the motivating factors are less contrived, the slapstick moment realer and grosser. It elicits from the viewer a sharper, realer laugh, but the humor is mixed with sadness and disgust. A sophisticated 2005 viewer would definitely react to this moment, but not entirely positively.

On the final episode of the first season of *The Comeback*, we see the moment when Valerie hits Paulie G and the subsequent vomiting—but through the lens of the reality show. The moment is stripped of context. To Valerie, it's shameful and embarrassing, but to the viewing public, it's just funny. Conclusion: Reality TV objectifies its participants into a different kind of light comedy.

If *Entourage* presents Los Angeles as a place of infinite power and glory for the taking, *The Comeback* explores it as a place where narrative is always controlling how much of that power and glory you have. *Entourage* shows us happy people in Los Angeles, but *The Comeback* shows us people in Los Angeles trying to tell the story of their own happiness by excluding the things that *Entourage* refuses to contemplate. Valerie wants to think about her TV show but not the water damage in her house. Paulie G wants to think of himself as a powerful Emmy-winning showrunner who gets blown by hot chicks, not a fat guy who had a childhood crush on Valerie. Valerie Cherish wants what Vinnie Chase has; it is perhaps her tragic flaw. She doesn't realize that Vinnie Chase's happiness is a thing that can exist only in fiction.

Andy Warhol said, "I love L.A. I love Hollywood. They're beautiful. Everybody's plastic, but I love plastic. I want to be plastic." Vinnie Chase is plastic. Valerie Cherish wants to be plastic. No human being can actually be plastic. Valerie Cherish is a fictitious character, but refusing to let Valerie be plastic imbues her with some of the magic of reality.

On *The Comeback*, Malin Akerman's character, Juna, is used to represent this misguided Hollywood dream. Juna is young, beautiful, and buzzy, just like Valerie used to be. Valerie covets all that Juna has, but every time we get a peek into Juna's perspective, we see someone with problems and indignities not so different from Valerie's. Valerie cannot imagine that Juna's it-girl status might fade like her own because she sees Juna as a flawless image of success—not a real, flawed, embattled person like Valerie has always known herself to be. Valerie never sees the water damage in Juna's house, so Valerie imagines her life is unsullied by such banalities. *The Comeback*'s central argument is that those banalities are important and beautiful, too.

We now laud *The Comeback* as a work of genius and tend to deride *Entourage* for its douchiness, but in 2005, that wasn't conventional wisdom. In the *New York Times* review of *The Comeback*, Alessandra Stanley contrasts the two: "'The Comeback' is interesting, but 'Entourage' is a more charming comedy: the missteps of actors on the way up are less painful to watch than the graceless freefall of actresses on the way down." Stanley sees it as a comedy's duty to protect her from the dangers of reality, but *The Comeback* argues that belief in the possibility of life without setbacks and complexity is the real danger.

The second season of *The Comeback* ends with a choice for Valerie: the image of clear, unalloyed happiness as she accepts an Emmy Award, or the complex, painful reality of going to the hospital room of her beloved hairdresser who's battling cancer. She chooses the latter, and for the first time in the series, she is represented not as someone *on-camera* but simply as a human being. She wins the Emmy, sure, but she accepts that the life she has off-camera matters more.

Entourage says L.A. is a comedy because everyone (we care about) is always succeeding. *The Comeback* says L.A. is a comedy because everyone is always failing, but in the end, they're all going to be fine.

✳

This is why I love L.A. My friend Ryan[5] once said, "Actors who go to New York want to act, and actors who come to L.A. want to be sexier versions of themselves." There's something so fun about being in a place where everyone's hungering for a thing they can't achieve and are always dissatisfied despite the fact that their lives are great, they're being paid to do fun things, and the sun is, at least 340 days out of the year, shining. But everyone in L.A. is a little bit sad because they're not as happy as Matt Bomer's head shot looks.

L.A. is particularly wonderful for a fat person. People are often confused by why I, a super-fat, not particularly physically attractive person, would want to live in West Hollywood, the ketamine-stoked crucible of shallow gay self-consciousness and derision. Let me answer that with a story.

My friend Matt Wilkas is insanely, ridiculously handsome. He has a square jaw, perfect abs, and luminous eyes. He and his Olympic-skier boyfriend[6] are regularly on lists of the hottest gay male couples. Matt sustained injuries during the course of playing Spider-Man on Broadway. He is a certifiable member of the gay-hot-person elite. When Matt moved from New York to West Hollywood, he complained about how inadequate he felt walking down the street in a tank top.

That is why I love L.A. I'm fat, I'm failing at L.A., but so is Matt Wilkas. So are Lisa Kudrow and Adrian Grenier and Matt Bomer. And in the end, we're all doing a lot better than anyone in Sacramento.

How much do I love Los Angeles? In 2014, we got a second chance to give *The Comeback*, Lisa Kudrow's greatest, purest performance, an Emmy. Nine years after our initial failure, we'd surely seen the error of our ways, given the series its very own comeback, and surrounded it with critical glory.

But we didn't.

We gave the Emmy to Julia Louis-Dreyfus, just one of the eleven

---

[5] This is the same gay Ryan.

[6] You know which one.

Emmys she'd received by then. Just one of the six she'd receive for the same role. The TV Academy not giving Lisa Kudrow an Emmy for *The Comeback* in 2014 is a grand lady in a ball gown slipping on a banana peel, picking herself up with as much dignity as she can recover, then slipping on the banana peel again. That's why I love L.A.

DURGA AND THE SLAYING
OF MAHISHASURA

EARLY IN THIS BOOK, I told you it was a survival guide.

It was a broad rhetorical gesture, intended to make you feel like you were going into something with powerful, life-and-death stakes. If I had really wanted to follow through on this premise, I probably should have ended each chapter with some suggested activities, possibly created some badges that could be earned for showing proficiency in various survival skills. I honestly thought there'd be more recipes for game meat and acorns in it. I should have at least told you guys how to build a lean-to.

This book isn't that kind of survival guide. This book is a guide to my own survival. I'm not telling you how to live your life, just detailing how I managed to make it through mine. It isn't a perfect or even an admirable life, but I thought you should have the chance to take a look at it and make your own judgments.

Once an interviewer asked Ruth Bader Ginsburg about her first legal job. Ginsburg was hired by a liberal New York law firm as a summer associate, but was not given an offer for a permanent position after graduation. The firm had hired a black woman as a lawyer, and didn't feel they needed to make any more gestures to prove their broad-mindedness. The interviewer asked if she was still angry about this dismissal of her skills. "Suppose they did offer me a job," Ginsburg responded. "Probably I would have climbed up the ladder and today I would be a retired partner." Instead she's a Supreme Court justice and one of the most successful oral advocates in American legal history. "So often in life," she continued, "things that you regard as an impediment turn out to be a great good fortune."

Ruth Bader Ginsburg certainly isn't saying oppression or discrimination are good things. They are not trials that ennoble us. What she's saying is life doesn't always follow the path you expected or hoped for, but everything you do, every skinned knee, every meltdown at a crush, every Secret Service raid on your house: They make you who you are, they give you strength and perspective.

And maybe along the way, you'll remember that you're a goddess.

Let me tell you the story of Durga.

There was this buffalo demon, Mahishasura, who was waging war against the Hindu gods. Well, he wasn't exactly a "demon"—that's a very Christian concept. He was this thing called an Asura, one of a group of powerful entities who were always waging war on the Devas, or, as we know them, gods. Mahishasura was a powerful warrior with the ability to shift shape, and he'd made Brahma, the god of creation, bless him so that no man could ever defeat him. Anytime the Devas would attack Mahishasura, he would just shift shape and defeat them. Vishnu tried turning into his incarnation as a man-lion, then as a boar, but Mahishasura always had a new and more powerful form. Shiva tried shooting a beam of destruction from his third eye, but nothing worked. Soon Mahishasura ruled over all of the world. Things weren't looking great for the Devas.

And the thing you need to know about Mahishasura is that he was pretty certain that all his powers and all of his invincibility meant he was king shit.

So all of the Hindu gods got together and realized the only way to defeat this powerful guy with the huge ego was to be a little selfless. They each took a piece of their female essence, called Shakti, and combined them. The combined energies became a blinding light, and then out of the light came an exquisitely beautiful woman with a thousand hands. This was Durga. The gods came forward, and each offered her their weapon. Shiva offered his trident, Vishnu his discus, Agni his spear, Vayu his bow and arrows. When all of her hands were filled with all the gods' weapons, Durga mounted a lion and rode to do battle with Mahishasura. When he heard about it, he laughed arrogantly. "She shall be my queen!" he said, and sent his generals to capture her. She cut both their heads off in a single stroke. He sent a thousand Asuras to bring down this proud woman, but she killed them all and drank their blood. One by one, Durga destroyed Mahishasura's henchmen until only he remained. This was to be Hinduism's greatest boss battle.

Mahishasura knew that no man could slay him, and he was pretty sure no woman was strong enough to do it. It was very Witch King of Angmar. He turned into a buffalo and charged at Durga. She threw a lasso around his neck and started strangling him, but Mahishasura transformed into an elephant and started uprooting rocks with his tusks and throwing at them at her. She shot the rocks out of the sky with her arrows. Then Mahishasura turned into a serpent, and Durga attacked with her sword. Finally, Mahishasura returned to his buffalo state and Durga lunged at him with her trident, the weapon of Shiva, the destroyer. Her attack was true—the trident plunged into Mahishasura's flank and unholy blood and bile gushed out. Durga, however, was untouched and resplendent. She returned with her trophies of victory to the adulations of the other gods, but she wasn't stuck up about it. Durga is the destruction of ego.

I hope she had a daiquiri in each and every one of those hands after saving the world from chaos and destruction. Even a goddess needs some "me" time.

Durga's name is frequently translated as "invincible" or "beyond reach." It comes from the roots *dur* (difficult) and *gam* (go through), and while I know absolutely nothing about ancient Sanskrit, it seems possible her name might not refer to how hard it is to go through her, but how hard the things she's gone through have been. Maybe both. Maybe those things are the same.

When I look back at the people and stories in this book, I feel a little bit like Durga. Not the resplendent, unbeatable beauty part, no, but the being formed from other people's essences. My mom and my dad, the women who played Tracy Turnblad, the kids who called me gay on the schoolyard, Eddie Murphy, Gurinder Chadha, Turtle from *Entourage*, the nation of Canada. Each of them gave me a weapon, a tool I could use to survive.

There is always a shape-shifting beast waiting for you: depression, oppression, even just bad luck ready to grind you into the dust and tell you that you don't get to be a hero. I am so astoundingly grateful for all the people who have given me the weapons to fight off those demons. And if Durga taught me anything, it's that just having the weapons isn't enough; it's being resourceful and agile enough to deploy the correct one at the correct time. These weapons, these skills, these fights: They are what made me.

They are my essence, and in the form of this book, I'm sharing my essence with you. (I know that coming from a man, that sounds semi-gross.) I hope that you can find some use for it; maybe it will provide some ammunition for your own arsenal, even if only as a literal weapon. This is nearly a hundred thousand words—you can do some serious blunt trauma with that.

Because being a goddess isn't just about slaying buffalo demons. It's also about imparting your essence and gifting your weapons. So now that you've read this book, this piece of me, you have to go figure out how to give a piece of yourself to the world.

ACKNOWLEDGMENTS

This work would not have been possible without my mother, Deborah Branum. Since I was born, Debbie taught me how to love, learn, and express myself. For that I am eternally in her debt. I must also thank my niece Olivia Allen, who is constantly bringing new culture to me, and challenging me to see the world in new ways.

I would not have written this book if my friend Kate Dresser hadn't insisted I meet her book agent friend. I would not have written this book if said agent, Robert Guinsler, hadn't lovingly goaded me for a year to write a book proposal. I wouldn't have written this book if Sara Weiss at Ballantine hadn't suggested I write a book that centered on pop culture (even though she didn't end up buying the book). I wouldn't have written this book if my manager, Zack Freedman, hadn't nudged me, every week for two years, first to finish my proposal, then to actually write the thing. And I most certainly wouldn't have written this book if my editor, Rakesh Satyal, hadn't breezily said "Oh, it's fine" after I missed every deadline. His guidance and enthusiasm were invaluable in this process.

I am indebted to the people who read this book and provided feedback while I was writing it: Rebecca Cohen, Louis Katz, and Annemarie Brentrup. I'm also very thankful for the people who read individual chapters to make sure they weren't dumb or offensive: Debra DiGiovanni, Allan Kustanovich, Arish Singh, and Karen Tongson.

And while we're talking about Karen Tongson, thanks to my podcasting sisters Wynter Mitchell, Margaret Wappler, and Oliver Wang. The insight and analysis you guys have shared with me on *Pop Rocket* over the past three years helped define the tone and content of this book as much as anything. Also thanks to Christian Dueñas, Laura Swisher, and Jesse Thorn for making *Pop Rocket* possible.

Mindy Kaling was kind enough to write my foreward when she had a two-month-old baby, two movies, and a TV show premiering. I certainly owe her thanks for that, and so much more. I also must thank Chelsea Handler, Kamau Bell, Billy Eichner, Wanda Sykes, and Page Hurwitz for all they have taught me.

I also owe an intellectual debt to four women from Northern California: Joan Didion, Pauline Kael, Greta Gerwig, and Karen Kilgariff. In different ways, but with united spirit, they showed me where I am from.

When I'm thinking about something and need a person to bounce ideas off, I frequently turn to Lindy West, Ryan Baber, and Riley Jess Silverman. Their hearts and minds were invaluable in this process.

I'd also like to thank Moshe Kasher, Natasha Leggero, Alex Koll, Ali Wong, Eliza Skinner, Sheng Wang, Vance Sanders, Robert Yasumura, Aparna Nancherla, Jackie Kashian, Laurie Kilmartin, Claudia Cogan, Kara Klenk, Chase Bernstein, and all the other stand-up comedians who have inspired me.

I would like to thank Art Alamo, Colin Dunn, Nigel Campbell, Ryan Dunn, Kevin Minnick, Michelle Buteau, and Kristin Smith for giving me shoulders to cry and/or sleep on.

And I would like to thank Solomon Georgio, Joel Kim Booster, Matt Rogers, Bowen Yang, Nick Sahoyah, Will Smalley, John Early, Casey Ley, Cole Escola, Chris Schleicher, Jeffery Self, and Louis Virtel for always having something scandalous to say.

I must also thank my not-book agent, Ayala Cohen, for always seeming breezy and amused. Also for keeping me gainfully employed.

Thanks also to Adam Ginivisian, Michael Grinspan, Taryn Ariel, and the rest of the guys at ICM.

And I'd like to thank the many other people who helped me out whom I've forgotten to thank. And Doris Gates. And Leto. And Durga. And you.

ABOUT THE AUTHOR

Guy Branum is the host and creator of *Talk Show the Game Show* on TruTV. He's also a comedian who was a regular on *Chelsea Lately*, and was named to *LA Weekly*, *Time Out Los Angeles*, and *New York* magazine's lists of comics to watch. He has written for *The Mindy Project*, *Another Period*, *Billy on the Street*, and *Awkward*. Mostly, he is a large, loud, gay Jew. He lives in West Hollywood with his beloved sourdough starter, Claire.

31901064396957